C-295   CAREER EXAMINATION SERIES

This is your
PASSBOOK for...

Commercial Driver's License (CDL)

Test Preparation Study Guide
Questions & Answers

COPYRIGHT NOTICE

This book is SOLELY intended for, is sold ONLY to, and its use is RESTRICTED to individual, bona fide applicants or candidates who qualify by virtue of having seriously filed applications for appropriate license, certificate, professional and/or promotional advancement, higher school matriculation, scholarship, or other legitimate requirements of education and/or governmental authorities.

This book is NOT intended for use, class instruction, tutoring, training, duplication, copying, reprinting, excerption, or adaptation, etc., by:

1) Other publishers
2) Proprietors and/or Instructors of "Coaching" and/or Preparatory Courses
3) Personnel and/or Training Divisions of commercial, industrial, and governmental organizations
4) Schools, colleges, or universities and/or their departments and staffs, including teachers and other personnel
5) Testing Agencies or Bureaus
6) Study groups which seek by the purchase of a single volume to copy and/or duplicate and/or adapt this material for use by the group as a whole without having purchased individual volumes for each of the members of the group
7) Et al.

Such persons would be in violation of appropriate Federal and State statutes.

PROVISION OF LICENSING AGREEMENTS – Recognized educational, commercial, industrial, and governmental institutions and organizations, and others legitimately engaged in educational pursuits, including training, testing, and measurement activities, may address request for a licensing agreement to the copyright owners, who will determine whether, and under what conditions, including fees and charges, the materials in this book may be used them. In other words, a licensing facility exists for the legitimate use of the material in this book on other than an individual basis. However, it is asseverated and affirmed here that the material in this book CANNOT be used without the receipt of the express permission of such a licensing agreement from the Publishers. Inquiries re licensing should be addressed to the company, attention rights and permissions department.

All rights reserved, including the right of reproduction in whole or in part, in any form or by any means, electronic or mechanical, including photocopying, recording, or by any information storage and retrieval system, without permission in writing from the Publisher.

Copyright © 2024 by
National Learning Corporation

212 Michael Drive, Syosset, NY 11791
(516) 921-8888 • www.passbooks.com
E-mail: info@passbooks.com

PUBLISHED IN THE UNITED STATES OF AMERICA

PASSBOOK® SERIES

THE *PASSBOOK® SERIES* has been created to prepare applicants and candidates for the ultimate academic battlefield – the examination room.

At some time in our lives, each and every one of us may be required to take an examination – for validation, matriculation, admission, qualification, registration, certification, or licensure.

Based on the assumption that every applicant or candidate has met the basic formal educational standards, has taken the required number of courses, and read the necessary texts, the *PASSBOOK® SERIES* furnishes the one special preparation which may assure passing with confidence, instead of failing with insecurity. Examination questions – together with answers – are furnished as the basic vehicle for study so that the mysteries of the examination and its compounding difficulties may be eliminated or diminished by a sure method.

This book is meant to help you pass your examination provided that you qualify and are serious in your objective.

The entire field is reviewed through the huge store of content information which is succinctly presented through a provocative and challenging approach – the question-and-answer method.

A climate of success is established by furnishing the correct answers at the end of each test.

You soon learn to recognize types of questions, forms of questions, and patterns of questioning. You may even begin to anticipate expected outcomes.

You perceive that many questions are repeated or adapted so that you can gain acute insights, which may enable you to score many sure points.

You learn how to confront new questions, or types of questions, and to attack them confidently and work out the correct answers.

You note objectives and emphases, and recognize pitfalls and dangers, so that you may make positive educational adjustments.

Moreover, you are kept fully informed in relation to new concepts, methods, practices, and directions in the field.

You discover that you are actually taking the examination all the time: you are preparing for the examination by "taking" an examination, not by reading extraneous and/or supererogatory textbooks.

In short, this PASSBOOK®, used directedly, should be an important factor in helping you to pass your test.

COMMERCIAL DRIVER'S LICENSE (CDL)

DUTIES
The Commercial Driver's License (CDL) is necessary for all those who seek to earn a living by operating a truck or tractor-trailer. All tractor trailer operators on interstate highways must possess a CDL or face heavy criminal penalties.

SCOPE OF THE WRITTEN TEST
The written test will be designed to test for knowledge, skills, and/or abilities in such areas as:
1. Operation and maintenance of motor vehicles, including tractor trailers; and
2. Motor vehicle laws, rules, regulations and safety.

HOW TO TAKE A TEST

I. YOU MUST PASS AN EXAMINATION

A. WHAT EVERY CANDIDATE SHOULD KNOW

Examination applicants often ask us for help in preparing for the written test. What can I study in advance? What kinds of questions will be asked? How will the test be given? How will the papers be graded?

As an applicant for a civil service examination, you may be wondering about some of these things. Our purpose here is to suggest effective methods of advance study and to describe civil service examinations.

Your chances for success on this examination can be increased if you know how to prepare. Those "pre-examination jitters" can be reduced if you know what to expect. You can even experience an adventure in good citizenship if you know why civil service exams are given.

B. WHY ARE CIVIL SERVICE EXAMINATIONS GIVEN?

Civil service examinations are important to you in two ways. As a citizen, you want public jobs filled by employees who know how to do their work. As a job seeker, you want a fair chance to compete for that job on an equal footing with other candidates. The best-known means of accomplishing this two-fold goal is the competitive examination.

Exams are widely publicized throughout the nation. They may be administered for jobs in federal, state, city, municipal, town or village governments or agencies.

Any citizen may apply, with some limitations, such as the age or residence of applicants. Your experience and education may be reviewed to see whether you meet the requirements for the particular examination. When these requirements exist, they are reasonable and applied consistently to all applicants. Thus, a competitive examination may cause you some uneasiness now, but it is your privilege and safeguard.

C. HOW ARE CIVIL SERVICE EXAMS DEVELOPED?

Examinations are carefully written by trained technicians who are specialists in the field known as "psychological measurement," in consultation with recognized authorities in the field of work that the test will cover. These experts recommend the subject matter areas or skills to be tested; only those knowledges or skills important to your success on the job are included. The most reliable books and source materials available are used as references. Together, the experts and technicians judge the difficulty level of the questions.

Test technicians know how to phrase questions so that the problem is clearly stated. Their ethics do not permit "trick" or "catch" questions. Questions may have been tried out on sample groups, or subjected to statistical analysis, to determine their usefulness.

Written tests are often used in combination with performance tests, ratings of training and experience, and oral interviews. All of these measures combine to form the best-known means of finding the right person for the right job.

II. HOW TO PASS THE WRITTEN TEST

A. NATURE OF THE EXAMINATION

To prepare intelligently for civil service examinations, you should know how they differ from school examinations you have taken. In school you were assigned certain definite pages to read or subjects to cover. The examination questions were quite detailed and usually emphasized memory. Civil service exams, on the other hand, try to discover your present ability to perform the duties of a position, plus your potentiality to learn these duties. In other words, a civil service exam attempts to predict how successful you will be. Questions cover such a broad area that they cannot be as minute and detailed as school exam questions.

In the public service similar kinds of work, or positions, are grouped together in one "class." This process is known as *position-classification*. All the positions in a class are paid according to the salary range for that class. One class title covers all of these positions, and they are all tested by the same examination.

B. FOUR BASIC STEPS

1) Study the announcement

How, then, can you know what subjects to study? Our best answer is: "Learn as much as possible about the class of positions for which you've applied." The exam will test the knowledge, skills and abilities needed to do the work.

Your most valuable source of information about the position you want is the official exam announcement. This announcement lists the training and experience qualifications. Check these standards and apply only if you come reasonably close to meeting them.

The brief description of the position in the examination announcement offers some clues to the subjects which will be tested. Think about the job itself. Review the duties in your mind. Can you perform them, or are there some in which you are rusty? Fill in the blank spots in your preparation.

Many jurisdictions preview the written test in the exam announcement by including a section called "Knowledge and Abilities Required," "Scope of the Examination," or some similar heading. Here you will find out specifically what fields will be tested.

2) Review your own background

Once you learn in general what the position is all about, and what you need to know to do the work, ask yourself which subjects you already know fairly well and which need improvement. You may wonder whether to concentrate on improving your strong areas or on building some background in your fields of weakness. When the announcement has specified "some knowledge" or "considerable knowledge," or has used adjectives like "beginning principles of..." or "advanced ... methods," you can get a clue as to the number and difficulty of questions to be asked in any given field. More questions, and hence broader coverage, would be included for those subjects which are more important in the work. Now weigh your strengths and weaknesses against the job requirements and prepare accordingly.

3) Determine the level of the position

Another way to tell how intensively you should prepare is to understand the level of the job for which you are applying. Is it the entering level? In other words, is this the position in which beginners in a field of work are hired? Or is it an intermediate or advanced level? Sometimes this is indicated by such words as "Junior" or "Senior" in the class title. Other jurisdictions use Roman numerals to designate the level – Clerk I, Clerk II, for example. The word "Supervisor" sometimes appears in the title. If the level is not indicated by the title, check the description of duties. Will you be working under very close supervision, or will you have responsibility for independent decisions in this work?

4) Choose appropriate study materials

Now that you know the subjects to be examined and the relative amount of each subject to be covered, you can choose suitable study materials. For beginning level jobs, or even advanced ones, if you have a pronounced weakness in some aspect of your training, read a modern, standard textbook in that field. Be sure it is up to date and has general coverage. Such books are normally available at your library, and the librarian will be glad to help you locate one. For entry-level positions, questions of appropriate difficulty are chosen – neither highly advanced questions, nor those too simple. Such questions require careful thought but not advanced training.

If the position for which you are applying is technical or advanced, you will read more advanced, specialized material. If you are already familiar with the basic principles of your field, elementary textbooks would waste your time. Concentrate on advanced textbooks and technical periodicals. Think through the concepts and review difficult problems in your field.

These are all general sources. You can get more ideas on your own initiative, following these leads. For example, training manuals and publications of the government agency which employs workers in your field can be useful, particularly for technical and professional positions. A letter or visit to the government department involved may result in more specific study suggestions, and certainly will provide you with a more definite idea of the exact nature of the position you are seeking.

III. KINDS OF TESTS

Tests are used for purposes other than measuring knowledge and ability to perform specified duties. For some positions, it is equally important to test ability to make adjustments to new situations or to profit from training. In others, basic mental abilities not dependent on information are essential. Questions which test these things may not appear as pertinent to the duties of the position as those which test for knowledge and information. Yet they are often highly important parts of a fair examination. For very general questions, it is almost impossible to help you direct your study efforts. What we can do is to point out some of the more common of these general abilities needed in public service positions and describe some typical questions.

1) General information

Broad, general information has been found useful for predicting job success in some kinds of work. This is tested in a variety of ways, from vocabulary lists to questions about current events. Basic background in some field of work, such as sociology or economics, may be sampled in a group of questions. Often these are principles which have become familiar to most persons through exposure rather than through formal training. It is difficult to advise you how to study for these questions; being alert to the world around you is our best suggestion.

2) Verbal ability

An example of an ability needed in many positions is verbal or language ability. Verbal ability is, in brief, the ability to use and understand words. Vocabulary and grammar tests are typical measures of this ability. Reading comprehension or paragraph interpretation questions are common in many kinds of civil service tests. You are given a paragraph of written material and asked to find its central meaning.

3) Numerical ability

Number skills can be tested by the familiar arithmetic problem, by checking paired lists of numbers to see which are alike and which are different, or by interpreting charts and graphs. In the latter test, a graph may be printed in the test booklet which you are asked to use as the basis for answering questions.

4) Observation

A popular test for law-enforcement positions is the observation test. A picture is shown to you for several minutes, then taken away. Questions about the picture test your ability to observe both details and larger elements.

5) Following directions

In many positions in the public service, the employee must be able to carry out written instructions dependably and accurately. You may be given a chart with several columns, each column listing a variety of information. The questions require you to carry out directions involving the information given in the chart.

6) Skills and aptitudes

Performance tests effectively measure some manual skills and aptitudes. When the skill is one in which you are trained, such as typing or shorthand, you can practice. These tests are often very much like those given in business school or high school courses. For many of the other skills and aptitudes, however, no short-time preparation can be made. Skills and abilities natural to you or that you have developed throughout your lifetime are being tested.

Many of the general questions just described provide all the data needed to answer the questions and ask you to use your reasoning ability to find the answers. Your best preparation for these tests, as well as for tests of facts and ideas, is to be at your physical and mental best. You, no doubt, have your own methods of getting into an exam-taking mood and keeping "in shape." The next section lists some ideas on this subject.

IV. KINDS OF QUESTIONS

Only rarely is the "essay" question, which you answer in narrative form, used in civil service tests. Civil service tests are usually of the short-answer type. Full instructions for answering these questions will be given to you at the examination. But in case this is your first experience with short-answer questions and separate answer sheets, here is what you need to know:

1) Multiple-choice Questions

Most popular of the short-answer questions is the "multiple choice" or "best answer" question. It can be used, for example, to test for factual knowledge, ability to solve problems or judgment in meeting situations found at work.

A multiple-choice question is normally one of three types—
- It can begin with an incomplete statement followed by several possible endings. You are to find the one ending which *best* completes the statement, although some of the others may not be entirely wrong.
- It can also be a complete statement in the form of a question which is answered by choosing one of the statements listed.

- It can be in the form of a problem – again you select the best answer.

Here is an example of a multiple-choice question with a discussion which should give you some clues as to the method for choosing the right answer:

When an employee has a complaint about his assignment, the action which will *best* help him overcome his difficulty is to
  A. discuss his difficulty with his coworkers
  B. take the problem to the head of the organization
  C. take the problem to the person who gave him the assignment
  D. say nothing to anyone about his complaint

In answering this question, you should study each of the choices to find which is best. Consider choice "A" – Certainly an employee may discuss his complaint with fellow employees, but no change or improvement can result, and the complaint remains unresolved. Choice "B" is a poor choice since the head of the organization probably does not know what assignment you have been given, and taking your problem to him is known as "going over the head" of the supervisor. The supervisor, or person who made the assignment, is the person who can clarify it or correct any injustice. Choice "C" is, therefore, correct. To say nothing, as in choice "D," is unwise. Supervisors have and interest in knowing the problems employees are facing, and the employee is seeking a solution to his problem.

2) True/False Questions

The "true/false" or "right/wrong" form of question is sometimes used. Here a complete statement is given. Your job is to decide whether the statement is right or wrong.

SAMPLE: A roaming cell-phone call to a nearby city costs less than a non-roaming call to a distant city.

This statement is wrong, or false, since roaming calls are more expensive.

This is not a complete list of all possible question forms, although most of the others are variations of these common types. You will always get complete directions for answering questions. Be sure you understand *how* to mark your answers – ask questions until you do.

V. RECORDING YOUR ANSWERS

Computer terminals are used more and more today for many different kinds of exams.
For an examination with very few applicants, you may be told to record your answers in the test booklet itself. Separate answer sheets are much more common. If this separate answer sheet is to be scored by machine – and this is often the case – it is highly important that you mark your answers correctly in order to get credit.
An electronic scoring machine is often used in civil service offices because of the speed with which papers can be scored. Machine-scored answer sheets must be marked with a pencil, which will be given to you. This pencil has a high graphite content which responds to the electronic scoring machine. As a matter of fact, stray dots may register as answers, so do not let your pencil rest on the answer sheet while you are pondering the correct answer. Also, if your pencil lead breaks or is otherwise defective, ask for another.

Since the answer sheet will be dropped in a slot in the scoring machine, be careful not to bend the corners or get the paper crumpled.

The answer sheet normally has five vertical columns of numbers, with 30 numbers to a column. These numbers correspond to the question numbers in your test booklet. After each number, going across the page are four or five pairs of dotted lines. These short dotted lines have small letters or numbers above them. The first two pairs may also have a "T" or "F" above the letters. This indicates that the first two pairs only are to be used if the questions are of the true-false type. If the questions are multiple choice, disregard the "T" and "F" and pay attention only to the small letters or numbers.

Answer your questions in the manner of the sample that follows:

32. The largest city in the United States is
    A. Washington, D.C.
    B. New York City
    C. Chicago
    D. Detroit
    E. San Francisco

1) Choose the answer you think is best. (New York City is the largest, so "B" is correct.)
2) Find the row of dotted lines numbered the same as the question you are answering. (Find row number 32)
3) Find the pair of dotted lines corresponding to the answer. (Find the pair of lines under the mark "B.")
4) Make a solid black mark between the dotted lines.

VI. BEFORE THE TEST

Common sense will help you find procedures to follow to get ready for an examination. Too many of us, however, overlook these sensible measures. Indeed, nervousness and fatigue have been found to be the most serious reasons why applicants fail to do their best on civil service tests. Here is a list of reminders:

- Begin your preparation early – Don't wait until the last minute to go scurrying around for books and materials or to find out what the position is all about.
- Prepare continuously – An hour a night for a week is better than an all-night cram session. This has been definitely established. What is more, a night a week for a month will return better dividends than crowding your study into a shorter period of time.
- Locate the place of the exam – You have been sent a notice telling you when and where to report for the examination. If the location is in a different town or otherwise unfamiliar to you, it would be well to inquire the best route and learn something about the building.
- Relax the night before the test – Allow your mind to rest. Do not study at all that night. Plan some mild recreation or diversion; then go to bed early and get a good night's sleep.
- Get up early enough to make a leisurely trip to the place for the test – This way unforeseen events, traffic snarls, unfamiliar buildings, etc. will not upset you.
- Dress comfortably – A written test is not a fashion show. You will be known by number and not by name, so wear something comfortable.

- Leave excess paraphernalia at home – Shopping bags and odd bundles will get in your way. You need bring only the items mentioned in the official notice you received; usually everything you need is provided. Do not bring reference books to the exam. They will only confuse those last minutes and be taken away from you when in the test room.
- Arrive somewhat ahead of time – If because of transportation schedules you must get there very early, bring a newspaper or magazine to take your mind off yourself while waiting.
- Locate the examination room – When you have found the proper room, you will be directed to the seat or part of the room where you will sit. Sometimes you are given a sheet of instructions to read while you are waiting. Do not fill out any forms until you are told to do so; just read them and be prepared.
- Relax and prepare to listen to the instructions
- If you have any physical problem that may keep you from doing your best, be sure to tell the test administrator. If you are sick or in poor health, you really cannot do your best on the exam. You can come back and take the test some other time.

VII. AT THE TEST

The day of the test is here and you have the test booklet in your hand. The temptation to get going is very strong. Caution! There is more to success than knowing the right answers. You must know how to identify your papers and understand variations in the type of short-answer question used in this particular examination. Follow these suggestions for maximum results from your efforts:

1) Cooperate with the monitor

The test administrator has a duty to create a situation in which you can be as much at ease as possible. He will give instructions, tell you when to begin, check to see that you are marking your answer sheet correctly, and so on. He is not there to guard you, although he will see that your competitors do not take unfair advantage. He wants to help you do your best.

2) Listen to all instructions

Don't jump the gun! Wait until you understand all directions. In most civil service tests you get more time than you need to answer the questions. So don't be in a hurry. Read each word of instructions until you clearly understand the meaning. Study the examples, listen to all announcements and follow directions. Ask questions if you do not understand what to do.

3) Identify your papers

Civil service exams are usually identified by number only. You will be assigned a number; you must not put your name on your test papers. Be sure to copy your number correctly. Since more than one exam may be given, copy your exact examination title.

4) Plan your time

Unless you are told that a test is a "speed" or "rate of work" test, speed itself is usually not important. Time enough to answer all the questions will be provided, but this does not mean that you have all day. An overall time limit has been set. Divide the total time (in minutes) by the number of questions to determine the approximate time you have for each question.

5) Do not linger over difficult questions

If you come across a difficult question, mark it with a paper clip (useful to have along) and come back to it when you have been through the booklet. One caution if you do this – be sure to skip a number on your answer sheet as well. Check often to be sure that you have not lost your place and that you are marking in the row numbered the same as the question you are answering.

6) Read the questions

Be sure you know what the question asks! Many capable people are unsuccessful because they failed to *read* the questions correctly.

7) Answer all questions

Unless you have been instructed that a penalty will be deducted for incorrect answers, it is better to guess than to omit a question.

8) Speed tests

It is often better NOT to guess on speed tests. It has been found that on timed tests people are tempted to spend the last few seconds before time is called in marking answers at random – without even reading them – in the hope of picking up a few extra points. To discourage this practice, the instructions may warn you that your score will be "corrected" for guessing. That is, a penalty will be applied. The incorrect answers will be deducted from the correct ones, or some other penalty formula will be used.

9) Review your answers

If you finish before time is called, go back to the questions you guessed or omitted to give them further thought. Review other answers if you have time.

10) Return your test materials

If you are ready to leave before others have finished or time is called, take ALL your materials to the monitor and leave quietly. Never take any test material with you. The monitor can discover whose papers are not complete, and taking a test booklet may be grounds for disqualification.

VIII. EXAMINATION TECHNIQUES

1) Read the general instructions carefully. These are usually printed on the first page of the exam booklet. As a rule, these instructions refer to the timing of the examination; the fact that you should not start work until the signal and must stop work at a signal, etc. If there are any *special* instructions, such as a choice of questions to be answered, make sure that you note this instruction carefully.

2) When you are ready to start work on the examination, that is as soon as the signal has been given, read the instructions to each question booklet, underline any key words or phrases, such as *least, best, outline, describe* and the like. In this way you will tend to answer as requested rather than discover on reviewing your paper that you *listed without describing*, that you selected the *worst* choice rather than the *best* choice, etc.

3) If the examination is of the objective or multiple-choice type – that is, each question will also give a series of possible answers: A, B, C or D, and you are called upon to select the best answer and write the letter next to that answer on your answer paper – it is advisable to start answering each question in turn. There may be anywhere from 50 to 100 such questions in the three or four hours allotted and you can see how much time would be taken if you read through all the questions before beginning to answer any. Furthermore, if you come across a question or group of questions which you know would be difficult to answer, it would undoubtedly affect your handling of all the other questions.

4) If the examination is of the essay type and contains but a few questions, it is a moot point as to whether you should read all the questions before starting to answer any one. Of course, if you are given a choice – say five out of seven and the like – then it is essential to read all the questions so you can eliminate the two that are most difficult. If, however, you are asked to answer all the questions, there may be danger in trying to answer the easiest one first because you may find that you will spend too much time on it. The best technique is to answer the first question, then proceed to the second, etc.

5) Time your answers. Before the exam begins, write down the time it started, then add the time allowed for the examination and write down the time it must be completed, then divide the time available somewhat as follows:
    - If 3-1/2 hours are allowed, that would be 210 minutes. If you have 80 objective-type questions, that would be an average of 2-1/2 minutes per question. Allow yourself no more than 2 minutes per question, or a total of 160 minutes, which will permit about 50 minutes to review.
    - If for the time allotment of 210 minutes there are 7 essay questions to answer, that would average about 30 minutes a question. Give yourself only 25 minutes per question so that you have about 35 minutes to review.

6) The most important instruction is to *read each question* and make sure you know what is wanted. The second most important instruction is to *time yourself properly* so that you answer every question. The third most important instruction is to *answer every question*. Guess if you have to but include something for each question. Remember that you will receive no credit for a blank and will probably receive some credit if you write something in answer to an essay question. If you guess a letter – say "B" for a multiple-choice question – you may have guessed right. If you leave a blank as an answer to a multiple-choice question, the examiners may respect your feelings but it will not add a point to your score. Some exams may penalize you for wrong answers, so in such cases *only*, you may not want to guess unless you have some basis for your answer.

7) Suggestions
    a. Objective-type questions
        1. Examine the question booklet for proper sequence of pages and questions
        2. Read all instructions carefully
        3. Skip any question which seems too difficult; return to it after all other questions have been answered
        4. Apportion your time properly; do not spend too much time on any single question or group of questions

5. Note and underline key words – *all, most, fewest, least, best, worst, same, opposite*, etc.
6. Pay particular attention to negatives
7. Note unusual option, e.g., unduly long, short, complex, different or similar in content to the body of the question
8. Observe the use of "hedging" words – *probably, may, most likely*, etc.
9. Make sure that your answer is put next to the same number as the question
10. Do not second-guess unless you have good reason to believe the second answer is definitely more correct
11. Cross out original answer if you decide another answer is more accurate; do not erase until you are ready to hand your paper in
12. Answer all questions; guess unless instructed otherwise
13. Leave time for review

b. Essay questions
1. Read each question carefully
2. Determine exactly what is wanted. Underline key words or phrases.
3. Decide on outline or paragraph answer
4. Include many different points and elements unless asked to develop any one or two points or elements
5. Show impartiality by giving pros and cons unless directed to select one side only
6. Make and write down any assumptions you find necessary to answer the questions
7. Watch your English, grammar, punctuation and choice of words
8. Time your answers; don't crowd material

8) Answering the essay question

Most essay questions can be answered by framing the specific response around several key words or ideas. Here are a few such key words or ideas:

M's: manpower, materials, methods, money, management
P's: purpose, program, policy, plan, procedure, practice, problems, pitfalls, personnel, public relations

a. Six basic steps in handling problems:
1. Preliminary plan and background development
2. Collect information, data and facts
3. Analyze and interpret information, data and facts
4. Analyze and develop solutions as well as make recommendations
5. Prepare report and sell recommendations
6. Install recommendations and follow up effectiveness

b. Pitfalls to avoid
1. *Taking things for granted* – A statement of the situation does not necessarily imply that each of the elements is necessarily true; for example, a complaint may be invalid and biased so that all that can be taken for granted is that a complaint has been registered

2. *Considering only one side of a situation* – Wherever possible, indicate several alternatives and then point out the reasons you selected the best one
3. *Failing to indicate follow up* – Whenever your answer indicates action on your part, make certain that you will take proper follow-up action to see how successful your recommendations, procedures or actions turn out to be
4. *Taking too long in answering any single question* – Remember to time your answers properly

IX. AFTER THE TEST

Scoring procedures differ in detail among civil service jurisdictions although the general principles are the same. Whether the papers are hand-scored or graded by machine we have described, they are nearly always graded by number. That is, the person who marks the paper knows only the number – never the name – of the applicant. Not until all the papers have been graded will they be matched with names. If other tests, such as training and experience or oral interview ratings have been given, scores will be combined. Different parts of the examination usually have different weights. For example, the written test might count 60 percent of the final grade, and a rating of training and experience 40 percent. In many jurisdictions, veterans will have a certain number of points added to their grades.

After the final grade has been determined, the names are placed in grade order and an eligible list is established. There are various methods for resolving ties between those who get the same final grade – probably the most common is to place first the name of the person whose application was received first. Job offers are made from the eligible list in the order the names appear on it. You will be notified of your grade and your rank as soon as all these computations have been made. This will be done as rapidly as possible.

People who are found to meet the requirements in the announcement are called "eligibles." Their names are put on a list of eligible candidates. An eligible's chances of getting a job depend on how high he stands on this list and how fast agencies are filling jobs from the list.

When a job is to be filled from a list of eligibles, the agency asks for the names of people on the list of eligibles for that job. When the civil service commission receives this request, it sends to the agency the names of the three people highest on this list. Or, if the job to be filled has specialized requirements, the office sends the agency the names of the top three persons who meet these requirements from the general list.

The appointing officer makes a choice from among the three people whose names were sent to him. If the selected person accepts the appointment, the names of the others are put back on the list to be considered for future openings.

That is the rule in hiring from all kinds of eligible lists, whether they are for typist, carpenter, chemist, or something else. For every vacancy, the appointing officer has his choice of any one of the top three eligibles on the list. This explains why the person whose name is on top of the list sometimes does not get an appointment when some of the persons lower on the list do. If the appointing officer chooses the second or third eligible, the No. 1 eligible does not get a job at once, but stays on the list until he is appointed or the list is terminated.

X. HOW TO PASS THE INTERVIEW TEST

The examination for which you applied requires an oral interview test. You have already taken the written test and you are now being called for the interview test – the final part of the formal examination.

You may think that it is not possible to prepare for an interview test and that there are no procedures to follow during an interview. Our purpose is to point out some things you can do in advance that will help you and some good rules to follow and pitfalls to avoid while you are being interviewed.

What is an interview supposed to test?

The written examination is designed to test the technical knowledge and competence of the candidate; the oral is designed to evaluate intangible qualities, not readily measured otherwise, and to establish a list showing the relative fitness of each candidate – as measured against his competitors – for the position sought. Scoring is not on the basis of "right" and "wrong," but on a sliding scale of values ranging from "not passable" to "outstanding." As a matter of fact, it is possible to achieve a relatively low score without a single "incorrect" answer because of evident weakness in the qualities being measured.

Occasionally, an examination may consist entirely of an oral test – either an individual or a group oral. In such cases, information is sought concerning the technical knowledges and abilities of the candidate, since there has been no written examination for this purpose. More commonly, however, an oral test is used to supplement a written examination.

Who conducts interviews?

The composition of oral boards varies among different jurisdictions. In nearly all, a representative of the personnel department serves as chairman. One of the members of the board may be a representative of the department in which the candidate would work. In some cases, "outside experts" are used, and, frequently, a businessman or some other representative of the general public is asked to serve. Labor and management or other special groups may be represented. The aim is to secure the services of experts in the appropriate field.

However the board is composed, it is a good idea (and not at all improper or unethical) to ascertain in advance of the interview who the members are and what groups they represent. When you are introduced to them, you will have some idea of their backgrounds and interests, and at least you will not stutter and stammer over their names.

What should be done before the interview?

While knowledge about the board members is useful and takes some of the surprise element out of the interview, there is other preparation which is more substantive. It *is* possible to prepare for an oral interview – in several ways:

1) Keep a copy of your application and review it carefully before the interview

This may be the only document before the oral board, and the starting point of the interview. Know what education and experience you have listed there, and the sequence and dates of all of it. Sometimes the board will ask you to review the highlights of your experience for them; you should not have to hem and haw doing it.

2) Study the class specification and the examination announcement

Usually, the oral board has one or both of these to guide them. The qualities, characteristics or knowledges required by the position sought are stated in these documents. They offer valuable clues as to the nature of the oral interview. For example, if the job involves supervisory responsibilities, the announcement will usually indicate that knowledge of modern supervisory methods and the qualifications of the candidate as a supervisor will be tested. If so, you can expect such questions, frequently in the form of a hypothetical situation which you are expected to solve. NEVER go into an oral without knowledge of the duties and responsibilities of the job you seek.

3) Think through each qualification required

Try to visualize the kind of questions you would ask if you were a board member. How well could you answer them? Try especially to appraise your own knowledge and background in each area, *measured against the job sought*, and identify any areas in which you are weak. Be critical and realistic – do not flatter yourself.

4) Do some general reading in areas in which you feel you may be weak

For example, if the job involves supervision and your past experience has NOT, some general reading in supervisory methods and practices, particularly in the field of human relations, might be useful. Do NOT study agency procedures or detailed manuals. The oral board will be testing your understanding and capacity, not your memory.

5) Get a good night's sleep and watch your general health and mental attitude

You will want a clear head at the interview. Take care of a cold or any other minor ailment, and of course, no hangovers.

What should be done on the day of the interview?

Now comes the day of the interview itself. Give yourself plenty of time to get there. Plan to arrive somewhat ahead of the scheduled time, particularly if your appointment is in the fore part of the day. If a previous candidate fails to appear, the board might be ready for you a bit early. By early afternoon an oral board is almost invariably behind schedule if there are many candidates, and you may have to wait. Take along a book or magazine to read, or your application to review, but leave any extraneous material in the waiting room when you go in for your interview. In any event, relax and compose yourself.

The matter of dress is important. The board is forming impressions about you – from your experience, your manners, your attitude, and your appearance. Give your personal appearance careful attention. Dress your best, but not your flashiest. Choose conservative, appropriate clothing, and be sure it is immaculate. This is a business interview, and your appearance should indicate that you regard it as such. Besides, being well groomed and properly dressed will help boost your confidence.

Sooner or later, someone will call your name and escort you into the interview room. *This is it.* From here on you are on your own. It is too late for any more preparation. But remember, you asked for this opportunity to prove your fitness, and you are here because your request was granted.

What happens when you go in?

The usual sequence of events will be as follows: The clerk (who is often the board stenographer) will introduce you to the chairman of the oral board, who will introduce you to the other members of the board. Acknowledge the introductions before you sit down. Do not be surprised if you find a microphone facing you or a stenotypist sitting by. Oral interviews are usually recorded in the event of an appeal or other review.

Usually the chairman of the board will open the interview by reviewing the highlights of your education and work experience from your application – primarily for the benefit of the other members of the board, as well as to get the material into the record. Do not interrupt or comment unless there is an error or significant misinterpretation; if that is the case, do not hesitate. But do not quibble about insignificant matters. Also, he will usually ask you some question about your education, experience or your present job – partly to get you to start talking and to establish the interviewing "rapport." He may start the actual questioning, or turn it over to one of the other members. Frequently, each member undertakes the questioning on a particular area, one in which he is perhaps most competent, so you can expect each member to participate in the examination. Because time is limited, you may also expect some rather abrupt switches in the direction the questioning takes, so do not be upset by it. Normally, a board member will not pursue a single line of questioning unless he discovers a particular strength or weakness.

After each member has participated, the chairman will usually ask whether any member has any further questions, then will ask you if you have anything you wish to add. Unless you are expecting this question, it may floor you. Worse, it may start you off on an extended, extemporaneous speech. The board is not usually seeking more information. The question is principally to offer you a last opportunity to present further qualifications or to indicate that you have nothing to add. So, if you feel that a significant qualification or characteristic has been overlooked, it is proper to point it out in a sentence or so. Do not compliment the board on the thoroughness of their examination – they have been sketchy, and you know it. If you wish, merely say, "No thank you, I have nothing further to add." This is a point where you can "talk yourself out" of a good impression or fail to present an important bit of information. Remember, *you close the interview yourself*.

The chairman will then say, "That is all, Mr. _____, thank you." Do not be startled; the interview is over, and quicker than you think. Thank him, gather your belongings and take your leave. Save your sigh of relief for the other side of the door.

How to put your best foot forward

Throughout this entire process, you may feel that the board individually and collectively is trying to pierce your defenses, seek out your hidden weaknesses and embarrass and confuse you. Actually, this is not true. They are obliged to make an appraisal of your qualifications for the job you are seeking, and they want to see you in your best light. Remember, they must interview all candidates and a non-cooperative candidate may become a failure in spite of their best efforts to bring out his qualifications. Here are 15 suggestions that will help you:

1) Be natural – Keep your attitude confident, not cocky

If you are not confident that you can do the job, do not expect the board to be. Do not apologize for your weaknesses, try to bring out your strong points. The board is interested in a positive, not negative, presentation. Cockiness will antagonize any board member and make him wonder if you are covering up a weakness by a false show of strength.

2) Get comfortable, but don't lounge or sprawl

Sit erectly but not stiffly. A careless posture may lead the board to conclude that you are careless in other things, or at least that you are not impressed by the importance of the occasion. Either conclusion is natural, even if incorrect. Do not fuss with your clothing, a pencil or an ashtray. Your hands may occasionally be useful to emphasize a point; do not let them become a point of distraction.

3) Do not wisecrack or make small talk

This is a serious situation, and your attitude should show that you consider it as such. Further, the time of the board is limited – they do not want to waste it, and neither should you.

4) Do not exaggerate your experience or abilities

In the first place, from information in the application or other interviews and sources, the board may know more about you than you think. Secondly, you probably will not get away with it. An experienced board is rather adept at spotting such a situation, so do not take the chance.

5) If you know a board member, do not make a point of it, yet do not hide it

Certainly you are not fooling him, and probably not the other members of the board. Do not try to take advantage of your acquaintanceship – it will probably do you little good.

6) Do not dominate the interview

Let the board do that. They will give you the clues – do not assume that you have to do all the talking. Realize that the board has a number of questions to ask you, and do not try to take up all the interview time by showing off your extensive knowledge of the answer to the first one.

7) Be attentive

You only have 20 minutes or so, and you should keep your attention at its sharpest throughout. When a member is addressing a problem or question to you, give him your undivided attention. Address your reply principally to him, but do not exclude the other board members.

8) Do not interrupt

A board member may be stating a problem for you to analyze. He will ask you a question when the time comes. Let him state the problem, and wait for the question.

9) Make sure you understand the question

Do not try to answer until you are sure what the question is. If it is not clear, restate it in your own words or ask the board member to clarify it for you. However, do not haggle about minor elements.

10) Reply promptly but not hastily

A common entry on oral board rating sheets is "candidate responded readily," or "candidate hesitated in replies." Respond as promptly and quickly as you can, but do not jump to a hasty, ill-considered answer.

11) Do not be peremptory in your answers

A brief answer is proper – but do not fire your answer back. That is a losing game from your point of view. The board member can probably ask questions much faster than you can answer them.

12) Do not try to create the answer you think the board member wants

He is interested in what kind of mind you have and how it works – not in playing games. Furthermore, he can usually spot this practice and will actually grade you down on it.

13) Do not switch sides in your reply merely to agree with a board member

Frequently, a member will take a contrary position merely to draw you out and to see if you are willing and able to defend your point of view. Do not start a debate, yet do not surrender a good position. If a position is worth taking, it is worth defending.

14) Do not be afraid to admit an error in judgment if you are shown to be wrong

The board knows that you are forced to reply without any opportunity for careful consideration. Your answer may be demonstrably wrong. If so, admit it and get on with the interview.

15) Do not dwell at length on your present job

The opening question may relate to your present assignment. Answer the question but do not go into an extended discussion. You are being examined for a *new* job, not your present one. As a matter of fact, try to phrase ALL your answers in terms of the job for which you are being examined.

Basis of Rating

Probably you will forget most of these "do's" and "don'ts" when you walk into the oral interview room. Even remembering them all will not ensure you a passing grade. Perhaps you did not have the qualifications in the first place. But remembering them will help you to put your best foot forward, without treading on the toes of the board members.

Rumor and popular opinion to the contrary notwithstanding, an oral board wants you to make the best appearance possible. They know you are under pressure – but they also want to see how you respond to it as a guide to what your reaction would be under the pressures of the job you seek. They will be influenced by the degree of poise you display, the personal traits you show and the manner in which you respond.

ABOUT THIS BOOK

This book contains tests divided into Examination Sections. Go through each test, answering every question in the margin. We have also attached a sample answer sheet at the back of the book that can be removed and used. At the end of each test look at the answer key and check your answers. On the ones you got wrong, look at the right answer choice and learn. Do not fill in the answers first. Do not memorize the questions and answers, but understand the answer and principles involved. On your test, the questions will likely be different from the samples. Questions are changed and new ones added. If you understand these past questions you should have success with any changes that arise. Tests may consist of several types of questions. We have additional books on each subject should more study be advisable or necessary for you. Finally, the more you study, the better prepared you will be. This book is intended to be the last thing you study before you walk into the examination room. Prior study of relevant texts is also recommended. NLC publishes some of these in our Fundamental Series. Knowledge and good sense are important factors in passing your exam. Good luck also helps. So now study this Passbook, absorb the material contained within and take that knowledge into the examination. Then do your best to pass that exam.

EXAMINATION SECTION

EXAMINATION SECTION
TEST 1

DIRECTIONS: Each question or incomplete statement is followed by several suggested answers or completions. Select the one that BEST answers the question or completes the statement. *PRINT THE LETTER OF THE CORRECT ANSWER IN THE SPACE AT THE RIGHT.*

1. The BEST way to check for loose lugs is to

    A. twist them by hand
    B. use a lug wrench
    C. look for space between the nuts and the rim
    D. none of the above

    1.____

2. Low tire pressure _____ chance of tire fire.

    A. improves handling and increases the
    B. makes handling more difficult, but lessens the
    C. makes handling more difficult and increases the
    D. none of the above

    2.____

3. Leaking wheel bearing lubricant is MOST likely to result in

    A. a wheel lock up   B. a tire fire
    C. loss of traction   D. all of the above

    3.____

4. In most vehicles, the brake low-air buzzer/alarm will come on when the air pressure is at _____ psi.

    A. 120   B. 60   C. 30   D. 40

    4.____

5. To check steering wheel free play on vehicles with power steering, the engine

    A. must be on   B. must be off
    C. may be either on or off D. none of the above

    5.____

6. With the engine off and the foot brake applied for one minute, the air pressure should drop no more than _____ to _____ psi.

    A. 3; 4   B. 7; 8   C. 10; 12   D. 13; 15

    6.____

7. With air brakes, it is wise to apply brake pressure _____ with hydraulic brakes.

    A. earlier than   B. later than
    C. at the same time as   D. none of the above

    7.____

8. Auxiliary brakes or speed retarders are designed to

    A. protect the engine   B. stop the vehicle
    C. slow the vehicle   D. none of the above

    8.____

9. On a long downhill grade,

    A. slowly apply and release the brakes
    B. use steady brake pressure
    C. fan the brakes
    D. none of the above

    9.____

10. To make a right turn, start the turn from the _____ lane.

    A. middle of your
    B. left
    C. left side of your
    D. none of the above

11. When carrying a load, start braking _____ when empty.

    A. sooner than
    B. at the same time as
    C. at the same time, but apply more pressure than
    D. none of the above

12. To make a normal stop in a truck equipped with air brakes,

    A. ease off the brake pedal as the vehicle slows
    B. maintain steady pressure on the brake pedal until the vehicle stops
    C. apply light pressure and increase pressure slightly as the vehicle slows
    D. none of the above

13. To take a curve, slow down _____ the curve.

    A. before entering
    B. before reaching the sharpest part of
    C. on entering the sharpest part of
    D. none of the above

14. When turning, the BEST way to keep others from trying to pass on the inside is to

    A. flash the brake lights
    B. put the turn signal on early
    C. keep speed up
    D. all of the above

15. On snow-packed roads, reduce normal driving speed by

    A. 2/3   B. 1/2   C. 1/4   D. 3/4

16. When the road is wet, you should reduce speed by

    A. a little over 1/2
    B. 1/2
    C. 1/4
    D. 3/4

17. Ice will be MOST slippery when the temperature is _____ freezing.

    A. almost at
    B. below
    C. well below
    D. above

18. On wet pavement, worn tread on front tractor tires is MOST likely to result in

    A. hydroplaning
    B. a blow out
    C. tire pressure loss
    D. none of the above

19. Hard acceleration on a slippery surface _____ traction.

    A. improves
    B. decreases
    C. does not affect
    D. none of the above

20. The vehicle trucks MOST often run into is the one

    A. in front
    B. to the left
    C. to the right
    D. none of the above

21. Before backing, check behind by

    A. using all mirrors
    B. using mirrors and leaning out of the cab
    C. getting out of the cab
    D. using left-hand signal

22. At night, low-beam headlights let you see ahead about _____ feet.

    A. 450
    B. 350
    C. 250
    D. 300

23. The image in a convex mirror will appear _____ it really is.

    A. closer than
    B. farther away than
    C. the distance
    D. none of the above

24. If you must slow down unexpectedly because the road ahead is blocked, warn drivers behind by

    A. turning on emergency flashers
    B. tapping the brake pedal
    C. motioning up and down with your hand
    D. stopping

25. After starting a lane change, you should

    A. move quickly into the new lane
    B. straddle the lane for a few seconds before continuing the lane change
    C. start the lane change and pause for a few seconds before entering the new lane
    D. none of the above

KEY (CORRECT ANSWERS)

1.	B	11.	A
2.	C	12.	A
3.	A	13.	A
4.	B	14.	B
5.	B	15.	B
6.	A	16.	C
7.	A	17.	A
8.	C	18.	A
9.	B	19.	B
10.	C	20.	C

21. C
22. C
23. B
24. B
25. C

TEST 2

DIRECTIONS: Each question or incomplete statement is followed by several suggested answers or completions. Select the one that BEST answers the question or completes the statement. *PRINT THE LETTER OF THE CORRECT ANSWER IN THE SPACE AT THE RIGHT.*

1. When meeting an on-coming vehicle, 1.____

    A. move away from the other vehicle as far as possible
    B. move toward the other vehicle to encourage it to give you space
    C. keep your vehicle centered in lane
    D. stop your vehicle

2. To turn at an intersection where there are two turning lanes, use _____ lane. 2.____

    A. the outside or far   B. the inside or near
    C. either   D. none of the above

3. When backing a loaded truck, you need a helper because 3.____

    A. mirrors don't let you see the full length of the trailer
    B. mirrors don't let you see directly behind
    C. both mirrors must be used for a complete view
    D. someone needs to stop oncoming traffic

4. When driving in the city, look ahead as far as_____ block(s). 4.____

    A. one full   B. one-half
    C. one-fourth   D. two

5. To drive safely, look ahead _____ to _____ seconds. 5.____

    A. 12; 15   B. 8; 10   C. 4; 6   D. 16; 20

6. Use emergency flashers to warn following drivers 6.____

    A. it is safe to pass
    B. they are following too closely
    C. your vehicle is stopped
    D. there is a traffic accident ahead

7. In an emergency, to STOP quickly and CONTROL the truck, you should 7.____

    A. lock the wheels and keep them locked
    B. use the trailer brakes only
    C. lock the wheels, release, and lock again
    D. none of the above

8. Use of escape ramps USUALLY 8.____

    A. damages the vehicle's suspension system
    B. damages the vehicle's frame
    C. causes little or no damage to the vehicle
    D. damages the vehicle's tires

9. In a STRAIGHT truck, front-wheel skids are often caused by cargo placed too   9._____

   A. far forward
   B. far back
   C. high in the cargo area
   D. far apart

10. To put out a fire, aim the fire extinguisher at the   10._____

    A. flame
    B. source of the fire
    C. area around the flame
    D. none of the above

11. In handling an emergency ahead, which of the following statements is MOST often correct?   11._____
    You

    A. can stop more quickly than you can turn
    B. can turn more quickly than you can stop
    C. cannot turn unless you first slow down
    D. cannot slow down unless you turn first

12. If the vehicle's air brakes fail, the FIRST thing to do is   12._____

    A. apply the emergency brake
    B. downshift
    C. pump the brakes to build pressure
    D. steer off the road

13. If you lock the rear wheels and begin to skid, the FIRST thing to do is   13._____

    A. accelerate quickly
    B. release the brake gradually
    C. release the brake immediately
    D. turn the vehicle into the skid

14. If you have to leave the road to avoid a collision, while off the road you should   14._____

    A. brake immediately
    B. avoid braking until slowed
    C. accelerate slightly
    D. get out of the cab

15. The BEST way to correct most trailer skids is to   15._____

    A. release the brake
    B. tap the trailer hand brake
    C. accelerate moderately
    D. apply the emergency brake

16. When requesting emergency assistance at an accident scene, the MOST important information to give is   16._____

    A. how the accident happened
    B. the location of the accident
    C. how many vehicles are involved
    D. your name

17. The BEST way to prevent fatigue is to schedule trips during

    A. daylight hours only
    B. hours you are normally awake
    C. weekdays only
    D. weekends only

18. Rust around lugs MOST often is a sign that the

    A. lug nuts are loose   B. rim is bent
    C. lug nuts are cracked   D. lug nuts are tight

19. *Thumping* a tire with a tire iron to check for proper air pressure

    A. is a quick and accurate method
    B. should only be done during enroute inspection
    C. is not an accurate method
    D. should be done daily

20. To check for air pressure loss in the brake system, watch the air pressure gauge while you

    A. apply the foot brake with the engine off
    B. apply the foot brake with the engine running
    C. run the engine without braking
    D. downshift

21. Steering wheel free play should be no more than _____ degrees.

    A. 30   B. 20   C. 10   D. 15

22. As cargo is unloaded, remaining cargo should be moved to

    A. the rear of the vehicle
    B. maintain an even load distribution
    C. increase the center of gravity
    D. the front of the vehicle

23. The PROPER procedure for inspecting air tanks for oil contamination is to

    A. check for oil leaks or smears around air hose, line and valve connections
    B. open the tank petcocks and allow the tanks to drain
    C. apply service brakes sharply at 5 to 7 mph and note any mushy feeling or delayed stopping
    D. none of the above

24. The governed cut-out pressure for an air brake system should be between _____ to _____ psi.

    A. 75; 100   B. 100; 125   C. 125; 150   D. 50; 75

25. As a vehicle's center of gravity is raised, the chance of rollover

    A. increases   B. decreases
    C. is not changed   D. none of the above

KEY (CORRECT ANSWERS)

1. C
2. A
3. B
4. A
5. A

6. C
7. C
8. C
9. A
10. B

11. B
12. B
13. C
14. B
15. A

16. B
17. B
18. A
19. C
20. A

21. C
22. B
23. B
24. B
25. A

TEST 3

DIRECTIONS: Each question or incomplete statement is followed by several suggested answers or completions. Select the one that BEST answers the question or completes the statement. *PRINT THE LETTER OF THE CORRECT ANSWER IN THE SPACE AT THE RIGHT.*

1. In vehicles equipped with air brakes, braking begins   1.____

    A. as your foot presses the pedal
    B. a short time after your foot presses the pedal
    C. only after maximum foot pressure is applied
    D. only while using the emergency brake

2. On downgrades, speed retarders are used to   2.____

    A. stop the vehicle
    B. help slow the vehicle
    C. save engine wear
    D. maintain air pressure in the tires

3. On a downgrade, it is BEST to   3.____

    A. shift slowly   B. avoid shifting
    C. shift quickly   D. use the emergency brake

4. To take a curve to the left, the front of the vehicle should be steered   4.____

    A. close to the center line
    B. close to the outside shoulder
    C. near the middle of your lane
    D. none of the above

5. On slippery roads, applying the trailer hand brake before the foot brake   5.____

    A. is likely to cause a jackknife
    B. keeps the rig straight, preventing a jackknife
    C. may lock the trailer wheels, but will prevent a jackknife
    D. will cause a tire blowout

6. The PROPER time to downshift for a curve is   6.____

    A. on entering it
    B. just before its sharpest part
    C. before entering it
    D. in its sharpest part

7. Gripping the steering wheel with the thumbs inside the wheel   7.____

    A. is the proper procedure
    B. can cause injury
    C. can cause loss of control
    D. should be done only on slippery roads

8. Braking skids are GENERALLY

    A. more dangerous than acceleration skids
    B. as dangerous as acceleration skids
    C. less dangerous than acceleration skids
    D. none of the above

9. Flash the brake lights to tell following drivers that

    A. you are about to slow down for a tight turn
    B. they are following too closely
    C. you are about to change lanes
    D. your vehicle is stopped

10. With air-brake equipped vehicles, when the warning device indicates low air pressure,

    A. stop as quickly as possible
    B. pump the brakes to build up pressure
    C. accelerate to generate more air pressure
    D. decelerate to generate more air pressure

11. On ice-covered roads, you should reduce your speed

    A. by two-thirds
    B. a little more than one-third
    C. almost one-third
    D. by three-quarters

12. When the temperature is right at 32 degrees, freezing is MOST likely to occur first on

    A. curves
    B. bridges
    C. hilltops
    D. highways

13. The road is MOST slippery

    A. just after it starts to rain
    B. after it rains long enough to *wash* the road
    C. just as the rain stops
    D. at night

14. When a vehicle hydroplanes, you should

    A. release the accelerator
    B. gently apply the brakes
    C. stab the brakes
    D. use emergency flashers

15. To alert others of your location, it is BEST to

    A. use a slight tap on the horn
    B. use a loud blast on the horn
    C. avoid using the horn
    D. use hand signals

16. MOST air brake failures occur because of	16._____

    A. improper adjustment	B. loss of air pressure
    C. wear to the brakes	D. *riding* the brake

17. In backing, you see the MOST area to the rear in	17._____

    A. the right mirror
    B. the left mirror
    C. both mirrors about the same
    D. none of the above

18. If you have a tough time spotting oncoming vehicles because of poor visibility, turn on	18._____

    A. low-beam headlights
    B. high-beam headlights
    C. identification or clearance lights
    D. emergency flashers

19. When backing into an alley, you can see BEST if you turn to	19._____

    A. your left side
    B. your right side
    C. the side with the shorter distance
    D. the side with the longer distance

20. For a lane change, check the mirrors at least _____ time(s)	20._____

    A. three	B. two	C. one	D. four

21. At night, if forced to stop on or near the road, the SAFEST practice is to turn emergency	21._____
    flashers on and

    A. put out reflective triangles and flares
    B. use identification and clearance lights
    C. leave your headlights and taillights on
    D. stand outside the cab

22. When approaching an oncoming vehicle on a narrow road, you should	22._____

    A. move to the left
    B. move to the right
    C. stay in the center of your lane
    D. none of the above

23. To make a left turn, start the turn	23._____

    A. as soon as you reach the intersection
    B. at the center of the intersection
    C. well before reaching the center of the intersection
    D. none of the above

24. To make a right turn in a straight truck, it is BEST to

    A. swing wide as you start the turn
    B. turn wide as you complete the turn
    C. start from the left side of the lane
    D. start from the right side of the lane

25. At highway speeds, look ahead as far as _____ mile.

    A. one-half
    B. one-quarter
    C. one-eighth
    D. three-quarters

KEY (CORRECT ANSWERS)

1.	B	11.	A
2.	B	12.	B
3.	B	13.	A
4.	B	14.	A
5.	A	15.	A
6.	C	16.	B
7.	B	17.	C
8.	A	18.	A
9.	A	19.	A
10.	A	20.	A

21. A
22. C
23. B
24. C
25. A

EXAMINATION SECTION
TEST 1

DIRECTIONS: Each question or incomplete statement is followed by several suggested answers or completions. Select the one that BEST answers the question or completes the statement. *PRINT THE LETTER OF THE CORRECT ANSWER IN THE SPACE AT THE RIGHT.*

1. Which statement is MOST correct about vehicle length and following distance? 1.____

    A. Vehicles 40 to 60 feet long require the same following distance from the vehicle ahead.
    B. Longer vehicles require more following distance from the vehicle ahead than shorter vehicles.
    C. Following distance depends more on the type of vehicle ahead than the length of the truck.
    D. Following distance depends upon the speed of the vehicle.

2. A general rule for following distance is to stay one second from the vehicle ahead for each _____ feet of your vehicle's length. 2.____

    A. 20   B. 10   C. 5   D. 2

3. To put out a fire, continue until the 3.____

    A. flame is gone   B. smoke is cleared
    C. object is cool   D. firetruck arrives

4. If there is a fire in the cargo area, doors should be 4.____

    A. kept closed   B. opened quickly
    C. opened slowly   D. opened only slightly

5. Vehicle skids MOST often are caused by 5.____

    A. wet road   B. driving too fast
    C. worn tires   D. loss of air pressure

6. In recovering from a rear-wheel braking skid, MOST drivers err by failing to steer 6.____

    A. in the right direction B. slowly enough
    C. quickly enough   D. none of the above

7. When coupling, the trailer should be positioned _____ than the tractor fifth wheel. 7.____

    A. slightly higher   B. slightly lower
    C. a great deal higher   D. a great deal lower

8. To support a trailer safely, lower the trailer landing gear with the crank until the 8.____

    A. gear touches the ground
    B. tractor stops rising
    C. tractor stops rising, and back off a turn
    D. gear touches the tractor

9. When turning a corner with a tractor-trailer, trailer rear wheels follow _____ the tractor rear wheels.

   A. a longer path than
   B. a shorter path than
   C. the same path as
   D. none of the above

10. To CORRECT a trailer drift when backing straight, turn the steering wheel

    A. away from the direction of the trailer drift
    B. in the same direction the trailer is drifting
    C. away from, then in, the direction the trailer is drifting
    D. in, then away from, the direction the trailer is drifting

11. To keep drivers from passing on the right when making a right turn with a tractor-trailer, position the

    A. tractor to block them
    B. trailer to block them
    C. tractor and trailer close to the curb line
    D. tractor and trailer away from the curb line

12. The BEST way to correct most trailer skids is to

    A. release the brake
    B. tap the trailer hand brake
    C. accelerate moderately
    D. turn into the skid

13. To check the fifth wheel coupling of a tractor-trailer, you must

    A. make a slow tight turn
    B. look under the rig
    C. move slowly backward
    D. make a fast left turn

14. A motor carrier who is also a driver (owner-operator)

    A. is not covered by the safety regulations which cover drivers
    B. must obey only those parts of the regulations which cover drivers
    C. must obey only those parts of the regulations which cover motor carriers
    D. must obey both the parts covering drivers and the parts covering motor carriers

15. With only a few exceptions, the Federal Motor Carrier Safety Regulations say a driver must be AT LEAST _____ years old.

    A. 18   B. 19   C. 20   D. 21

16. A driver cannot drive a motor vehicle for one year after a first-offense conviction for

    A. a felony involving a commercial motor vehicle operated by the driver
    B. driving a commercial vehicle under the influence of alcohol or narcotics
    C. leaving the scene of an accident which resulted in personal injury or death
    D. any of the above

17. Every driver applicant must fill out an application form giving a list of _____ during the previous three years.

    A. all vehicle accidents
    B. all motor vehicle violation convictions and bond forfeits (except for parking)
    C. names and addresses of all employers
    D. all of the above

18. At least once a year, a driver must fill out a form listing all motor vehicle violations (except parking) occurring during the previous 12 months.
    The driver must fill out the form

    A. even if there were no violations
    B. only if convicted
    C. only if convicted or had forfeited bond or collateral
    D. only if the carrier requires it

19. If a driver applicant has a valid certificate showing successful completion of a driver's road test, the carrier

    A. must accept it
    B. may still require the applicant to take a road test
    C. cannot accept it
    D. may request a road test waiver from the Bureau of Motor Carrier Safety

20. A person with breathing problems which may affect safe driving cannot

    A. drive
    B. drive unless the vehicle has an emergency oxygen supply
    C. drive unless another driver is along
    D. drive except on short runs

21. Persons with arthritis, rheumatism, or any such condition which may affect safe driving cannot

    A. drive unless they are checked by a doctor before each trip
    B. drive
    C. drive on long runs
    D. drive without monthly medical examinations

22. Persons who have ever had epilepsy cannot

    A. drive unless another driver is along
    B. drive
    C. drive on long runs
    D. drive without monthly medical examinations

23. In order to be able to drive, a driver must NOT

    A. have any mental, nervous, or physical problem likely to affect safe driving
    B. use an amphetamine, narcotic, or any habit-forming drug
    C. have a current alcoholism problem
    D. have or use any of the above

24. If a driver gets an injury or illness serious enough to affect the ability to perform duties, the driver 24.____

    A. must report it at the next scheduled physical
    B. cannot drive again
    C. must take another physical and be recertified before driving again
    D. must wait at least 1 month after recovery before driving again

25. A driver may not drive faster than posted speed limits 25.____

    A. unless the driver is sick and must complete the run quickly
    B. at any time
    C. unless the driver is passing another vehicle
    D. unless the driver is late and must make a scheduled arrival

---

KEY (CORRECT ANSWERS)

1.	B	11.	B
2.	B	12.	A
3.	C	13.	B
4.	A	14.	D
5.	B	15.	D
6.	C	16.	D
7.	B	17.	D
8.	B	18.	A
9.	B	19.	B
10.	B	20.	A

21.	B
22.	B
23.	D
24.	C
25.	B

TEST 2

DIRECTIONS: Each question or incomplete statement is followed by several suggested answers or completions. Select the one that BEST answers the question or completes the statement. *PRINT THE LETTER OF THE CORRECT ANSWER IN THE SPACE AT THE RIGHT.*

1. When a driver's physical condition while on a trip requires the driver to stop driving, but stopping would not be safe, the driver   1.____

    A. must stop anyway
    B. may try to complete the trip, but as quickly as possible
    C. may continue to drive to the home terminal
    D. may continue to drive, but must stop at the nearest safe place

2. A driver may not drink or be under the influence of any alcoholic beverage (regardless of alcoholic content) within _____ hours before going on duty or driving.   2.____

    A. 4   B. 6   C. 8   D. 12

3. A driver must be satisfied that service and parking brakes, tires, lights and reflectors, mirrors, coupling and other devices are in good working order   3.____

    A. at the end of each trip
    B. before the vehicle may be driven
    C. only when the driver considers it necessary
    D. according to the schedules set by the carrier

4. The following must be in place and ready for use before a vehicle can be driven: 4.____

    A. at least one spare fuse or other overload protector of each type used on the vehicle
    B. a tool kit containing a specified list of hand tools
    C. at least one spare tire for every four wheels
    D. a set of spark plugs

5. If any part of the cargo or anything else blocks a driver's front or side views, arm or leg movements, or the driver's access to emergency equipment, the driver   5.____

    A. can drive the vehicle, but must report the problem at the end of the trip
    B. cannot drive the vehicle
    C. can drive the vehicle, but only at speeds under 40 miles per hour
    D. can drive the vehicle, but only on secondary roads

6. Any driver who needs glasses to meet the minimum visual requirements must   6.____

    A. drive only during daylight hours
    B. always wear glasses when driving
    C. always carry a spare pair of glasses
    D. not drive a motor vehicle

7. A driver may drive with a hearing aid if

   A. the driver always has it turned on while driving
   B. the driver always carries a spare power source for it
   C. the driver can meet the hearing requirements when the hearing aid is turned on
   D. all of the above requirements are met

8. A driver required to stop at a railroad crossing should bring the vehicle to a stop no closer to the tracks than _____ feet.

   A. 5   B. 10   C. 15   D. 20

9. Shifting gears is not permitted when

   A. traveling faster than 35 miles per hour
   B. moving across any bridge
   C. crossing railroad tracks
   D. traveling down a hill steeper than 10 degrees

10. A driver of a motor vehicle, not required to stop at drawbridges without signals, must

    A. drive at a rate of speed which will permit a stop before reaching the lip of the draw
    B. sound the horn before crossing
    C. proceed across without reducing speed
    D. slow down only if directed by an attendant

11. When turning a vehicle, a driver should begin flashing the turn signals AT LEAST_____ feet before turning.

    A. 50   B. 60   C. 75   D. 100

12. Which of the following is TRUE?

    A. If a seat belt is installed in the vehicle, a driver must have it fastened before beginning to drive.
    B. A driver may or may not use the seat belt, depending on the driver's judgment.
    C. Seat belts are not necessary on heavier vehicles.
    D. A driver must use the seat belt only if required by the carrier.

13. When a motor vehicle cannot be stopped off the traveled part of the highway, the driver

    A. must keep driving
    B. may stop, but shall get as far off the traveled part of the highway as possible
    C. may stop, but shall make sure that the vehicle can be seen as far as possible to its front and rear
    D. may stop if the driver has to, but should do both B and C above

14. If a vehicle has a breakdown, the driver must place one emergency signal

    A. 100 feet in front of the vehicle in the center of the lane it occupies
    B. 100 feet in back of the vehicle in the center of the lane it occupies
    C. 10 feet in front or back on the traffic side
    D. at all of the above locations

15. If a vehicle has a breakdown on a poorly lit street or highway, the driver shall place on the traffic side a   15.____

    A. reflective triangle
    B. lighted red electric lantern
    C. red reflector
    D. any one of the above

16. No emergency signals are required for a vehicle with a breakdown if the street or highway lighting is bright enough so it can be seen at a distance of _____ feet.   16.____

    A. 100   B. 200   C. 500   D. 750

17. If a vehicle has a breakdown and stops on a poorly lit DIVIDED or ONE-WAY HIGHWAY, the driver must place one emergency signal   17.____

    A. 200 feet in back of the vehicle in the center of the lane it occupies
    B. 100 feet in back of the vehicle on the traffic side of the vehicle
    C. 10 feet in back of the vehicle on the traffic side of the vehicle
    D. at all of the above locations

18. Lighted flame-producing emergency signals, including fuses, may not be used with   18.____

    A. vehicles carrying Class A or B explosives
    B. tank vehicles, loaded or empty, which are used to carry flammable liquids or gas
    C. any vehicle using compressed gas as a fuel
    D. any of the above

19. A driver is required to turn on vehicle lights from   19.____

    A. one-half hour before sunset to one-half hour before sunrise
    B. one-half hour before sunset to sunrise
    C. one-half hour after sunset to one-half hour before sunrise
    D. sunset to one-half hour before sunrise

20. When lights are required on the highway, a driver shall use the high beam EXCEPT when within _____ feet of an oncoming vehicle or a vehicle the driver is following.   20.____

    A. 500   B. 400   C. 200   D. 100

21. When lights are required, a driver may use lower beam lights when   21.____

    A. fog, dust, or other such conditions exist
    B. approaching tunnels or bridges
    C. driving on one-way highways
    D. within 1000 feet of business areas or where people live

22. Every driver involved in an accident must follow the safety regulation procedures whenever an injury or death is involved or if   22.____

    A. the accident is caused by the driver and property damage of over $2000 results
    B. property damage of over $2000 results, no matter who is at fault
    C. property damage of over $100 results
    D. property damage of any kind results

23. If a driver strikes a parked vehicle, the driver should FIRST stop and   23.____

    A. call the local police
    B. call the carrier
    C. try to find the driver or owner of the parked vehicle
    D. estimate the damages

24. When a driver receives notice of license or permit revocation, suspension or other withdrawal action, the driver must   24.____

    A. notify the carrier within 72 hours
    B. notify the carrier within one week
    C. notify the carrier before the end of the next business day
    D. take no action since the carrier will get a notice

25. Except in emergencies, no driver shall allow a vehicle to be driven by any other person   25.____

    A. except by those the driver knows are capable
    B. except on roads with little or no traffic
    C. except by those allowed by the carrier to do it
    D. unless the driver goes along with the person driving

KEY (CORRECT ANSWERS)

1.	D	11.	D
2.	A	12.	A
3.	B	13.	D
4.	A	14.	D
5.	B	15.	D
6.	B	16.	C
7.	D	17.	D
8.	C	18.	D
9.	C	19.	C
10.	A	20.	A

21. A
22. D
23. C
24. C
25. C

TEST 3

DIRECTIONS: Each question or incomplete statement is followed by several suggested answers or completions. Select the one that BEST answers the question or completes the statement. *PRINT THE LETTER OF THE CORRECT ANSWER IN THE SPACE AT THE RIGHT.*

1. A person may ride inside a vehicle's closed body or trailer ONLY 1.____

    A. on short runs
    B. if there is an easy way to get out from the inside
    C. if the inside of the body or trailer is lighted
    D. if there is no cargo in it

2. If carbon monoxide is inside a vehicle or if a mechanical problem may produce a carbon monoxide danger, the vehicle may 2.____

    A. be sent out and driven so long as the windows are left open
    B. not be sent out or driven
    C. be sent out and driven only if the carrier decides the vehicle has to be used
    D. be sent out and driven on short runs

3. No motor vehicle shall be operated out of gear EXCEPT 3.____

    A. when fuel must be saved
    B. on hills which are less than 20 degrees
    C. when it is necessary for stopping or shifting gears
    D. when the vehicle's speed is under 25 miles per hour

4. Under the Federal Motor Carrier Safety Regulations, no vehicle may be driven 4.____

    A. until a list of all missing or defective equipment has been prepared and given to the carrier
    B. until all equipment has been inspected and replacements for defective parts have been ordered
    C. unless all missing equipment is to be replaced no later than the end of the vehicle's next run
    D. until it meets all of the equipment requirements of the regulations

5. Minimum requirements for lighting, reflecting and electrical equipment and devices on buses and trucks are 5.____

    A. set by the vehicle makers
    B. set by the National Safety Council
    C. specified in the safety regulations
    D. set by the trucking associations

6. Every motor vehicle which has a load sticking out over its sides must be specifically marked with flags and lamps. 6.____
Additional flags and lamps must be added if the load or tailgate sticks out beyond the rear of the vehicle by more than _____ feet.

    A. 2   B. 4   C. 6   D. 8

7. Every vehicle shall have a parking brake system which will hold it, no matter what its load, on

   A. any grade on which it is operated which is free from ice and snow
   B. all grades under 15 degrees which are free from ice and snow
   C. all grades under 20 degrees which are free from ice and snow
   D. all grades under 25 degrees which are free from ice and snow

8. A portable heater may NOT be used in any vehicle cab

   A. unless the heater is secured
   B. unless the heater is of the electric filament type
   C. at any time
   D. without approval from the carrier

9. A driver is not generally allowed to drive for more than _____ hours following 8 straight hours off duty.

   A. 6   B. 8   C. 10   D. 12

10. Most drivers of large vehicles are NOT allowed to drive after they have been *on duty* for _____ hours.

    A. 16   B. 15   C. 14   D. 12

11. Generally, a driver may not be *on duty* for more than _____ hours in any 7 straight days.

    A. 40   B. 50   C. 60   D. 70

12. When a driver is riding in a vehicle, but is not driving and has no other responsibility, such time shall be counted as on-duty

    A. time
    B. time unless the driver is allowed 8 straight hours off duty upon arrival at the destination
    C. time unless the driver is allowed 6 straight hours off duty upon arrival at the destination
    D. time unless the driver is allowed 4 straight hours off duty upon arrival at the destination

13. Every driver must prepare an original and one copy of the driver's record of duty status which must be kept current by updating it

    A. every time a change of duty status is made
    B. every 24 hours
    C. every 8 hours
    D. at the end of each trip

14. Except for the name and main address of the carrier, all entries relating to the driver's record of duty status must be

    A. printed in ink or typed
    B. made by the carrier dispatcher
    C. made in front of a witness
    D. in the driver's handwriting

15. Which of the following is NOT required to be put in a driver's record of duty status? 15.____

    A. Time spent in a sleeper berth
    B. Total hours in each duty status
    C. Origin and destination
    D. The name and make of the vehicle

16. If any emergency delays a run which could normally have been completed within hours of service limits, the driver 16.____

    A. must still stop driving when the hours of service limits is reached
    B. may drive for 1 extra hour
    C. may drive for 2 extra hours
    D. may finish the run without violation

17. A driver declared *Out of Service* 17.____

    A. must take a road test before driving again
    B. must wait 72 hours before driving again
    C. must appeal to the Director of the Bureau of Motor Carrier Safety to drive
    D. can drive again only after hours of service requirements are met

18. If a vehicle on a trip is in a condition likely to cause an accident or breakdown, the driver should 18.____

    A. report it at the end of the run so repairs can be made
    B. drive at lower speeds for the rest of the run
    C. stop immediately unless going on to the nearest repair shop is safer than stopping
    D. change the route so as to get away from heavily traveled roads

19. If authorized federal inspectors find a vehicle which is likely to cause an accident or breakdown, it will be 19.____

    A. reported to the carrier for repair as soon as the vehicle is not scheduled
    B. reported to the carrier for repair at the end of the trip
    C. marked with an *out of service vehicle* sticker and not driven until repairs are made
    D. the driver will be held responsible and declared *out of service*

20. If the driver personally makes repairs on an *out of service* vehicle, the 20.____

    A. work must be approved by a mechanic
    B. driver must complete and sign a *Certification of Repairman* form
    C. work must be approved by a supervisor
    D. work must be approved by a federal inspector

21. Department of Transportation regulations covering the driving and parking of vehicles containing hazardous materials 21.____

    A. replace state and local laws
    B. prevent states and cities from having their own laws
    C. must be obeyed even if state or local laws are less strict or disagree
    D. should not be obeyed if state or local laws disagree

22. A vehicle which contains hazardous materials other than Class A or B explosives must be attended at all times by the

   A. driver
   B. driver, except when involved in other driver duties
   C. driver or a person chosen by the driver
   D. driver or a police officer

23. A vehicle containing Class A or B explosives or other hazardous materials on a trip is *attended*

   A. when the person in charge is anywhere within 100 feet of the vehicle
   B. as long as the driver can see the vehicle from 200 feet away
   C. when the person in charge is within 100 feet and has a clear view of the vehicle
   D. when the person in charge is resting in the berth

24. Except for short periods when operations make it necessary, trucks carrying Class A or B explosives cannot be parked any closer to bridges, tunnels, buildings or crowds of people than _____ feet.

   A. 50   B. 100   C. 200   D. 300

25. Smoking or carrying a lighted cigarette, cigar, or pipe near a vehicle which contains explosives, oxidizing or flammable materials is not allowed EXCEPT

   A. in the closed cab of the vehicle
   B. when the vehicle is moving
   C. at a distance of 25 feet or more from the vehicle
   D. when approved by the carrier

KEY (CORRECT ANSWERS)

1.	B	11.	C
2.	B	12.	B
3.	C	13.	A
4.	D	14.	D
5.	C	15.	D
6.	B	16.	D
7.	A	17.	D
8.	C	18.	C
9.	C	19.	C
10.	B	20.	B

21. C
22. B
23. C
24. D
25. C

EXAMINATION SECTION
TEST 1

DIRECTIONS: Each question or incomplete statement is followed by several suggested answers or completions. Select the one that BEST answers the question or completes the statement. *PRINT THE LETTER OF THE CORRECT ANSWER IN THE SPACE AT THE RIGHT.*

Questions 1-5.

DIRECTIONS: Questions 1 to 5 are to be answered ONLY on the basis of information given in the following statement.

Fatigue can make a driver incompetent. He may become less vigilant. He may lose judgment as to the speed and distance of other cars. His reaction time is likely to be slowed down, and he is less able to resist glare. With increasing fatigue, driving efficiency falls. Finally, nodding at the wheel results, from which accidents follow almost invariably.

Accidents that occur with the driver asleep at the wheel are generally very serious. With the driver unconscious, no effort is made either to prevent the accident or to lessen its seriousness. Accidents increase as day wears on and reach their peak in the early evening and during the first half of the night. Driver fatigue undoubtedly plays a significant part in causing these frequent night accidents.

1. Among the results of fatigue, the statement does NOT indicate   1.____

    A. lessened hearing effectiveness
    B. lessened vigilance
    C. loss of driving efficiency
    D. increased reaction time

2. According to the statement, accidents almost always follow as a result of   2.____

    A. fatigue
    B. slowed down reaction time
    C. nodding at the wheel
    D. lessened vigilance

3. According to the statement, accidents that occur in the early evening and during the first half of the night are   3.____

    A. always caused by driver fatigue
    B. very frequently the result of lessened resistance to glare
    C. usually due to falling asleep at the wheel
    D. more frequent than accidents in the afternoon

4. According to the statement, very serious accidents result from   4.____

    A. falling asleep at the wheel
    B. poor driving
    C. lack of judgment
    D. poor vision

27

5. Referring to the statement, which of the following conclusions is NOT correct?

    A. There are only two paragraphs in the entire statement.
    B. One paragraph contains four sentences.
    C. There are six words in the first sentence.
    D. There is no sentence of less than six words.

Questions 6-8.

DIRECTIONS: Questions 6 to 8 are to be answered ONLY on the basis of the information contained in the following chart.

CHART "A"
Mileage between New York and points in Nearby Connecticut

	New York	Bridgeport	Danbury	Hartford	New Haven	New London	Stamford	Waterbury
New York	--	61	66	115	80	132	39	91
Bridgeport	61	--	27	54	19	71	22	30
Danbury	66	27	--	57	33	85	31	30
Hartford	115	54	57	--	37	44	76	27
New Haven	80	19	33	37	--	52	41	21
New London	132	71	85	44	52	--	93	62
Stamford	39	22	31	76	41	93	--	52
Waterbury	91	30	30	27	21	62	52	--

6. According to Chart "A", the total mileage on a continuous trip from New York to Danbury, to Waterbury, to New London, to New York would be _____ miles.

    A. 280   B. 290   C. 316   D. 294

7. According to Chart "A", the mileage between New Haven and New London is the same as the mileage between

    A. Danbury and Hartford   B. Hartford and New London
    C. Stamford and New Haven   D. Waterbury and Stamford

8. According to Chart "A", which of the following pairs of cities are CLOSEST to each other?

    A. Bridgeport and Hartford   B. New York and Bridgeport
    C. Hartford and Danbury   D. New Haven and New London

9. If you drove a car for three quarters of an hour and kept it at a steady speed of 30 miles per hour for half an hour, and a steady speed of 40 miles per hour the rest of the time, you would have traveled _____ miles.

    A. 20   B. 25   C. 30   D. 35

10. The length of curb available for the parking of cars on a certain street is 435 feet on the south side and 405 feet on the north side. Assuming that the bumper to bumper length of the average car to be parked is 15 feet, the total number of cars that can be parked bumper to bumper on both sides of the street will be

    A. 56   B. 58   C. 60   D. 61

11. If the charges against a certain vehicle total $2,000 a year, and 74%, of this is for repairs and maintenance, then the annual cost of repairs and maintenance for that vehicle is

    A. $50   B. $100   C. $150   D. $300

12. The list price of truck A is $13,500 and that of truck B is $12,000. If the discount on truck A is 20% and the discount on truck B is 10%, how much cheaper would it be to buy truck A instead of truck B? _____ cheaper.

    A. $900   B. $450   C. $400   D. no

13. There are three garages located in a single block. Garage A has 3/4 of the capacity of Garage B and 2/3 of the capacity of Garage C. If 88 cars can be parked in Garage B, the total number of cars that can be parked in all of the three garages is

    A. 186   B. 205   C. 238   D. 253

14. The city purchases 5 vehicles costing $6,000 each, 3 vehicles costing $8,000 each, and 2 vehicles costing $13,000 each.
    The total cost of these vehicles is

    A. $67,000   B. $26,000   C. $80,000   D. $84,000

15. A car that averages 15 miles per gallon of gas is driven 135 miles. The gas tank is then filled to capacity by pumping in 12 gallons of gas. If the gas tank holds 18 gallons when full, the amount of gas in the tank at the beginning of the 135 mile trip must have been _____ gallons.

    A. 6   B. 9   C. 12   D. 15

16. The PROPER way to make a right turn from a two-way road into a one-way road is shown in Diagram

    A.

    B.

    C.

    D.

17. Traffic signs have standard shapes for certain types of information.

    For instance, a round sign indicat'es a railroad crossing

    The shape of signs giving general traffic information, such as "No Parking" and "Do Not Enter", is USUALLY

    A. Rectangular
    B. Octagona
    C. Triangular
    D. Diamond

17.____

18. The so-called "blind spot" in motor vehicle operation refers to the region

    A. to the left of the driver where vision is obstructed by the left car pillar
    B. immediately to the right of the driver where vision is obstructed by the right car pillar
    C. immediately to the rear right of the car
    D. immediately to the rear left of the car

18.____

19. The MOST desirable manner of driving around a curve on a highway is to

    A. slow the car down before reaching the curve, start around the curve, and accelerate just before entering the straight-away
    B. accelerate at the start of the curve and slow down just before entering the straight-away
    C. start into the curve at normal straight-away speed and apply the brakes if necessary
    D. slow the car down before reaching the curve, put the car into neutral, and coast around the curve

19.____

20. At a speed of 40 miles per hour, a driver is NOT considered to be "tailgating" (following too closely) until the distance between his car and the car he is following is less than _____ feet.

    A. 120   B. 60   C. 30   D. 0

20.____

21. You are driving alongside and to the rear of a large truck or bus as you approach and pass through an intersection. It is GOOD driving practice to

    A. accelerate   B. stay alongside
    C. blow your horn   D. stop

21.____

22. In approaching a traffic light such as the one shown at the right, you see that both left and right arrows are showing yellow. You should expect that shortly the right arrow light will go
    A. red, and the left arrow light will go green
    B. green, and the left arrow light will go red
    C. red, and the left arrow light will go red
    D. green, and the left arrow light will go green

22.____

23. With an automatic transmission, it is NOT desirable to shift from the "Drive" to the "Intermediate" or "Low" position when driving down a steep hill because

    A. there will be no increase in the braking power of the engine
    B. the gears will not engage while the car is in motion
    C. the low speed gears may engage with the low speed gears and wreck the transmission
    D. the car may skid if the road is slippery

23.____

24. When entering a two-way street from a private garage driveway, you

    A. do not have the right of way over traffic approaching from the right but only over traffic approaching from the left
    B. have the right of way over traffic approaching only from the right
    C. have the right of way over traffic approaching from both right and left
    D. do not have the right of way over traffic approaching from either right or left

24.____

25. In the state, a report need not be made to the Department of Motor Vehicles of any motor vehicle accident in which there is

    A. personal injury only
    B. personal injury and property damage of less than $100
    C. property damage of more than $100 but no personal injury
    D. injury to a horse or a dog

25.____

26. When the level of the liquid in a battery gets too low, it is necessary to put in some more

    A. battery acid   B. hydroxide
    C. distilled water   D. tap water

26.____

27. When the temperature indicator shows the engine running cold, even after the car has been driven for about ten minutes, the trouble is USUALLY caused by

    A. a broken fan belt
    B. a thermostat out of order
    C. a frozen radiator
    D. too little liquid in the cooling system

27.____

28. If you had to choose the oil for the crankcase of a new model passenger car motor, it would be SAFEST to use

    A. machine oil   B. transmission oil
    C. S.A.E. 20-20W oil   D. S.A.E. 50 oil

28.____

29. Inspection of your car's front tires shows that the tread is greatly worn on both the outer and inner edges of both tires. This is USUALLY a sign of

    A. underinflation
    B. overinflation
    C. misalignment
    D. unbalance

30. In washing the outside of a dirty car, the MOST effective cleanser is

    A. gasoline
    B. soap and water
    C. a detergent cleanser and water
    D. benzine

31. The MOST probable cause of a complete loss of oil pressure while driving is

    A. a crankcase oil level which is too low
    B. a crankcase oil level which is too high
    C. the use of too thick an oil
    D. an obstruction in the oil line

32. Proper tire inflation pressures are measured BEST by the

    A. eye; the tire should have the same shape on bottom as on top
    B. tire wear; the tire should wear evenly
    C. use of a tire gage
    D. hardness of the tire

33. In order to change a tire MOST safely and effectively, it is sufficient to have a

    A. jack, lug wrench, screwdriver, and wheel blocks
    B. screwdriver, lug wrench, and jack
    C. jack, screwdriver, hammer, and tire gage
    D. screwdriver, wheel blocks, and jack

34. While traveling on a two-way roadway having two traffic lanes in each direction and hearing the siren and seeing the flashing red light of a fire truck approaching from the rear, the driver of a motor vehicle should

    A. stop immediately
    B. pull over to the right-hand side of the roadway and proceed slowly in order not to block traffic
    C. pull over into the nearest intersection and stop
    D. pull over to the right-hand side of the roadway and stop

35. For the sole purpose of discharging a passenger, it is illegal to stop a motor vehicle

    A. within 10 feet of a fire hydrant during daylight hours
    B. in a marked bus stop when no bus is in sight
    C. in a zone marked "No Standing"
    D. in a zone marked "No Stopping"

36. The Vehicle and Traffic Law states that every motor vehicle must have its headlamps lit when being driven upon a public highway between

    A. dusk and dawn
    B. sunset and sunrise
    C. one-half hour before sunset and one-half hour after sunrise
    D. one-half hour after sunset and one-half hour before sunrise

37. With regard to "Stop" signs at intersections, which of the following statements is CORRECT?

    A. A motorist approaching a "Stop" sign need not come to a complete stop, but he must slow down before driving through the intersection or he loses the right of way.
    B. At an intersection with a "Stop" sign, a police officer directing traffic can wave on a motorist to permit him to pass through the intersection without stopping.
    C. At an intersection with a "Stop" sign, a motorist must stop no matter what the police officer who is directing traffic there signals him to do.
    D. After stopping for a "Stop" sign at an intersection, the driver of the stopped car has the right of way over all cars in, or approaching, the intersection.

38. You are driving straight ahead on a state highway marked with a double solid line down the middle (=========).
    You may

    A. nor cross this line
    B. cross from either side if there is no oncoming traffic
    C. cross only from right to left
    D. cross only from left to right

39. You are driving straight ahead on a state highway marked with a solid and broken double line down the middle (----------).
    You may

    A. not cross the line from either side
    B. cross the line from either side at any time with caution
    C. cross the line from the broken line side only
    D. cross the line from the solid line side only with extreme caution if traffic permits

40. It is LEAST correct to say that a broken line (----------) painted along the length of a state highway

    A. defines traffic lanes
    B. may not be crossed at any time
    C. may be crossed from either side
    D. may be crossed only if crossing will not interfere with traffic

41. When traveling at 30 miles per hour, a car with four wheel brakes MUST be able to stop within _____ feet.

    A. 45   B. 180   C. 67   D. 100

42. Square road traffic signs mean

    A. caution B. stop
    C. reduce speed D. danger

43. Statistics show that drivers under 20 years of age have a higher accident rate than other age groups. This is probably due to the fact that

    A. younger drivers are not as quick-witted as older ones
    B. it takes about seven years to develop good driving ability
    C. youthful drivers are inclined to take more chances
    D. most drivers are under 20 years of age

44. The MOST serious type of accident is caused by

    A. a rear-end collision
    B. a moving vehicle hitting a parked car
    C. the blowout of a tire
    D. a head-on collision

45. License plates MUST be fastened to a motor vehicle

    A. at least 12 inches from the top of the vehicle
    B. about 48 inches from the ground
    C. between 12 and 48 inches from the ground
    D. so as to be visible at 350 feet

46. The one of the following which may NOT be crossed at any time is a

    A. single solid line B. broken line
    C. solid and broken line D. double solid line

47. A "defensive driver" is one who

    A. makes allowances for the weaknesses of other drivers
    B. is always apologizing for his poor driving
    C. blames the other driver when he is involved in an accident
    D. drives very slowly at the extreme right side of the road

48. The height of a vehicle from the under side of the tire to the top of the vehicle, including load, may NOT be more than _____ feet.

    A. 15 B. 10 C. 8 D. 13

49. The one of the following which is NOT classed as a crime is

    A. parking overtime
    B. operating an unregistered motor vehicle
    C. driving without a license
    D. removing a serial number on an automobile engine

50. When a car starts to skid,

    A. the brakes should be applied forcefully
    B. the wheels should be turned in the opposite direction
    C. accelerate gently
    D. put the gears in neutral

50.____

KEY (CORRECT ANSWERS)

1.	A	11.	C	21.	B	31.	A	41.	C
2.	C	12.	D	22.	C	32.	C	42.	A
3.	D	13.	D	23.	D	33.	A	43.	C
4.	A	14.	C	24.	D	34.	D	44.	D
5.	D	15.	D	25.	D	35.	D	45.	C
6.	B	16.	D	26.	C	36.	D	46.	D
7.	D	17.	A	27.	B	37.	B	47.	A
8.	D	18.	D	28.	C	38.	A	48.	D
9.	B	19.	A	29.	A	39.	C	49.	A
10.	A	20.	B	30.	C	40.	B	50.	C

TEST 2

DIRECTIONS: Each question or incomplete statement is followed by several suggested answers or completions. Select the one that BEST answers the question or completes the statement. *PRINT THE LETTER OF THE CORRECT ANSWER IN THE SPACE AT THE RIGHT.*

1. Garage floors are to be kept free of oil and grease. The MAIN reason for such a rule is that oil and grease spots on a garage floor

    A. are breeding places for germs
    B. develop an unpleasant odor
    C. increase the chance of accidents
    D. show poor maintenance of vehicles

    1.____

2. After you return from lunch, you find that the new city car, which you parked at the curb, has a big scratch on the right front door. There is no one around.
The BEST thing for you to do is to

    A. get the license number of the vehicle that did the damage
    B. lay out some money for touch-up enamel and make the repair
    C. question passersby to find someone who will be willing to be a witness for the city
    D. report the damage to the garage foreman when you get back to the garage

    2.____

3. Suppose that the dispatcher has assigned you to drive a diesel truck during the regular operator's vacation. You have never operated this type of vehicle.
For you to tell this to the dispatcher would be

    A. foolish, because the dispatcher will think you do not want to cooperate
    B. sensible, because an inexperienced operator may damage the equipment
    C. foolish, because this is a good chance to learn how to operate a diesel truck
    D. sensible, because your regular assignment is an easier job than operation of the truck

    3.____

4. A motor vehicle operator is assigned to drive another city employee who is delivering several bulky packages to a city building. Upon arrival at the building, it would be MOST desirable for the motor vehicle operator to

    A. ask the other employee if he can give him any help in carrying the packages into the building
    B. leave for the garage as soon as the packages have been unloaded onto the sidewalk
    C. load the packages onto the employee's arms and go with him into the building in case he should need any assistance
    D. wait inside the vehicle for a few minutes and then leave

    4.____

5. When the light at an intersection changes from red to green, the driver of the car nearest the corner does not go ahead because he is waiting for pedestrians to clear the crosswalk.
If the driver of the car behind starts to blow his horn, the driver of the first car should

    A. call a policeman to give the horn-blower a ticket for making unnecessary noise
    B. get out of his vehicle so that he can explain why he could not go ahead

    5.____

C. pay no attention to the horn-blower and go ahead after the pedestrians are out of the way
D. lean out the window and shout angrily to the driver behind to stop blowing his horn

6. When he returns to the garage after driving several passengers during the day, a motor vehicle operator finds a set of keys on the floor of his vehicle.
The BEST thing for the operator to do is to

   A. keep the keys in case he sees any of these passengers again
   B. take the keys to the police department's lost property unit
   C. telephone each passenger to find out who lost the keys
   D. turn the keys over to his supervisor

7. The garage foreman has asked the motor vehicle operators in your garage to try out a new system for making out daily mileage reports.
Suppose that you do not think the new system is necessary. You should

   A. continue to use the old system to make out your daily mileage reports
   B. make out no reports until after the foreman decides on a final system
   C. use the new system even though you think the change is not necessary
   D. write a complaint to the foreman's supervisor that the new system is unnecessary

8. Recently, the city has been carrying on an anti-jaywalking drive for pedestrians.
The success of this drive is important to motorists MAINLY because

   A. the pedestrian will then be just as much at fault as the driver if there is an accident
   B. there will be less chance of a vehicle hitting a pedestrian
   C. traffic will move more quickly
   D. vehicles will then have the right of way

9. After you have driven a city official to an office building, he asks you to wait in the parked car saying that he will be out in fifteen minutes.
When, after twenty-five minutes, he still hasn't come out, it would be BEST for you to

   A. call the garage and ask what to do
   B. continue to wait in the car until he comes out
   C. enter the building to find the official and tell him that fifteen minutes are past and he may be late for other appointments
   D. go for a cup of coffee since he seems to be delayed, but come right back

10. A motor vehicle operator who does NOT clearly understand the dispatcher's route instruction should first

    A. ask an experienced motor vehicle operator the best route to follow
    B. ask the American Automobile Association to recommend a route
    C. ask the dispatcher to explain the route more fully
    D. figure out his own route using an official map

Questions 11-13.

DIRECTIONS: Answer Questions 11 to 13 ONLY on the basis of the information given in the following paragraph.

A National Safety Council study of 685,000 traffic accidents reveals that most accidents happen under "safe" conditions - in clear, dry weather, on straight roads, and when traffic volumes are low. The point is, most accidents can be attributed to lapses on the part of the drivers rather than traffic or road conditions or deliberate law violations. Most drivers try to avoid accidents. Why, then, do so many get into trouble? A major cause is the average motorist's failure to recognize a hazard soon enough to avoid it entirely. He does not, by habit, notice the clues that are there for him to see. He takes constant risks in traffic without even knowing it. These faulty seeing habits plus the common distractions that all drivers must deal with, such as hurry, worry, daydreaming, impatience, concentration on route problems, add up to a guaranteed answer - an accident.

11. According to a study by the National Safety Council, MOST accidents can be blamed on

    A. curving, hilly roads
    B. errors made by drivers
    C. heavy streams of traffic
    D. wet, foggy weather

12. According to the above paragraph, an IMPORTANT reason why the average motorist gets into an accident is that he

    A. does not see the danger of an accident soon enough
    B. does not try to avoid accidents
    C. drives at too great a speed
    D. purposely takes reckless chances

13. According to the above paragraph, it is NOT reasonable to say that drivers are distracted from their driving and possibly involved in an accident because they

    A. are impatient about something
    B. concentrate on the road ahead
    C. hurry to get to where they are going
    D. worry about some problem

Questions 14-17.

DIRECTIONS: Answer Questions 14 to 17 ONLY on the basis of the information given in the following paragraph.

If a good automobile map is studied thoroughly before a trip is started, much useful information can be learned. This information may help to decrease the cost of and the time required for the trip and, at the same time, increase the safety and comfort of the trip. The legend found on the face of the map explains symbols and markings and the kind of roads on various routes. The legend also explains how to tell by width, color, or type of line whether the road is dual- or multiple-lane, and whether it is paved, all-weather, graded, earth, under construction, or proposed for construction. Federal routes are usually shown by a number within a shield and state routes by a number within a circle. The legend also shows scale of miles on a bar marked to indicate the distance each portion of the bar represents on the earth's surface. Distances between locations on the map are shown by plain numerals beside the route lines; they indicate mileage between marked points or intersections. Add the mileage numbers shown along a route to determine distances.

14. According to the above paragraph, the markings on the road map will show   14.____

    A. a different color for a road proposed for construction than for one under construction
    B. a double line if a road is a dual-lane road
    C. what part of a road is damaged or being repaired
    D. which roads on state routes have more than two lanes

15. The above paragraph does NOT mention as a possible advantage of studying a good   15.____
    road map before beginning a trip the

    A. increase in interest of the trip
    B. reduction in the chance of an accident on the trip
    C. saving of money
    D. saving of time

16. According to the above paragraph, in order to find the total mileage of a certain route, a   16.____
    motorist should add the numbers

    A. on the bar scale in the legend
    B. between marked points beside the route lines
    C. inside a shield along the route
    D. within a circle along the route

17. According to the above paragraph, the legend on a road map includes information which   17.____
    a motorist could use to

    A. choose the best paved route
    B. figure the toll charges
    C. find the allowable speed limits
    D. learn the location of bridges

Questions 18-22.

DIRECTIONS: The following report is similar to those used in departments for reporting accidents. Read it carefully, then answer Questions 18 to 22 using ONLY the information given in the report.

REPORT OF ACCIDENT

Date of Accident: 3/21
Department Vehicle

Date of Report: 3/24
Time: 3:43 P.M.
Vehicle No. 2

Operator's Name: James Doe
Title: Motor Vehicle Operator
Vehicle Code No.: 22-187
License Plate No.: 3N-1234

Operator's Name: Richard Roe
Operator's Address: 841 W. 68th St.
Owner's Name: Jane Roe
Owner's Address: 2792 Beal Ave.
License Plate No.: 8Y-6789

Damage to Vehicle: right rear
fender ripped, hubcap dented,
rear bumper twisted.
Place of Accident: 8th Ave. &
48th Street

Damage to Vehicle: grill, radiator
right side of front bumper,
front fender and headlight crushed.

Description of Accident: I was driving east on 48th Street with the green light. I was almost across 8th Avenue when Ford panel truck started north and crashed into my rear right fender. Driver of Ford used abussive language and accused me of rolling into his truck.

Persons Injured

Name Richard Roe   Address 841 W. 68th Street

Name _____   Address _____

Name _____   Address _____

Witnesses

Name Richard Roe   Address 841 W. 68th Street

Name John Brown   Address 226 South Avenue

Name Mary Green   Address 42 East Street

Report Prepared by James Doe

Title MVO   Badge No. 11346

18. Of the following words used in the report, the one spelled INCORRECTLY is

    A. abussive   B. accused   C. radiator   D. twisted

19. The city vehicle involved in this accident can BEST be identified

    A. as a panel truck
    B. as a passenger car
    C. by the badge number of the operator
    D. by the vehicle code number

20. According to the information in the report, the right of way belonged to

    A. neither vehicle   B. the Department vehicle
    C. the vehicle that took it   D. vehicle No. 2

21. An entry on the report that seems to be INCORRECT is the

    A. first witness   B. second witness
    C. third witness   D. owner's name

22. According to the description of the accident, the diagram that would BEST show how and where the vehicles crashed is:

Questions 23-24.

DIRECTIONS: Answer Questions 23 and 24 ONLY on the basis of the information given in the following paragraph.

When heavy rain beats on your windshield, it becomes hard for you to see ahead and even harder to see objects to the side - despite good windshield wipers. Also, the danger zone 'becomes longer when it is raining because the car takes longer to stop on wet streets. Remember that the danger zone of your car is the distance within which you can't stop after you have seen something on the road ahead of your car. The way to reduce the length of the danger zone of your car while driving is to reduce speed.

23. From the information in the above paragraph, you cannot tell if the danger zone of your car

    A. can be made smaller
    B. is greater on a rainy day
    C. is greater on cloudy days than on clear days
    D. is the distance in back of the car or in front of the car

24. According to the above paragraph, the danger zone of a moving car is affected by

    A. the condition of the street and the speed of the car
    B. many things which cannot be pinned down, in addition to the mechanical condition of the car
    C. the number of objects to the front and to the side
    D. visibility of the road and the reaction time of the driver

25. In the city it is not permissible for the operator to drive in any direction on a one-way street if he is operating a

   A. fire department vehicle in response to an alarm
   B. police department vehicle in response to a radio call
   C. hospital department ambulance in response to a call on that street
   D. United States mail truck while collecting mail

26. In the city, a flashing yellow light at an intersection indicates that the driver should

   A. blow his horn before making a left or right turn
   B. come to a full stop, then proceed with caution
   C. not make any turns but may proceed directly ahead
   D. proceed through the intersection with caution

27. A driver of a passenger vehicle would be guilty of a violation of city traffic regulations if he

   A. parked his car in an area marked "1 Hour Parking" and proceeded to wash the car
   B. remained in the driver's seat while the car stood alongside a fire hydrant during the daytime
   C. stopped in an area marked "Taxi Stand" to discharge a passenger
   D. stopped to pick up a passenger in an area marked "No Standing"

28. According to the State Vehicle and Traffic Law, when there is a motor accident in which a person is injured, an accident report MUST be filed with the Bureau of Motor Vehicles by

   A. both the driver and owner of the car responsible for the accident
   B. each driver separately if more than one car was involved
   C. the driver of only the car responsible for the accident
   D. the injured person or his representative

29. In the city, a driver is allowed to park in a metered area without putting a coin in the parking meter if the

   A. car being parked is a city vehicle
   B. driver stays in the car
   C. meter is covered with a bag marked "out of order"
   D. meter shows there is still unused time on it

30. A traffic sign cannot be read because the printing on it is covered with snow. A motor vehicle operator should bring his vehicle to a full stop when he reaches this sign if it is shaped like

   A. △   B. □   C. ◇   D. ⬡

Questions 31-34.

DIRECTIONS: Questions 31 to 34 are diagrams of road markings used in the state. From Column I, select the traffic rule that applies to each road marking. Indicate your answer in the space at the right.

COLUMN I

31.

A. crossing allowed from either dotted line side

31._____

B. crossing allowed from either side at any time

32.

C. crossing allowed from either side at any time

32._____

D. line may be crossed cautiously except in the city

33.

E. no crossing allowed from either side at any time

33._____

34.

34._____

35. Keeping the gas tank of a car well-filled is a good practice MAINLY because it helps

35._____

    A. add weight to the car, resulting in smoother riding
    B. avoid frequent stops for gasoline
    C. prevent watering of the gasoline due to excess condensation of moisture
    D. the operator to keep a close check on gas consumption of the vehicle

36. The odometer is the instrument on a motor vehicle which indicates the

36._____

    A. amount of electric current flowing to or from the battery
    B. number of miles the car has traveled
    C. oil pressure needed to pump lubricating oil to the engine
    D. speed, in miles per hour, at which the car is traveling

37. You can think of a car as made of two major units: A - the engine; B - the body and chassis. The one of the following which is used to disconnect the power of A from B while keeping the car in gear is the

37._____

    A. clutch   B. differential
    C. transmission   D. universal

38. Of the following, the MAIN purpose of the fan connected to the automobile engine is to cool the   38._____

   A. air as it goes into the engine
   B. engine oil as it goes through the oil filter
   C. exhaust manifold
   D. water in the radiator

Questions 39-48.

DIRECTIONS: Answers to Questions 39 to 48, inclusive, are based on the map appearing on Page 10.

39. To drive from the courthouse to the railroad station, the MOST direct allowable route is   39._____

    A. across 2nd Street, Avenue A, 1st Street
    B. through the underpass in Square Park
    C. 2nd Street, Park Drive, and 1st Street
    D. 2nd Street, Park Drive, and 3rd Street

40. A left turn is prohibited at   40._____

    A. 1st Street and Cross Avenue
    B. 1st Street and Park Drive
    C. Avenue C and 2nd Street
    D. 4th Street and Transverse Boulevard

41. The direction of traffic on Front Street is   41._____

    A. east and west
    B. northwest and southeast
    C. southwest and northeast
    D. the same as on Transverse Boulevard

42. When driving from the Y.M.C.A. to the dock by the SHORTEST allowable route, the direction of travel would be, in order,   42._____

    A. east, south, west
    B. southwest, west, south
    C. southwest, south
    D. west, south

43. When driving from the post office to the movie by the SHORTEST allowable route, the direction of travel would be, in order,   43._____

    A. north, east, south, east
    B. south, east, south, west
    C. south, southeast, north, east
    D. south, southeast, east

44. The two buildings which face on both Cross Avenue and Avenue D are the   44._____

    A. bank and the department store
    B. department store and the hotel
    C. department store and the library
    D. library and the museum

45. The MOST direct allowable route that a truck may take from the factory to the bus terminal is Avenue A and   45._____

    A. 2nd Street, Avenue B, 5th Street
    B. 3rd Street, Transverse Boulevard, 5th Street
    C. 5th Street
    D. Transverse Boulevard, 5th Street, 2nd Street

46. The SHORTEST allowable route from the office building on 1st Street to the parking lot is 1st Street,

    A. Avenue E
    B. Avenue F
    C. Park Drive, 2nd Street, Avenue E
    D. Park Drive, Main Street, Avenue F

47. In driving from the museum to the theatre, the MOST direct route allowable for a passenger car is 3rd Street,

    A. Avenue C
    B. Park Drive, 1st Street, Avenue C
    C. Park Drive, 1st Street, Cross Avenue
    D. Square Park underpass, 1st Street, Avenue C

48. The shopping center is on a street where traffic is

    A. one way, north
    B. one way, south
    C. two ways, east and west
    D. two ways, north and south

49. Of the following, the MAIN disadvantage of using alcohol as an anti-freeze in the cooling system of a motor vehicle is that alcohol

    A. is poisonous and cannot be handled safely
    B. is thin and finds holes in the cooling system
    C. boils and evaporates at an undesirably high temperature
    D. boils and evaporates at an undesirably low temperature

50. To keep the clutch pedal fully down while starting the engine of a gearshift car is

    A. *bad* practice because it wears out the clutch
    B. *good* practice because it reduces the work required of the starter
    C. *bad* practice because it will cause the car to jerk forward if it is in gear
    D. *good* practice because it saves fuel

KEY (CORRECT ANSWERS)

1. C	11. B	21. A	31. C	41. B
2. D	12. A	22. A	32. E	42. C
3. B	13. B	23. C	33. A	43. B
4. A	14. D	24. A	34. D	44. C
5. C	15. A	25. D	35. C	45. B
6. D	16. B	26. D	36. B	46. C
7. C	17. A	27. A	37. A	47. B
8. B	18. A	28. B	38. D	48. D
9. B	19. D	29. D	39. C	49. D
10. C	20. B	30. D	40. A	50. B

EXAMINATION SECTION
TEST 1

DIRECTIONS: Each question or incomplete statement is followed by several suggested answers or completions. Select the one that BEST answers the question or completes the statement. *PRINT THE LETTER OF THE CORRECT ANSWER IN THE SPACE AT THE RIGHT.*

1. The state has set up a system of rigid controls for the licensing of drivers. The MAIN reason for these controls is to
   A. insure that people using the highways carry proper identification
   B. make sure that cars are regularly inspected to prevent accidents due to mechanical failure
   C. maintain up-to-date records of the number of cars using the roads
   D. protect the public from irresponsible and dangerous drivers

2. A traffic regulation of the department of traffic states that the driver of any vehicle shall not turn such vehicle so as to proceed in the opposite direction upon any street in a business district.
   According to this regulation, you are prohibited from
   A. making a U-turn on any street
   B. making a U-turn on a street in the business district
   C. backing your car to park on a business street
   D. backing your car on any street where there is traffic

3. Often, when parking regulations in an area are changed, it is the custom for the first day or two of the change to issue warnings to violators, rather than summonses
   Of the following, the MAIN reason for issuing warnings rather than summonses is to
   A. give motorists a chance to become acquainted with the new regulations
   B. judge public reaction to the change
   C. show the public that the new regulations will be strictly and impartially enforced
   D. see if the new regulations will work

4. Employees who deal with the public may sometimes be required to take an action, in accordance with the rules and regulations of their department, which may cause a citizen to become angry or resentful.
   In order to keep good public relations in such a situation, it would be MOST preferable for the employee to say to the citizen:
   A. "My job is to uphold the rules and regulations even if you don't like them."
   B. "Rules and regulations are made to be obeyed by everyone."
   C. "Let me explain as best I can the reasons for my action."
   D. "I'm only doing the job I'm getting paid for, so don't get made at me."

5. Assume that as a city employee on official business, you have parked a city vehicle at a metered parking space. When you come back later, you see a police officer writing out a summons and the red flag (parking time expired) shows on the parking meter.
In this situation, you should
   A. point out to the police officer that the car's license plate shows that this is a city car
   B. explain to the police officer in a polite manner that you are on city business and ask him not to give you the summons
   C. accept the summons as you are obviously illegally parked
   D. call your supervisor, explain what is going on, and ask him what you should do

5.____

6. One day, during the absence of your regular supervisor, your temporary supervisor assigns you to some work that you have done before but instructs you to do it a different way than you have done it in the past.
Of the following, it would be BEST for you to
   A. do the work the way you have been doing it in the past since this is a better method
   B. explain to your temporary supervisor the method you have used in the past
   C. follow the instructions of your temporary supervisor without question
   D. speak to other employees to see if they have been assigned to this work and how they are doing it

6.____

7. The BEST reason for requiring employees to learn the rules and regulations of their jobs is to
   A. help them do their work safely and correctly
   B. prepare them for future promotion to higher positions
   C. develop their study habits
   D. test their alertness

7.____

8. Departments generally require that an employee who is ill and cannot report to work call his supervisor to tell him that he is ill.
Of the following, the BEST reason for having such a requirement is to make it possible for the supervisor to
   A. keep an accurate record of absences
   B. make plans, if necessary, to cover the work of the absent employee
   C. call the absent employee back to make sure that he is really at home
   D. mail important instructions to the absent employee

8.____

9. If you find that there isn't enough room on a required department form to include all the information you want to give, it would be BEST to
   A. not use the form
   B. write as much as will fit on the form and tell your supervisor orally about the rest of the information
   C. leave out some of the less important information
   D. attach another sheet with the additional information written on it

9.____

10. A *scofflaw* is a term applied to a person who has
    A. accumulated many unanswered traffic summonses
    B. his driver's license revoked by the state commissioner of motor vehicles
    C. insufficient automobile liability insurance
    D. failed to renew his driver's license but continues to drive a car

11. A flashing red traffic signal means
    A. stop and then proceed with caution
    B. slow down and proceed with caution
    C. street closed to traffic
    D. wait for green

12. Which one of the following shapes of road traffic signs would you LEAST expect to find in the city?
    A. ▽   B. ▭   C. ⬡   D. ◯

13. An intersection with a flashing yellow traffic signal means MOST NEARLY
    A. *Do Not Enter the Intersection*
    B. *Proceed With Caution*
    C. *Watch Out For Pedestrians Crossing*
    D. *Reduce Speed and Stop*

14. Suppose you are driving straight ahead at moderate speed on a two-way street and have entered an intersection when the traffic light facing you changes from green to red and green.
    In this situation, it would be BEST for you to
    A. come to a stop
    B. back up out of the intersection
    C. blow your horn and speed up
    D. continue across the intersection

15. Peach Street is one-way northbound and is crossed by Apple Street which is a one-way eastbound.
    If there are no traffic or other directional signals at the intersection, it would be CORRECT to make a
    A. right turn from Apple Street into Peach Street
    B. left turn from Peach Street into Apple Street
    C. right turn from Peach Street into Apple Street
    D. left or right turn from either street if there is no cross traffic

16. You are driving a car. In front of you is a moving car with its trunk lid in the air.
    Of the following, the CHIEF traffic hazard in this situation is the
    A. excessively slow precautionary driving speed of driver in front of you
    B. poor rear visibility for the driver in front of you
    C. poor visibility ahead for you
    D. possibility of some contents of the open trunk falling onto the roadway

17. If you have a blowout while driving at 50 miles an hour on an expressway, the BEST thing for you to do is to
    A. steer the car at a sharp angle onto the shoulder of the road and coast to a stop
    B. put the car in low gear, turn off the ignition, and apply the brakes slowly
    C. turn off the ignition, put the car in neutral gear, and coast to a stop
    D. grip the steering wheel tightly to keep the car steady, let up on the gas pedal, and brake slowly

17.____

18. If you are driving a car with automatic transmission and the rear end of the car begins to skid to the right, the BEST way to get out of the skid is to steer the car to the
    A. right, avoid any hard braking, and keep the car in *drive*
    B. left, pump the brake smoothly, and keep the car in *drive*
    C. right, pump the brake smoothly, and put the car in *neutral*
    D. left, avoid any hard braking, and put the car in *neutral*

18.____

19. Most cars have automatic chokes which help to start a cold engine.
    The choke performs this function by
    A. regulating battery current to produce a hot spark
    B. pre-heating the gasoline before it enters the engine
    C. reducing the amount of air going to the carburetor
    D. directing the current from the generator directly to the starting motor

19.____

20. Driving with a window open is recommended MAINLY in order to prevent the accumulation inside the car of an excess of
    A. moisture   B. carbon monoxide
    C. sulfur dioxide contaminants   D. battery acid fumes

20.____

21. The MAIN reason for requiring cars to be parked parallel to and as close to a curb as possible is to
    A. allow drivers to get out without stepping onto the roadway
    B. leave the greatest amount of space open for passing traffic
    C. provide parking space for the greatest number of cars
    D. reduce damage to parked cars

21.____

22. The MAIN purpose of extending the program of *alternate side of the street parking* to many residential areas is to
    A. relieve traffic congestion
    B. make it easier to clean the streets
    C. reduce the number of traffic accidents
    D. reduce the number of cars parked on the streets overnight

22.____

23. The CHIEF reason for installing a *progressive system* of traffic lights on the main one-way streets in Manhattan is to
    A. reduce speeding
    B. speed up the loading and unloading of trucks
    C. reduce the volume of traffic using these streets
    D. move more traffic with less delay

23.____

5 (#1)

Questions 24-35.

DIRECTIONS: The following is an accident report similar to those used by city departments for reporting accidents. Questions 24 through 35 are to be answered ONLY on the basis of the information contained in this accident report.

ACCIDENT REPORT

Date of Accident: April 12,...
Place of Accident: 17th Ave. & 22nd Street
Time of Accident: 10:15 A.M.
City Vehicle:
  Operator's Name: John Smith
  Title: Motor Vehicle Operator
  Badge, No. 17-5427
  Operator License No.: S2874-7513-3984
  Vehicle Code No.: B7-8213
  License Plate No. BK-4782
  Damage to Vehicle: Left front fender dented; broken left front headlight and parking light; windshield wipers not operating

Date of Report: April 15,...Friday

Vehicle No. 2
  Operator's Name: James Jones
  Operator's Address: 427 E. 198th St.
  Operator's License No.: J0836-0882-7851
  Owner's Name: Michael Greene
  Owner's Address: 582 E. 92nd St.
  License Plate No.: 6Y-3916
  Damage to Vehicle: Left front bumper bent inward; broken left front headlight; grille broken in three places

DESCRIPTION OF ACCIDENT: I was driving on 17th Avenue, a southbound one-way street, and made a slow, wide turn west into 22nd Street, a two-way street, because a moving van was parked near the corner on 22nd Street. As I completed my turn, a station wagon going east on 22nd Street hit me. The driver of the station wagon said he put on his brakes but he skidded on some oil that was on the street. The driver of the van saw the accident from his cab and told me that the station wagon skidded as he put on his brakes. Patrolman Jack Reed, Badge No 24578, who was at the southeast corner of the intersection, saw what happened and made some notes in his memo book.

Persons Injured - Names and Addresses. If none, state NONE.

Witnesses – Names and Addresses. If none, state NONE.
    Jack Reed, 33-47 83rd Drive
    Thomas Quinn, 527 Flatlands Avenue

                                      Report Prepared By: John Smith
                                      Title: Motor Vehicle Operator

24. According to the report, the accident happened on   24._____
    A. Friday, between 6:00 A.M. and 12:00 Noon
    B. Friday, between 12:00 Noon and 6:00 P.M.
    C. Tuesday, between 6:00 A.M. and 12:00 Noon
    D. Monday, between 12:00 Noon and 6:00 P.M.

25. Which one of the following numbers is part of the driver's license of the   25._____
    operator of the city vehicle?
       A. 3984   B. 5247   C. 4782   D. 7851

26. The address of the driver of the city vehicle is   26._____
       A. not given in the report   B. 427 E. 198th Street
       C. 582 E. 92nd Street   D. 33-47 83rd Drive

27. A section of the report that is NOT properly filled out is   27._____
       A. Witnesses   B. Description of the Accident
       C. Persons Injured   D. Damage to Vehicle

28. According to the accident report, if the only witnesses were the patrolman   28._____
    and the van driver, then the van driver's name is
       A. Reed   B. Quinn   C. Jones   D. Greene

29. According to the report, the diagram that would BEST show where the cars   29._____
    collided and where the moving van ( ) was parked at the time of the accident
    is

30. According to the information in the report, it would be MOST correct to say that   30._____
    Michael Greene was
       A. the driver of the station wagon   B. a passenger in the station wagon
       C. the owner of the moving van   D. the owner of the station wagon

31. According to the information in the report, a factor which contributed to the   31._____
    accident was
       A. a slippery road condition
       B. bad brakes of one car
       C. obstructed view of traffic light caused by parked van
       D. windshield wipers on the city car not operated properly

32. When a driver makes a report such as this, it is MOST important that he
    A. print the information so that his supervisor can read it quickly
    B. keep it short because a long report makes it look as though he is hiding a mistake
    C. show clearly why the accident isn't his fault
    D. give all the facts accurately and completely

33. The first two letters or numbers in the vehicle code number indicate the type of vehicle. Two letters indicate an 8 passenger-8 cylinder car; two numbers indicate a 6 passenger-8 cylinder car; a letter followed by a number indicates a 6 passenger-6 cylinder car; a number followed by a letter indicates an 8 cylinder station wagon.
    The car involved in this accident is, therefore, a(n)
    A. 8 cylinder station wagon
    B. 6 passenger-6 cylinder car
    C. 6 passenger-8 cylinder car
    D. 8 passenger-8 cylinder car

34. From the information in the report, the driver of the city vehicle may have been partially at fault because he
    A. appears to have begun his turn from the wrong lane
    B. appears to have entered the wrong lane of traffic
    C. did not blow his horn as he made the turn
    D. should have braked as he made the turn

35. What evidence is there in the report that the two vehicles collided in front, drivers' side?
    A. The description of the accident
    B. There is no such evidence
    C. The type of damage to the vehicles
    D. The van driver's statement

Questions 36-42.

DIRECTIONS: Questions 36 through 42 are to be answered SOLELY according to the information given in the following passage.

The parking meter was designed many years ago primarily as a mechanism to assist in reducing overtime parking at the curb, to increase parking turnover, and to facilitate enforcement of parking regulations. That the meter has accomplished these basic functions is attested to by its use in an increasing number of cities.

A recent survey of cities in the United States indicates that overtime parking was reduced 75% or more in 47% of the cities surveyed, and to a lesser degree in 43% of the cities surveyed, making a total of 90% of the cities surveyed where the parking meter was found to be effective in reducing overtime parking at the curb.

A side effect of the reduction in overtime parking is the increase in parking turnover. Approximately 89% of the places surveyed found meters useful in this respect. Meters also encourage even spacing of cars at the curb. Unmetered curb parking is often so irregular that it wastes space or makes parking and departure difficult.

The effectiveness of parking meters, in the final analysis, rests upon the enforcement of regulations by squads of enforcement agents who will diligently patrol the metered area. The task of checking parking time is made easier with meters since violations can be checked from a moving vehicle or by visual sightings of an agent on foot patrol, and the laborious process of chalking tigress is greatly reduced. It is reported that, after meters have been installed, it takes on the average only 25% of the time formerly required to patrol the same area.

The fact that a parker activates a mechanism that immediately begins to count time, that will indicate exactly when the parking time has expired, and that will advertise such fact by showing a red flag, tends to make a parker more conscious of his parking responsibilities than the hit and miss system of possible detection by a patrolman.

36. According to the above passage, when the parking meter was introduced, one of its major purposes was NOT to
    A. cut down overtime curb parking
    B. make curb parking available to more parkers
    C. bring in revenue from parking fees
    D. make it easier to enforce parking regulations

37. In the cities surveyed, how effective was the installation of parking meters in cutting down overtime parking?
    A. It was effective to some degree in all the cities surveyed.
    B. It was ineffective in only one out of every ten cities surveyed.
    C. It reduced overtime parking at least 75% in most cities surveyed.
    D. There was only a small reduction in overtime parking in 43% of the cities surveyed.

38. When overtime parking is reduced by the installation of parking meters, an accompanying result is
    A. an increase in the amount of parking space
    B. the use of the available parking spaces by more cars
    C. the faster movement of traffic
    D. a decrease in the number of squads required to enforce traffic regulations

39. According to the above passage, on streets which have parking meters, as compared with streets which are unmetered,
    A. there is less waste of parking space
    B. parking is more difficult
    C. parking time limits are irregular
    D. drivers waste more time looking for an empty parking space

40. According to the above passage, the use of parking meters will NOT be effective unless
    A. parking areas are patrolled in automobiles
    B. it is combined with the chalking of tires
    C. the public cooperates
    D. there is strict enforcement of parking regulations

41. According to the above passage, one reason why there is greater compliance with parking regulations when parking time is regulated by meters rather than by a foot patrolman chalking tires is that
    A. overtime parking becomes glaringly evident to everyone
    B. the parker is himself responsible for operating the timing mechanism
    C. there is no personal relationship between parker and enforcing officer
    D. the timing of elapsed parking time is accurate

42. In the last paragraph of the above passage, the words *a parker activates a mechanism* refers to the fact that a motorist
    A. starts the timing device of the meter working
    B. parks his car
    C. checks whether is meter is working
    D. starts the engine of his car

Questions 43-45.

DIRECTIONS: Questions 43 through 45 are to be answered SOLELY according to the information given in the following passage.

When markings upon the curb or the pavement of a street designate parking space, no person shall stand or park a vehicle in such designated parking space so that any part of such vehicle occupies more than one such space or protrudes beyond the markings designating such a space, except that a vehicle which is a size too large to be parked within a single designated parking space shall be parked with the front bumper at the front of the space with the rear of the vehicle extending as little as possible into the adjoining space to the rear, or vice-versa.

43. The regulation quoted above applies to parking at any
    A. curb or pavement
    B. metered spaces
    C. street where parking is permitted
    D. parking spaces with marked boundaries

44. The regulation quoted above prohibits the occupying of more than one indicated parking space by
    A. any vehicle
    B. large vehicles
    C. small vehicles
    D. vehicles in spaces partially occupied

45. In the regulation quoted above, the term vice-versa refers to a vehicle of a size too large parked with
    A. front bumper flush with front of parking space it occupies
    B. front of vehicle extending into front of parking space
    C. rear bumper flush with rear of parking space it occupies
    D. rear of vehicle protruding into adjoining parking space

KEY (CORRECT ANSWERS)

1. D	11. A	21. B	31. A	41. A
2. B	12. D	22. B	32. D	42. A
3. A	13. B	23. D	33. B	43. D
4. C	14. D	24. C	34. B	44. C
5. C	15. C	25. A	35. C	45. C
6. B	16. B	26. A	36. C	
7. A	17. D	27. C	37. B	
8. B	18. A	28. B	38. B	
9. D	19. C	29. D	39. A	
10. A	20. B	30. D	40. D	

TEST 2

DIRECTIONS: Each question or incomplete statement is followed by several suggested answers or completions. Select the one that BEST answers the question or completes the statement. *PRINT THE LETTER OF THE CORRECT ANSWER IN THE SPACE AT THE RIGHT.*

Questions 1-3.

DIRECTIONS: Questions 1 through 3 are to be answered SOLELY on the basis of the information given in the following passage.

Drivers and pedestrians face additional traffic hazards during the fall months. Changing autumn weather conditions, longer hours of darkness, and the abrupt nightfall during the evening rush hour can mean more traffic deaths and injuries unless drivers and pedestrians exercise greater care and alertness. Drivers must adjust to changing light conditions; they cannot use the same driving habits and attitudes at dusk as they do during daylight. Moderate speed and continual alertness are imperative for safe driving at this time of year.

1. According to the above passage, two new traffic risks which motorists face in the fall are
    A. changing weather conditions and more traffic during the evening rush hour
    B. fewer hours of daylight and sudden nightfall
    C. less care by pedestrians and a change in autumn weather conditions
    D. more pedestrians on the street and longer hours of darkness

1._____

2. According to the above passage, there may be more traffic deaths and injuries in the fall MAINLY because both pedestrians and drivers are
    A. distracted by car lights being turned on earlier
    B. hurrying to get home from work in the evening
    C. confronted with more traffic dangers
    D. using the streets in greater numbers

2._____

3. According to the above passage, an essential requirement of driving safely in the Fall is
    A. eyes down on the road at all times
    B. very slow speed
    C. no passing
    D. reasonable speed

3._____

Questions 4-6.

DIRECTIONS: Questions 4 through 6 are to be answered SOLELY according to the information given in the following passage.

A traffic sign is a device mounted on a fixed or portable support through which a specific message is conveyed by means of words or symbols. It is erected by legal authority for the purpose of regulating, warning, or guiding traffic.

A regulatory sign is used to indicate the required method of traffic movement or the permitted use of a highway. It gives notice of traffic regulations that apply only at specific places or at specific times that would not otherwise be apparent.

A warning sign is used to call attention to conditions on or near a road that are actually or potentially hazardous to the safe movement of traffic.

A guide sign is used to direct traffic along a route or toward a destination, or to give directions, distances, or information concerning places or points of interest.

4. According to the above passage, which one of the following is NOT a *regulatory* sign?
    A. Right turn on red signal permitted
    B. Trucks use right lane
    C. Slippery when wet
    D. Speed limit 60

5. According to the above passage, which one of the following LEAST fits the description of a *warning* sign?
    A. No right turn
    B. Falling rock zone
    C. Low clearance 12 ft. 6 in.
    D. Merging traffic

6. According to the above passage, which one of the following messages is LEAST likely to be conveyed by a *guide* sign?
    A. South bound
    B. Signal ahead
    C. Bridge next exit
    D. Entering city

Questions 7-8.

DIRECTIONS: Questions 7 and 8 are to be answered SOLELY on the basis of the information given in the following passage.

The State Vehicle and Traffic law provides for all new driving licenses to be issued on a six-month probationary basis. The probationary license will be cancelled if during this six-month period the driver is found guilty of tailgating, speeding, reckless driving, or driving while his ability is impaired by alcohol. The license will also be cancelled if the driver is found guilty of two other moving traffic violations. If a probationary license is cancelled, the driver must wait for sixty days after the date of cancellation before applying for another license, and if the application is approved, the applicant must meet certain additional requirements, including a new road test, before a new license will be issued.

7. It is MOST reasonable to assume that the main purpose of the law referred to above was to
    A. find out who is responsible for most traffic accidents
    B. make the road tests more difficult for new drivers to pass
    C. make it harder to get a driver's license
    D. serve as a further check on the competence of new drivers

3 (#2)

8. According to the above passage, we may assume that a probationary license will NOT be cancelled if a driver is found guilty of   8._____
   A. passing a red light and failing to keep to the right on a road
   B. following another vehicle too closely
   C. overtime parking at a meter on two or more occasions
   D. driving at 60 miles an hour on a road where the speed limit is 50 miles an hour

9. At a certain garage, there are 216 cars. Of these, half are assigned to Department P, one-third to Department Q, one-ninth to Department R, and the rest to Department S.   9._____
   How many cars are assigned to Department S?
   A. 9   B. 12   C. 18   D. 24

10. In August, a car travels 572 miles; in September, 438 miles; in October, 898 miles; and in December, it travels 609 miles.   10._____
    If the five-month average from August through December was 673 miles traveled a month, then the number of miles traveled in November was
    A. 638   B. 706   C. 774   D. 848

11. Suppose the Units R, S, and T gave out a total of 1,715 parking tickets.   11._____
    If Unit R gave out twice as many tickets as Unit S, and Unit T gave out twice as many tickets as Unit R, the number of tickets given out by Unit S is
    A. 270   B. 255   C. 245   D. 225

12. A car travels at the average rate of 40 miles an hour on the highway.   12._____
    If it takes 5 hours to make a trip of 150 miles, 2/3 of which is on the highway and the rest on city streets, what was the average rate of speed of the car on city streets?
    A. 20   B. 25   C. 30   D. 35

13. A motorist uses 27 gallons of gas on a trip of 351 miles.   13._____
    How many gallons of gas would he use if he took a trip of 624 miles under the same condition?
    A. 45   B. 46   C. 47   D 48

14. If the taxi rate in the city is $1.75 for the first 1/5 of a mile and 25¢ for each additional 1/5 of a mile, a passenger whose fare was $4.75 traveled _____ miles.   14._____
    A. $2^1/_5$ B. $2^3/_5$ C. $3^2/_5$ D. $3^4/_6$

Questions 15-20.

DIRECTIONS: Questions 15 through 20 are to be answered SOLELY on the basis of the information given in the following table.

RIVER CITY – WEEKLY REPORT – WEEK ENDING 7/17				
	No. of Parking Meters		No. of Summonses Issued	
	On Streets	In Parking Lots	Overtime Parking	Other Violations
Zone P	840	1,680	460	130
Zone Q	1,400	420	1,200	480
Zone R	920	460	520	180
Zone S	1,550	620	800	200
Zone T	750	2,250	400	120

15. Compared to the total number of parking meters *On Streets*, the total number of parking meters in *In Parking Lots* is
    A. 30 less B. 60 less C. 90 more D. 30 more

16. Of all the summonses given out in Zone S during the week, what percent were for *Other Violations*?
    A. 25 B. 20 C. 15 D. 5

17. The average number of summonses issued for *Overtime Parking* in each Zone during the week is MOST NEARLY
    A. 225 B. 340 C. 675 D. 1,090

18. Suppose that an employee can check 40 meters an hour on the streets and 3 times that number in a parking lot.
    If an employee works 7 hours a day, excluding a lunch period, and each meter is checked twice a day, how many employees must be assigned daily to Zone P to check all the meters?
    A. 7 B. 8 C. 10 D. 12

19. Suppose that a new parking lot is to be built in Zone Q.
    How many metered spaces must there be in this new parking lot so that Zone Q will have the same ratio of street meters to parking lot meters as Zone R?
    A. 700 B. 440 C. 350 D. 280

20. Comparing the total number of parking meters with the total of summonses issued, it is CORRECT to state that the zone with the _____ number of meters issued the _____ number of summonses.
    A. smallest; smallest
    B. largest; largest
    C. smallest; largest
    D. largest; smallest

21. Of the following, the one which is NOT a part of the ignition system of an automobile is the
    A. battery
    B. distributor
    C. master cylinder
    D. spark plugs

22. Of the following, the BEST practice to follow when driving is to stay at least
    A. one car length behind the vehicle directly in front for each 20 miles per hour of speed of your own vehicle
    B. 20 feet behind the vehicle directly in front for each 10 miles per hour of speed of your own vehicle
    C. twice as far behind the vehicle directly in front on expressways as on city streets
    D. two car lengths behind the vehicle directly in front at any speed on city streets

23. When applied to a motor vehicle, the term *wheel alignment* USUALLY refers to the adjustment of the _____ wheel(s).
    A. front
    B. rear
    C. front and rear
    D. steering

24. As an automobile makes a sharp turn, the rear wheel which is on the inside of the turn
    A. rotates at a faster speed than the outside rear wheel
    B. rotates at a slower speed than the outside rear wheel
    C. rotates at the same speed as the outside rear wheel
    D. slips slightly while the outside rear wheel does not slip

25. The MOST accurate of the following statements about driving and driving practices is that
    A. an angry driver is more likely to have an accident than a calm driver
    B. high beam headlights penetrate fog better than low beam headlights
    C. letting air out of the tires greatly improves traction on snow
    D. wearing tinted glasses makes night driving safer by reducing the light from oncoming vehicles

26. In driving, you hear a fire siren behind you.
    The procedure to follow is
    A. decrease your speed slowly, coming to a full stop
    B. increase your speed to keep well ahead of the fire apparatus
    C. pull over to the right as far as possible and stop
    D. turn off at the first available intersection

27. When you are approaching an intersection with the lights, you see another vehicle traveling against the lights about to cross your path.
    The PROPER thing for you to do is
    A. call a traffic policeman at once and tell him the situation
    B. continue on your way even if an accident should occur since you have the right of way
    C. give the proper signal and stop immediately

28. The tail light of a passenger car MUST be visible at night for a distance of _____ feet.
    A. 350
    B. 400
    C. 450
    D. 500

29. The headlights of a passenger car MUST be able to show up objects at a distance of _____ feet.
    A. 350   B. 400   C. 450   D. 500

30. A broken white line on a city street indicates
    A. separate traffic lanes which may be crossed if they do not interfere with traffic
    B. no crossing from the solid line side of the road but crossing is allowed from the broken line side with proper precaution
    C. separate opposing traffic lanes where no crossing is allowed
    D. separate opposing traffic lanes where crossing is allowed under favorable conditions

31. A solid and broken line indicates
    A. separate traffic lanes which may be crossed if they do not interfere with traffic
    B. no crossing from the solid line side of the road but crossing is allowed from the broken side with proper caution
    C. separate opposing traffic lanes where no crossing is allowed
    D. separate opposing traffic lanes where crossing is allowed under favorable conditions

32. A double solid line indicates
    A. separate traffic lanes which may be crossed if they do not interfere with traffic
    B. no crossing from the solid line side of the road but crossing is allowed from the broken line side with proper caution
    C. separate opposing traffic lanes where no crossing is allowed
    D. separate opposing traffic lanes where crossing is allowed under favorable conditions

33. The BEST reason for NOT passing another car when going up a hill is that
    A. the car you are passing is being slowed down by the steepness of the grade
    B. the strain of speeding up your car may damage your engine
    C. you can't get the additional speed while climbing a hill
    D. you can't see beyond the crest while climbing it

34. The BEST reason for driving slowly when approaching a busy intersection is that
    A. a bus stop is frequently found at a busy intersection
    B. busy intersections provide more opportunity for accidents
    C. a policeman is assigned to regulate traffic at such an intersection
    D. traffic controls must be observed

7 (#2)

35. While waiting in traffic for a red light to change, the PROPER procedure is to
    A. pull up your handbrake and move over to the curb
    B. put your gears into neutral ready to shift into low
    C. race your motor to be sure it doesn't stall
    D. turn off your ignition while keeping the foot brake on

35.____

36. If a driver loses his operator's license, the PROPER procedure is to
    A. apply for a new license
    B. drive without a license until it is time to renew the lost one
    C. get a letter from the police department explaining the entire situation
    D. use a friend's license when he must drive

36.____

37. If the accelerator on a car you are driving fails to shut off while the car is in motion after you have removed your foot from the pedal, you should
    A. blow your horn to warn vehicles and pedestrians in front of you to clear the road
    B. call a patrolman to give you assistance
    C. drive to the garage for expert help
    D. release the clutch and turn off the ignition immediately

37.____

38. Shock, a condition often brought on by a serious injury to any part of the body, is dangerous MAINLY because
    A. body temperature rises too high
    B. blood pressure becomes very high
    C. the injured person remains unconscious for a long time
    D. there is a reduction in the flow of blood to the vital organs

38.____

39. If a little battery fluid accidentally gets into a person's eye, the FIRST thing to do is to
    A. call a doctor or ambulance
    B. find out what safety rule was broken
    C. put several drops of clean olive oil in the eye
    D. wash the eye with large quantities of plain water

39.____

40. If an unconscious person is found on the sidewalk, the BEST of the following to do right away is to
    A. cover him to keep him warm
    B. give him sips of hot tea or coffee
    C. move him into the nearest building
    D. shake him gently to arouse him

40.____

41. To keep germs from entering a wound, it is BEST to
    A. apply a sterilized dressing to the wound
    B. put an antiseptic on the wound
    C. squeeze the wound gently to make it bleed
    D. wash the wound with soap and hot water

41.____

42. If several persons are injured in an accident, the one who should be treated FIRST is the person who
    A. has a compound fracture
    B. has severe burns
    C. is bleeding seriously
    D. is in the greatest pain

    42._____

43. Suppose that a car ran a total of 9,888 miles in a four-month period from September through December, inclusive. It used 234 gallons of gas in September, 203 gallons in October, 191 gallons in November, and 196 gallons in December.
    The average number of miles it traveled per gallon of gasoline was
    A. 10   B. 11   C. 12   D. 12½

    43._____

44. A government agency has a policy of replacing 1/3 of its vehicles each year. Of the twenty vehicles the agency is requesting in the budget, 95% are replacements.
    If the request is granted, the total number of vehicles in the agency will be
    A. 19   B. 27   C. 58   D. 61

    44._____

45. Car A averaged 21 miles to a gallon of gas. Car B averaged 18 miles to a gallon of gas. Each car used 14 gallons of gas.
    Car A traveled _____ miles more than Car B.
    A. 42   B. 39   C. 28   D. 14

    45._____

46. A garage has a gas tank with a capacity of 500 gallons. During the week, 210 gallons were used, and 340 gallons were delivered at the end of the week to fill the tank.
    How many gallons of gas were in the tank at the beginning of the week?
    A. 160   B. 210   C. 340   D. 370

    46._____

47. The list price of Vehicle A is $42,000 and that of Vehicle B is $38,000. The city can get a discount of 20% of the list price on Vehicle A and 10% of the list price on Vehicle B.
    How much cheaper can the city buy Vehicle than Vehicle B?
    A. $200   B. $600   C. $2,000   D. $6,000

    47._____

48. In a certain bureau, there are four employees who each earn $2,500 a month, twelve employees who each earn $3,000 a month, and two employees who each earn $3,500 a month.
    The monthly payroll for all these employees is
    A. $49,000   B. $51,000   C. $53,000   D. $55,000

    48._____

49. If the average passenger car needs 120 square feet of parking space, the LARGEST number of such cars that could be parked in a garage with a usable floor area that measures 70 feet by 100 feet is
    A. 52   B. 54   C. 56   D. 58

    49._____

50. On a certain bridge, the toll for a motorcycle is 5/7 the toll for a passenger 50.____
car, and 1/3 the toll for a truck.
If the toll for a passenger car is $1.75, then the toll for a truck on this bridge is
A. $2.50   B. $3.75   C. $5.00   D. $6.25

KEY (CORRECT ANSWERS)

1.	B	11.	C	21.	C	31.	B	41.	C
2.	C	12.	A	22.	B	32.	C	42.	C
3.	D	13.	D	23.	A	33.	D	43.	C
4.	C	14.	B	24.	B	34.	B	44.	C
5.	A	15.	A	25.	A	35.	B	45.	A
6.	B	16.	B	26.	C	36.	A	46.	D
7.	D	17.	C	27.	C	37.	D	47.	B
8.	C	18.	C	28.	D	38.	B	48.	C
9.	B	19.	D	29.	A	39.	D	49.	D
10.	D	20.	D	30.	A	40.	D	50.	B

TEST 3

DIRECTIONS: Each question or incomplete statement is followed by several suggested answers or completions. Select the one that BEST answers the question or completes the statement. *PRINT THE LETTER OF THE CORRECT ANSWER IN THE SPACE AT THE RIGHT.*

1. To straighten out a car in which the rear wheels have started to skid to the right, the recommended procedure is for the driver to steer to the
   A. left, take the car out of gear, and apply the brakes gently
   B. right, ease up on the accelerator pedal, and apply the brakes firmly
   C. left, ease up on the accelerator pedal, and avoid braking
   D. right, east up on the accelerator pedal, and avoid braking

   1.____

2. When driving in heavy traffic for a long distance on a four-lane one-way avenue, it is GOOD practice to
   A. drive in the left lane
   B. drive in the middle lane
   C. drive in the right lane
   D. change from one lane to another from time to time

   2.____

3. According to the state vehicle and traffic law and good driving practice, the distance between wheels and curb when a car is parked parallel to the curb should be NO more than _____ inches.
   A. 12   B. 10   C. 8   D. 6

   3.____

4. Poor driving is indicates when a driver
   A. gives up the right of way to allow another car to enter a stream of traffic in front of him
   B. positions his car so as to prevent a possible accident to a following car unable to see the danger
   C. in his desire to be careful, drives slowly in both the right-hand lane and in the passing lane
   D. frequently gives up the right of way to show his courtesy

   4.____

Questions 5-6.

DIRECTIONS: Questions 5 and 6 are to be answered SOLELY on the information contained in the following passage.

Many experiments have been made on the effects of alcoholic beverages. These studies show that alcohol decreases alertness and efficiency. It decreases self-consciousness and, at the same time, increases confidence and feelings of ease and relaxation. It impairs attention and judgment. It destroys fear of consequences. Usual cautions are thrown to the winds. Habit systems become disorganized. The driver who uses alcohol tends to disregard his usual safety practices. He many not even be aware that he is disregarding them. His reaction time slows down; normally quick reactions are not possible for him. To make matters worse, he may not realize he is slower. His eye muscles may be so affected that his vision is not normal. He cannot correctly judge the speed of his car or of any other car. He cannot correctly estimate distances being covered by each. He becomes a highway menace.

5. The paragraph states that the drinking of alcohol makes a driver
   A. more alert
   B. less confident
   C. more efficient
   D. less attentive

6. From the above passage, it is reasonable to assume that a driver may overcome the bad effects of drinking alcohol by
   A. being more cautious
   B. relying on his good driving habits to a greater extent than normally
   C. watching the road more carefully
   D. waiting for the alcohol to wear off before driving

7. For better driving effectiveness on snowy and icy streets in winter driving, it is BEST to drive as usual but with
   A. slower speeds and without sudden speed or direction change
   B. slightly deflated tires for better traction
   C. tighter brakes than usual to permit more positive stops
   D. tighter steering than usual to give more positive control

8. In night driving, when passing oncoming cars that have bright headlights, it is wise to
   A. use colored glasses to help cut down the glare
   B. slow down and fix your eyes on the right-hand side of the road to cut down the glare
   C. speed up so as to pass quickly and reduce the effect of the glare
   D. switch on your high beam lights to see clearly enough to pass safely

9. When making a left turn from a one-way street into a one-way avenue, you should approach the turn in the
   A. left lane of the street and turn so as to leave the intersection in the left lane of the avenue
   B. right lane of the street and turn so as to leave the intersection in the left lane of the avenue
   C. right lane of the street and turn so as to leave the intersection in the lane to the right of the middle of the avenue
   D. left lane of the street and turn so as to leave the intersection in the lane to the right of the middle of the avenue

10. According to good driving practice, the MINIMUM distance for signaling your intention to make a turn is _____ feet.
    A. 20   B. 40   C. 70   D. 100

11. When a tire blows out while you are driving, the recommended procedure for stopping safely is to grip the steering wheel hard to control the car, let up on the accelerator, and
    A. put the car into neutral and apply a firm hard pressure on the brake pedal
    B. keep the car in gear and apply a firm hard pressure on the brake pedal
    C. keep the car in gear and apply the brakes very gently and slowly
    D. put the car into neutral and apply the brakes very gently and slowly

12. When a hand signal is used by a driver to indicate a stop or a decrease in speed of his vehicle, the hand and arm should be extended
    A. horizontally with palm forward
    B. horizontally with palm down
    C. upward
    D. downward

13. You are driving north on the East River Drive and as you start around a curve, you see that something has happened ahead, and all northbound traffic has come to a stop about 300 feet ahead of you.
    You should
    A. step hard on the brake to stop your car immediately
    B. maintain your speed, roll down your window, extend your arm, and wave it as a warning to the drivers behind you
    C. maintain your speed and make a quick stop when you reach the line of cars if they are still stopped
    D. pump your brake pedal and bring your car to a stop slowly

14. The MOST serious result of driving through flooded sections of streets or highways is USUALLY
    A. wet brakes
    B. a wet exhaust system
    C. a wet master cylinder
    D. a wet intake manifold

15. When you have to drive at night in a dense fog, it is MOST desirable to drive
    A. slowly, using the low beam of the headlights
    B. slowly, using parking lights only
    C. slowly, using the high beam of the headlights
    D. very slowly, using the high beam of the headlights and blowing your horn steadily

16. The length of roadway needed by the average driver when stopping in a hurry from a speed of 60 miles per hour while traveling on a superhighway is MOST NEARLY _____ feet.
    A. 150
    B. 60
    C. 300
    D. 200

17. Driving with a car window partly open at all times, regardless of the weather or season of the year, is advisable MAINLY to
    A. maintain a reasonable car temperature
    B. prevent fogging of the car windows
    C. permit the escape of unpleasant odors from the interior
    D. maintain proper ventilation of the interior

18. When using an acceleration lane to enter a main traffic lane of a highway on which the speed limit is 60 miles per hour, it is DESIRABLE to
    A. enter the main traffic lane at the speed of the vehicles using the main traffic lane
    B. enter the main traffic lane at about one-half the speed of the vehicles using the main traffic lane
    C. enter the main traffic lane slowly but without stopping
    D. come to a complete stop before entering the main traffic lane

19. You are driving at the speed limit on a four-lane one-way avenue, and a driver behind you sounds his horn and starts to pass you.
    The PROPER procedure for you to follow is to
    A. block him to keep him from exceeding the speed limit
    B. let him pass and overtake him later
    C. decrease your speed slightly and let him go by
    D. increase your speed so as to get out of his way

20. Driving at night is more dangerous than driving in the daytime because
    A. there are more cars on the road at night
    B. visibility is poorer at night than during the day
    C. drunken drivers are more numerous
    D. most drivers drive faster at night than during the day

21. A manufacturer recommends a tire pressure of 26 pounds for a certain tire. For a LONGEST life and even tread wear, it is desirable to use an actual tire pressure of _____ pounds.
    A. 23   B. 26   C. 30   D. 35

22. If brakes squeak when they are being applied, the MOST probable cause is
    A. worn brake linings
    B. improperly lubricated brake linings
    C. too little brake fluid in the system
    D. a stiff master cylinder piston

23. When you pull off the road to investigate trouble with your engine, you must be careful not to touch the exhaust manifold because you may
    A. upset the engine timing   B. upset the air-fuel ratio
    C. get a severe electrical shock   D. get a severe burn

24. The liquid level in an automobile storage battery should always be above the plates.
    It is good practice, however, to maintain the liquid level in the battery at a
    A. low level throughout the year – just above the plates
    B. higher level in the summer than in winter
    C. up to the very top throughout the year
    D. higher level in the winter than in summer

25. *Shimmy* of the front wheels of an automobile USUALLY occurs as a result of
    A. tire unbalance   B. over-lubricated wheel bearings
    C. a broken shock absorber   D. a broken front spring

26. After starting an engine in cold weather, to warm it up as fast as possible with least harm, the BEST of the following techniques would be to
    A. pump the accelerator pedal up and down for about a minute before driving off at normal speed
    B. hold down the accelerator steadily for about 10 seconds before driving off at normal speed

C. let the engine idle normally for about a minute before driving off at normal speed
D. let the engine idle normally for about a minute before driving off at slow speed

27. The MAIN purpose of a carburetor is to
    A. keep the engine from overheating
    B. cool the engine oil
    C. control the circulation of cooling water
    D. mix gasoline with air

27.____

28. A driver should understand the term *right of way* to be the
    A. description of any roadway
    B. description of the extreme right-hand lane of any roadway
    C. privilege of passing a slower driver on the right of the roadway
    D. privilege of the immediate use of the roadway

28.____

29. The horn on a motor vehicle is being used properly when it is sounded to
    A. hasten the movement of slowly moving traffic at an intersection
    B. indicate to the driver behind you that you wish to pass
    C. warn a pedestrian of possible danger
    D. clear a crosswalk of pedestrians so as to permit the turning of cars on a green light

29.____

30. When you leave your vehicle unattended while it is parked in a proper parking space, it is legal to have the engine
    A. running with the transmission lever in neutral as long as the brake is set
    B. stopped with the key in the ignition lock and without the brake set as long as the car is in reverse gear
    C. stopped, the ignition locked by removal of the ignition key, the brake set, and the car windows open
    D. stopped, the ignition locked by removal of the ignition key, the car in reverse gear instead of set brakes, and all windows closed with all doors locked

30.____

31. If you are driving south, in a business district, on a two-way avenue and you wish to make a turn to go back north on the same avenue, the PROPER way to make the turn is to
    A. drive around a block and turn north into the avenue
    B. keep to the right, back into a one-way west street, and then turn north into the avenue
    C. keep to the center of the avenue, turn left into a one-way east street, back into the avenue heading north
    D. wait until the flow of traffic permits, and then make a simple U-turn

31.____

32. In the city, when the use of lights is required while driving any motor vehicle other than an authorized emergency vehicle, it is illegal to use
    A. white parking lights
    B. low beam white headlights
    C. low beam yellow headlights
    D. white or yellow multiple beam headlights

33. A properly posted *Play Street* sign indicates that the street is
    A. closed to all vehicular traffic
    B. closed to all vehicular traffic except to those drivers who have business or who reside on the street
    C. open to all traffic, but extreme caution is to be used in driving
    D. open to passenger vehicles but not to trucks

34. Except where official signs indicate a different maximum speed limit, the speed limit in the city is _____ miles per hour.
    A. 25   B. 28   C. 30   D. 35

35. Parking regulations are being violated in a parking meter space during the hours in which the posted parking meter regulations are in force if
    A. upon parking, a coin is not deposited because of an unexpired time interval still showing on the meter
    B. after parking and depositing a coin, a second coin is deposited later to extend the period of parking the car
    C. a large commercial vehicle occupies more than a single parking space and a coin has been deposited only in the forward meter
    D. a coin has been properly deposited, but the car has been parked for the purpose of changing a tire

36. While driving on a one-way street, you find that you must stop because a large moving van is blocking the way while the driver is jockeying the vehicle back and forth in order to park it. Cars accumulate behind you, and the drivers begin blowing their horns.
    You should
    A. start blowing your horn in the hope of attracting a policeman
    B. get out of the car and look for a policeman to clear the traffic jam
    C. signal to the cars in back of you to back up so that all cars can back out of the street
    D. wait until there is sufficient clearance to drive safely past the van

37. You are returning to the garage after having dropped a passenger off near his office. The passenger and his office are well known to you since you frequently drive him about the city. You suddenly discover that he forgot his glasses on the seat of the car.
    You should
    A. telephone him to tell him that his glasses have been found and can be picked up at the garage
    B. hold on to the glasses so that you can return them the next time you drive him

C. drive on and turn the glasses in at the garage
D. drive right back to his office to give him the glasses

38. You have left the garage and have stopped at your first place of call to pick up a passenger. On opening the car door for him, you see a briefcase on the floor of the car.
You should
    A. excuse yourself and return immediately to the garage with the briefcase
    B. telephone your dispatcher as soon as you can and tell him what you found
    C. open the briefcase as soon as you can to find out who owns it so that you can return it
    D. be patient and wait until you return to the garage at the end of the day to turn the briefcase in

38.____

39. You have been sent to a city office to pick up an important package. When you arrive at 9:30 A.M., you learn that the only person authorized to give you the package will not be in until noon.
You should
    A. return to the garage immediately
    B. try to talk someone else into giving you the package
    C. telephone your dispatcher immediately
    D. wait for the authorized person to arrive

39.____

40. A dispatcher gives you instructions to travel a certain route in an assignment with a strict time schedule. You know that a large emergency evacuation is causing long delays on the route.
You should
    A. tell the dispatcher about the probable delay
    B. choose a different route which will get you to your destination on time
    C. follow the given route and attempt to make up time before and after the delay
    D. follow the given route and explain why you were late at your destination

40.____

41. You have driven a city executive to a meeting in the morning, and you have to wait a half-hour for him to come out to drive him to his next appointment. Parking is permitted in the area but there is no open space available except by a fire hydrant.
Of the following, the BEST thing for you to do is to
    A. double park, remain in the driver's seat, and keep the motor running
    B. park by the hydrant, remain in the driver's seat, and keep the motor running
    C. park by the hydrant, remain in the driver's seat, and shut the motor off
    D. park by the hydrant, shut the motor off, get out of the car but remain in the immediate vicinity

41.____

42. Upon the complete loss of oil pressure while a car is in operation, it is BEST that the car be
    A. pulled over to the side of the road and the engine stopped immediately for inspection
    B. pulled over to the side of the road, and a repair truck called to install a new oil pump
    C. driven four miles to the department repair shop for inspection and repair
    D. driven on its usual rounds and the incident reported to the department garage at the end of the day

43. If the *charge and discharge* indicator, whether a meter or a light, suddenly indicates *discharge* while a car is in normal operation, it is BEST that the car be
    A. stopped immediately and then be towed to the department repair shop for repairs
    B. stopped immediately and a repair truck called to install a new battery
    C. drive on its usual round and the incident reported to the department garage at the end of the day
    D. drive four miles to the department repair shop for inspection and repair

44. The causes of MOST automobile accidents can be traced to
    A. heavy traffic conditions
    B. mistakes made by drivers
    C. mechanical failure of vehicles
    D. bad weather conditions

45. While you are driving a city official, you see a car up ahead suddenly swerve sharply to the right, climb the sidewalk, and crash into a store front. As your car is slowed, you see a crowd gather, and you notice that a policeman appears.
    You should
    A. pull over and help get the injured driver out of his car
    B. get the attention of the policeman and tell him who was at fault
    C. copy the car's license number
    D. drive on to your destination

Questions 46-50.

DIRECTIONS: Questions 46 through 50 are to be answered SOLELY on the basis of the information contained in the following accident report.

9 (#3)

REPORT OF ACCIDENT

Date of Accident: Nov. 27 — Time: 2:20 P.M. — Date of Report: 11/28

Department Vehicle
Operator's Name: John Doe
Title: Motor Vehicle Operator
Vehicle Code No.: 17-129
License Plate No: IN-2345
Damage to Vehicle: Crumpled and torn front left fender, broken left headlight, front bumper bent outward on left side left front hubcap dented badly and torn off.

Vehicle No. 2
Operator's Name: Richard Roe
Operator's Address: 983 E. 84 St.
Owner's Name: Robert Roe
Owner's Address: 983 E. 84 St.
License Plate No.: 9Y-8765
Damage to Vehicle: Crumpled right front fender, broken right headlight and parking light, right side of front bumper badly bent.

Place of Accident: 71st & 3rd Ave.

Description of Accident: I was driving west on 71st Street and started to turn north into 3rd Avenue since the light was still green for me. I stopped at the crosswalk because a woman was in the middle of 3rd Avenue crossing from west to east. She had just cleared by car when a Ford sedan, going north, crashed into my left front fender. The light was green on 3rd Avenue when he hit me. The woman who had crossed the avenue in front of me, and whose name I got as a witness, was standing on the corner when I got out of the car.

Persons Injured

_____   _____

_____   _____

Mrs. Mary Brown   Witness   215 E. 71st Street

Report prepared by John Doe
Title: Motor Vehicle Operator
Badge #17832

10 (#3)

46. According to the description of the accident, the diagram that would BEST show how and where the vehicles crashed and the position of the witness (X) is
    A. A   B. B   C. C   D. D

47. The pedestrian mentioned in the description of the accident was
    A. an unknown woman
    B. Mary Brown
    C. an unknown man
    D. Robert Roe

48. According to the information in the report, the one of the following statements which is INCORRECT is:
    A. Both cars were moving when the accident happened
    B. One car was moving when the accident happened
    C. The department car was headed northwest when the accident happened
    D. The traffic lights had changed just before the accident happened

49. From the description of the accident as given in the report, the accident would PROBABLY be classified as
    A. premeditated
    B. calamitous
    C. minor
    D. fatal

50. From a reading of the accident report, it can be seen that
    A. the witness was completely unfamiliar with the neighborhood in which the accident took place
    B. the accident occurred in the early hours of the morning
    C. neither driver owned the vehicle he was driving
    D. it was raining when the accident took place

KEY (CORRECT ANSWERS)

1.	D	11.	C	21.	B	31.	A	41.	C
2.	B	12.	D	22.	A	32.	A	42.	A
3.	A	13.	D	23.	D	33.	B	43.	D
4.	C	14.	A	24.	B	34.	A	44.	B
5.	D	15.	A	25.	A	35.	B	45.	D
6.	D	16.	C	26.	D	36.	D	46.	C
7.	A	17.	D	27.	D	37.	D	47.	B
8.	B	18.	A	28.	D	38.	B	48.	A
9.	A	19.	C	29.	C	39.	C	49.	C
10.	D	20.	B	30.	C	40.	A	50.	C

EXAMINATION SECTION
TEST 1

DIRECTIONS: Each question or incomplete statement is followed by several suggested answers or completions. Select the one that BEST answers the question or completes the statement. *PRINT THE LETTER OF THE CORRECT ANSWER IN THE SPACE AT THE RIGHT.*

1. Your car's brakes transform one type of energy into another. Which of the following BEST describes the change?   1._____

    A. Kinetic energy into heat
    B. Centrifugal force into force of impact
    C. Gravity into kinetic energy
    D. Centrifugal force into heat

2. Which of the following qualities is MOST important in driving a motor vehicle?   2._____

    A. Fast reaction time
    B. Courage
    C. Skill
    D. Judgment

3. Glaring headlights add to night driving hazards. Which of the following should you NOT do?   3._____

    A. Lower your headlight beams in advance of meeting other cars
    B. Reduce your speed when facing headlight glare
    C. Focus your eyes downward on the center line of the road instead of up into the oncoming lights
    D. Lower your headlight beams when following another car

4. The following institutions lend money for the purchase of cars. Which charges the LOWEST rate of interest?   4._____

    A. Banks
    B. Pawnshops
    C. Installment finance companies
    D. Personal loan companies

5. Under what conditions do we find the GREATEST traction?   5._____

    A. Wet concrete pavement
    B. Dry concrete pavement
    C. Dry concrete pavement with sand on it
    D. Bumpy, uneven pavement

6. Your danger zone is   6._____

    A. the longest distance at which you can see and recognize danger
    B. your stopping distance
    C. the distance at which a vehicle in back of your car is following
    D. your braking distance

7. For sound financing of a purchase of an automobile, you would have to raise a down payment of AT LEAST _____ of the value of the car.

   A. 10 percent
   B. 25 percent
   C. one-third
   D. one-half

8. Which of the following is characteristic of older paved roads and not of modern highways?

   A. Median strips
   B. High road crowns
   C. Road banking
   D. Long sight distances

9. Designed especially for slowing down to prepare to leave the freeway is the

   A. deceleration lane
   B. median strip
   C. ramp
   D. road shoulder

10. When you find yourself getting very sleepy while driving on a long trip, the BEST remedy is

    A. black coffee
    B. fresh air
    C. Benzedrine
    D. sleep

11. Which of these four types of insurance does a bank or other lender require the purchaser to have?

    A. Collision
    B. Comprehensive
    C. Liability
    D. Medical payment

12. The professional specialist who plans the operation of highways is the

    A. Commissioner of Motor Vehicles
    B. highway engineer
    C. traffic engineer
    D. Commissioner of State Police

13. Which of the following is the CORRECT formula?

    A. Braking distance + stopping distance = reaction distance
    B. Reaction distance + stopping distance = braking distance
    C. Reaction distance + braking distance = stopping distance
    D. Reaction distance + danger zone = stopping distance

14. Which of the following is a YIELD sign?

15. When you drive around a curve, which of the following helps you to do it safely?

    A. Centrifugal force
    B. Friction
    C. Kinetic energy
    D. Force of impact

16. If you are involved in an accident, which of the following things should you NOT do? 16.____
    A. Show your driver's license and vehicle registration card and make note of the information on those of the driver of the other car.
    B. If any person seems to be seriously injured, place him in your car immediately and proceed at once to the nearest hospital.
    C. Submit accident reports as indicated by your state and local regulations.
    D. Notify your insurance company.

17. No person should drive in dense fog unless it is absolutely necessary. When it does prove necessary, he should use 17.____
    A. parking lights
    B. high-beam headlights
    C. low-beam headlights
    D. no lights, to avoid distortion of vision

18. Under which of the following would you classify the wearing of glasses to aid vision? 18.____
    A. Compensation   B. Field of vision
    C. Correction   D. Adjustment

19. The key words for driving on a slippery surface are 19.____
    A. firmly and accurately   B. gently and gradually
    C. strongly and steadily   D. quickly and surely

20. Which of the following types of insurance is MOST important to a car owner? 20.____
    A. Collision   B. Liability
    C. Comprehensive   D. Medical payment

KEY (CORRECT ANSWERS)

1.	C	11.	A
2.	D	12.	C
3.	D	13.	C
4.	A	14.	D
5.	B	15.	A
6.	B	16.	B
7.	C	17.	C
8.	B	18.	C
9.	A	19.	B
10.	D	20.	B

TEST 2

DIRECTIONS: Each question or incomplete statement is followed by several suggested answers or completions. Select the one that BEST answers the question or completes the statement. *PRINT THE LETTER OF THE CORRECT ANSWER IN THE SPACE AT THE RIGHT.*

1. Which of these four items is a *grade separation*? 1.____

   A. A divided highway
   B. A change in the slope of a hill
   C. Bushes planted between two roadways on which traffic moves in opposite directions
   D. A cloverleaf

2. Which of the following blood alcohol concentrations should be used to establish that a driver is *under the influence of alcohol*? 2.____

   A. 0.05%   B. 0.10%   C. 0.15%   D. 0.6%

3. Three of the following four statements are true of freeways. Which statement is NOT true? 3.____

   A. They have a limited number of interchanges at which vehicles may enter or leave the freeway.
   B. They have a limited number of STOP and GO signals.
   C. Traffic moving in opposite directions is not separated by a median strip.
   D. Crossing the median strip is not permitted.

4. To correct a skid, you should 4.____

   A. steer in the direction in which the rear of the car is skidding
   B. steer in the direction opposite that in which the rear of the car is skidding
   C. hold the steering wheel firmly in the straight-ahead position
   D. use the parking or handbrake so that only the rear wheels will lock while the front wheels turn freely

5. The MOST dangerous effects of alcohol on the driver are those concerned with 5.____

   A. vision
   B. reaction time
   C. behavior
   D. coordination and driving skill

6. The *Three E's* of traffic safety are included in the following four words. Which of them is NOT one of the *Three E's*? 6.____

   A. Education   B. Engineering
   C. Enforcement   D. Efficiency

7. Which of the following BEST describes the true meaning of the word *courage*? 7.____

   A. Ability to overcome fear
   B. Absence of fear
   C. Taking chances to gain a reputation as a daredevil
   D. Lack of realization of the true nature of danger

8. Which of the following types of insurance is of GREATEST importance to you when you own a car?

   A. Liability
   B. Collision
   C. Comprehensive
   D. Medical payment

   8.____

9. Which of the following statements is NOT correct?

   A. Most states have legalized the use of electric directional signals to signal turns.
   B. Overheating is always due to failures in the cooling system.
   C. Power brakes do not decrease the stopping distance.
   D. The horn should never be sounded except in the interest of safety.

   9.____

10. Three of the following are good safety features. Which is NOT a safety feature?

    A. Door locks
    B. Rear-view mirror inside the car
    C. Eye-level outside mirror
    D. Ventilation of the inside of the car

    10.____

11. The MOST important factor in good car maintenance is

    A. an honest, dependable service station or garage
    B. a skilled mechanic
    C. high quality, reliable parts
    D. a responsible car owner

    11.____

12. Three of the following procedures will add to tire traction in starting your car on ice. Which one will NOT help?

    A. Letting some air out of the rear tires
    B. Sprinkling sand on the ice
    C. Slipping the clutch
    D. Feeding gas more gently and more gradually

    12.____

13. The four-stroke cycle includes THREE of the following. Which of the following is NOT part of the cycle? _____ stroke.

    A. Intake
    B. Compression
    C. Power
    D. Completion

    13.____

14. Vehicles A, C, and D in the illustration shown at the right have stopped to allow vehicle B to turn.
    Which vehicle, A, C, or D, would be the FIRST to cross the intersection, considering right-of-way rules?

    A. A
    B. C
    C. D
    D. None of the above

    14.____

81

15. What part of the cost of planning, designing, and constructing the National System of Interstate and Defense Highways is paid for by Federal-aid funds?

    A. 90%   B. 50%   C. 10%   D. 100%

16. When you leave a freeway and drive on a city street, you must check your speed frequently because you may be

    A. accelerated
    B. suffering from highway hypnosis
    C. velocitized
    D. suffering impairment of vision due to carbon monoxide

17. Which of the following statements is CORRECT?

    A. Certain drugs, like Benzedrine in *keep-awake* pills, actually make driving at night safe.
    B. A driver should trust no one but a physician to determine whether or not he should drive after taking any kind of drug.
    C. The Federal Food and Drug Act does not permit the sale of any drug dangerous to a driver without a prescription from a registered physician.
    D. The individual driver must rely entirely upon his judgment and knowledge of how a specific drug will affect him.

18. Three of the following four maintenance procedures are good.
    Which is NOT a good procedure?

    A. Rotate your tires to avoid uneven wear.
    B. Avoid letting oil or gasoline come into contact with your tires.
    C. For driving in very hot weather, underinflate your tires to avoid building up excessive pressure in them.
    D. Keep the battery terminals covered with a light layer of grease.

19. Drivers should be able to recognize traffic signs by their shape.
    Which of the following signs warns drivers that they are approaching a railroad grade crossing?

    A.   B.   C.   D.

20. Imagine that the steering wheel is the face of a clock.
    The driver's hands should grasp it at _____ and _____ o'clock.

    A. 8; 4   B. 9; 3   C. 10; 2   D. 11; 1

KEY (CORRECT ANSWERS)

1.	D	11.	C
2.	A	12.	A
3.	B	13.	D
4.	A	14.	C
5.	D	15.	A
6.	C	16.	C
7.	A	17.	B
8.	A	18.	C
9.	B	19.	B
10.	C	20.	C

BASIC FUNDAMENTALS OF DRIVING

CONTENTS

		Page
I.	WHAT TO WATCH OUT FOR IN YOUR VEHICLE	1
	A. Brakes	1
	B. Tires	1
	C. Steering	1
	D. Lights	1
	E. Windshield	1
	F. Wipers	2
	G. Mirrors	2
	H. Wheel Alignment	2
II.	RULES OF THE ROAD	2
	A. Right-of-Way	2
	B. Keep to the Right	2
	C. Passing	3
	D. Turning	4
	E. A Place to Park	5
III.	GUIDE POSTS	5
	A. Traffic Signs	5
	B. Pavement Markings	6
	C. Traffic Signals	7
IV.	SENSIBLE DRIVING	8
	A. Safe Driving	8
V.	OTHER ROAD CITIZENS	10
	A. Pedestrians	10
VI.	IN CASE OF ACCIDENT	11
	A. If you are involved	11
	B. If you are first at the scene	13
VII.	SUMMARY OF BASIC DRIVER'S RULES	13
VIII.	SUMMARY OF DRIVING SKILLS	16

BASIC FUNDAMENTALS OF DRIVING

I. **WHAT TO WATCH OUT FOR IN YOUR VEHICLE**

   A. BRAKES
   Brakes become worn and the linings must be replaced. Oil or grease may seep in and cause slipping or binding. Water may set in during wet weather. Dirt from dusty roads may filter in and make them grab. They may get out of adjustment and not apply evenly to all wheels. (You can test this by stopping your car suddenly on a level, hard-surfaced road. If your car pulls in one direction or another, adjustment is needed. But make this test only at a slow speed when no other cars are nearby.) If your car has hydraulic brakes, have the fluid checked frequently to maintain the proper amount in the system. Constant loss of fluid or the brake pedal going down too far indicates a leak in the system which should be repaired immediately. If you have four-wheel brakes, you must be able to stop after applying the brakes within 30 feet at 20 miles per hour, 67 feet at 30 miles per hour, 120 feet at 40 miles per hour, and 190 feet at 50 miles per hour.

   B. TIRES
   It is extremely dangerous to use tires after tread is worn off or if the sidewalls have been cut or slashed. Make certain they are inflated to the recommended pressure to take advantage of their safety factors. If a tire blows out, take your foot off the accelerator and hold the steering wheel as steadily as possible. Do not disengage your clutch or use your brakes until speed has been reduced considerably.
   Danger Signs: If your car wanders or steers hard, or if your tires are smooth or worn unevenly, or if there is a "break" in the sidewall, have the tires checked immediately.

   C. STEERING
   Proper steering is essential for safe driving. If the front end of your car shakes or shimmies, or if your steering wheel has excessive "play" it seems to turn farther than usual before the front wheels react to your turn) or if the mechanism doesn't respond normally to your steering, you should have the steering mechanism checked immediately.

   D. LIGHTS
   You need all the light you can get, within the limits set by law, in order to see as far ahead as possible at night. For your protection, keep headlights at top efficiency, aimed properly, and replace them as they grow dim or burn out. Carry a box of extra fuses for replacement in an emergency. Each time you drive at night, first walk around your car to be sure your lights are working properly.

   E. WINDSHIELD
   Your windshield should be kept clean of dirt in summer and snow or ice in winter. It should be free of discoloration and pockmarks. Stickers, except those authorized by the Commissioner of Motor Vehicles, may not be used on front or back windows.

F. WIPERS
Your windshield wiper should be in good operating condition at all times. You should replace blades frequently.

G. MIRRORS
All cars must have rear view mirrors. These should be adjusted to give you a clear view of the road behind you.

H. WHEEL ALIGNMENT
At least once a year have your wheel alignment checked. Poor alignment can reduce tire life and cause excessive wear, looseness, and failure of the king pins as well as the components of the independent front wheel suspension system and tie rod ends. Such a condition is expensive to repair and is extremely dangerous in operating the vehicle.

II. RULES OF THE ROAD

A. RIGHT-OF WAY
The "right" in "right-of-way" is the key to most situations you will come across when reaching intersections. In general, the vehicle on your right has the privilege of proceeding before you do.
Exceptions: There are several situations when the general rule does not apply. They are:
1. When you approach an intersection, yield the right-of-way to a vehicle coming from the opposite direction which is within the intersection or so close as to be an immediate hazard. Other vehicles coming from the opposite direction must yield the right-of-way to you, if you already are in the intersection. This rule does not apply when both vehicles are halted outside of the intersection and both are to start at the same time. In this case, the car going straight ahead has the right-of-way.
2. If you notice an approaching fire engine, ambulance, or other emergency vehicle displaying a red light and an audible signal, you must yield right-of-way to that vehicle and immediately drive to a position parallel to, and as close as possible to, the right-hand edge or curb of the roadway and stop until the emergency vehicle has passed. On a one-way road, three or more lanes in width, you may drive to either edge or curb and halt. You must keep clear of intersections.
3. If you are about to enter or cross a highway from a private road or driveway, you must yield the right-of-way to all vehicles on the highway.
4. You must give the right-of-way to pedestrians in crosswalks.
Remember: The right-of-way is easy to give another driver. It doesn't cost you a penny. But it may cost your life if you try to grab it even when it is rightfully yours and the other fellow is taking it away.

B. KEEP TO THE RIGHT
The Safe Way: Driving on the wrong side of the road is one of the major causes of accidents. Your failure to keep on your own side may not get you into an accident, but may force the other driver off the road or cause him to lose control while avoiding you.

<u>Keep to the Right</u>: In the United States and Canada, traffic drives on the right-hand side of the road in most circumstances

<u>Exceptions</u>: There are several situations where this rule does not apply. They are:
1. When overtaking and passing another vehicle proceeding in the same direction as you are.
2. When passing pedestrians, animals, or obstructions in the right lane.
3. When you are on a road, or certain lanes of it, marked for one-way traffic.

<u>Musts</u>: You must stay on the right-hand side of the road in these situations:
1. When you are approaching the crest of a hill.
2. When you are approaching a curve and you cannot see around it.
3. When you are within 100 feet of a railroad grade crossing.
4. When your view is obstructed and you are within 100 feet of a bridge, viaduct, or tunnel.
5. When you are traveling slowly, in comparison with other traffic.
6. Do not speed up when other vehicles start to pass you.
7. When pavement markings prohibit driving on the left.

C. PASSING

<u>Pass on the Left</u>: The general rule is to pass other vehicles going in the same direction as you are on the left, allowing plenty of distance to clear the overtaken vehicle. Never pass unless you are sure you have enough time and space to get back in line. You must return to the right lane as soon as practical and safe. And signal before you pass and before you return to the right-hand lane, either with your hand or mechanical turn signals.

<u>Exceptions</u>: You may pass on the right under certain limited circumstances, so long as you do not drive off the pavement. These are:
1. When the vehicle ahead is making a left turn.
2. When you are traveling on a one-way road wide enough for two cars, provided such passing is not forbidden by signs.
3. When you are traveling on a road with unobstructed pavement and room for two or more lanes of traffic in each direction, provided such passing is not forbidden by signs.

<u>Don't Pass</u>: Passing is forbidden in certain circumstances. These include:
1. You may not pass a vehicle stopped at a crosswalk to allow a pedestrian to cross.
2. You may not pass from either direction a school bus which has halted to load or unload passengers, even when the highway is divided by a center mall. Such vehicles are marked "School Bus," and will have red lights flashing. You must stop before reaching the bus and wait for the bus to start, unless you are waved on by the driver or a police officer.

<u>Tips on Passing</u>: Danger is always present when you pass another vehicle. Always be sure any vehicles behind you are not attempting to pass, and that cars from the opposite direction are far enough away so you won't get involved in a difficult traffic situation. Don't cut back into the right-hand lane too quickly and risk hitting the overtaken car.

<u>When a Car Passes You</u>: Stay to your right as far as possible without going off the pavement and slow up slightly. Be alert if the other driver cuts back too quickly.

D. TURNING

Make Your Intentions Known: The first thing to do when changing directions or turning is to look around and behind your car. Be sure that you have an unobstructed path for the turn you are about to make. All turns should be made with caution and reduced speed. Let the other drivers know your intentions. Your car is probably equipped with mechanical turn signals, and you must use them or the recommended arm signals for at least 100 feet before you make your turn. Always be sure your mechanical signals are switched off after the turn as been completed.

Hand Signals: The prescribed hand signals, which you may wish to use, are:

    Left Turn: Arm and hand extended horizontally;

    Right Turn: Hand and arm extended upward with arm folded in right angle at the elbow;

    Slow or Stop: Hand and arm extended downward.

Making Right Turn: Both the approach and the turn should be made as close as practicable to the right-hand curb or edge of the road.

Left Turn on Two-Way Road: Approach the turn with your left wheels as close to the center line of the road as possible. After entering the intersection, make the left turn so that you keep to the left of the center of intersection and leave the intersection to the right of the center of the road you are entering.

Left Turn From Two-Way Road into One-Way Road: Approach the turn with your left wheels close to the center line of the road. Turn before reaching the center of the intersection and leave the intersection to the right of the center of the road you are entering.

Left Turn From One-Way Road into One-Way Road: Approach the turn in the left lane. After entering the intersection, turn so as to leave the intersection as nearly as possible in the left-hand lane of the road you are entering.

On Any Left Turn into Approaching Traffic: If oncoming traffic prevents you from making the turn as soon as you reach the intersection, do not wait behind edge of crosswalk. Proceed into the intersection and wait there for traffic to clear so that you may complete your turn. Traffic behind you can then often proceed on your right.

Right Turn: Approach the turn as far to the right as possible, and make the turn as close as possible to the right curb or edge of the road.

Left Turn From One-Way Road into Two-Way Road: Approach the turn in the left lane. Make the turn to the left of the center of the intersection and leave the intersection to the right of the center of the road you are entering.

Left Turn From a One-Way Road into One-Way Road: Approach the turn in the left lane. After entering the intersection, turn so as to leave the intersection as nearly as possible in the left-hand lane of the road you are entering.

Left Turn From Two-Way Road into Two-Way Road: Approach the turn with your left wheels as close as possible to the center line of the road. After entering the intersection, make the left turn, when possible, to the left of the center of the intersection. (Old law required vehicles to pass to the right of the center of the road.) the left turn has to be made so that you leave the intersection to the right of the center of the road you are entering.

Left Turn From Two-Way Road into One-Way Road: Approach the turn with your left wheels as close to the center line of the road as possible. Make the turn before

reaching the center of the intersection and leave the intersection as nearly as possible in the left-hand lane of the road you are entering.
Left Turn: Hand and arm extended horizontally.
Right Turn: Hand and arm extended upward.
Stop or Decrease Speed: Hand and arm extended downward.

E. A PLACE TO PARK

Why Parking is Limited: Parking is regulated and sometimes forbidden in certain locations. Usually this is done as a safety measure, and to allow rapid, smooth flow of traffic.

"No Parking" Signs: These mean that you may stop a vehicle in that space only temporarily to actually load or unload merchandise or passengers.

"No Stopping" Signs: These mean you may not stop a vehicle in that space for any purpose except when necessary to avoid conflict with other traffic or in compliance with the directions of a police officer.

"No Standing" Signs: These mean you may stop a vehicle in that space only temporarily to actually receive or discharge passengers.

No Stopping Here:
1. On a Sidewalk: In front of a driveway.
2. On a Crosswalk: Alongside or opposite any road excavation or obstruction.
3. On the road side of a parked vehicle.

No Stopping Here Either:
1. Within an intersection unless permitted by signs or parking meters.
2. Within 15 feet of a fire hydrant (unless a different distance is indicated by a sign), except when a licensed operator is in the front seat who can move the vehicle in case of emergency.

No Standing Here: Unless indicated otherwise by signs or parking meters:
1. Within 10 feet of a crosswalk at an intersection.
2. Within 30 feet on the approach to a traffic signal or "stop" sign at the side of the roadway.
3. Between a safety zone and the curb.
4. Within 50 feet of a railroad crossing.
5. On a bridge or in a tunnel.

Parallel Parking: Except where angle parking is permitted, you must park parallel where there are curbs—wheels within 12 inches of the curb. On two-way roads, you should park, stand or stop with the right wheels parallel to the right-hand curb; on one-way roads parallel to nearest curb.

For Safety's Sake: For the safety of your car and the safety of others, never park where it will be a hazard to traffic.

III. **GUIDE POSTS**

A. TRAFFIC SIGNS

Special Meanings: State highway signs have special shapes and colors, and these shapes and colors have special meanings for drivers. Red and white, black and white, yellow and black, or white and green are used in places where danger exists. They indicate the particular danger ahead.

Stop: This is an eight-sided sign with a red background. It means you must come to a full stop at a stop line if one is marked on the highway. If there is none, then stop at the crosswalk. If there is neither a stop line nor a crosswalk, stop at the point nearest the intersecting road where you can see approaching traffic in both directions. Proceed with caution after yielding the right-of-way to any vehicle which has entered the intersection from another road or which is so close as to be an "immediate hazard." (The older yellow "Stop" signs have the same meaning.)

Railroad: This is a round sign containing an "X" and the letters "RR" on a yellow background. It means you are approaching a railroad crossing. Buses and certain trucks must stop at grade crossings; other vehicles must use caution.

Yield Right-of-Way: Relatively new on many state highways, this sign varies slightly in shape from an inverted pyramid and in wording, but one word, "YIELD" always appears on it. It may say "Yield Right-of-Way" or just "Yield" and it may be white or black letters on a red or yellow background, but in any case it means you should approach such a sign with caution. A complete stop is not required unless there is traffic on the intersecting road. You must give the other traffic the right-of-way.

Other Signs: Diamond-shaped signs tell you of permanent physical hazards such as curves, steep hills, or narrow bridges. Rectangular signs are used to post regulations and to warn of possible operating hazards.

B. PAVEMENT MARKINGS

Lines and Lanes: State highways are marked with white or yellow lines. Each of these lines has a meaning of its own. Here is what the markings mean:

1. Broken Line: This line defines traffic lanes. You may cross it if crossing will not interfere with traffic.
2. Solid Line: Separates opposing traffic lanes. You should keep to the right of it, but may cross it if conditions permit, unless this is forbidden by local ordinance. Be especially cautious in crossing this line, however.
3. Solid and Broken Double Line: If the broken line is on your side, you may cross if traffic permits. If the solid line is on your side, you may cross except for a left turn from or into a road or driveway.
4. Double Solid Line: You should never cross this line except to turn into or from a road or driveway.
5. Crosswalk Line: This line, usually at a right angle to the curb, designates the area in which a pedestrian always has the right of way, provided he is not crossing against a red light.
6. "Stop" Line: This is a line across a highway usually at right angles to the curb at an intersection. If a stop is required at the intersection, you should stop in back of the line. Make a full stop, and start up only when it is safe to do so.
7. Arrows: These are painted on some highways, especially where there are multiple lanes, to help guide into proper lanes.
8. Broken Line: Defines traffic lanes. You may cross it if crossing will not interfere with traffic.
9. Solid Line: Separates opposing traffic lanes. You should keep in line but you may cross it when conditions are favorable for you to do so. BE CAUTIOUS.

10. Solid and Broken Line: Do not cross from the solid line side of the road, except for turn from or into private roads. You may cross from the broken line side, exercising EXTREME CAUTION.
11. Double Solid Line: No crossing allowed except for left turn from or into private roads.
12. Use of Double Line on Hills: The motorist often sees double line markings on a hill. A motorist on the right, who is climbing the hill, and who cannot see beyond the crest, is forbidden to start to pass by the solid line on his side, which he must not cross. A motorist coming down the hill can see a reasonable distance and is therefore free to use his judgment. Because the broken line is on his side, he may cross it if the road is clear ahead.
13. Reduction in Pavement Widths: The point at which a pavement narrows in width is dangerous because a lane which may be used by traffic on the wide pavement, disappears on the narrow pavement. To avoid confusion, traffic in this lane is shunted to the right.

C. TRAFFIC SIGNALS

<u>Red, Green and Amber</u>: These are among the most effective traffic devices for preventing accidents and tie-ups at intersections. Here is what the standard red, green and yellow indications mean:
1. Green Alone: You may proceed through the intersection or make a turn, unless a sign prohibits such a turn. But you must yield the right of way to other vehicles and pedestrians lawfully within the intersection or an adjacent crosswalk at the time the light changed.
2. Steady Yellow Alone: This warns you that the red signal will follow immediately, and that you may not enter or still be crossing the intersection when the signal turns red.
3. Steady Red Alone: This means stop before entering the intersection or one of its crosswalks. You must wait for the green light or arrow. The same rules apply here as for a stop sign as to where you should stop.
4. Dark Period, or Red-Green Combined When Shown Following Green: This period, on two-color signals, warns you that the red signal will follow immediately and that you may not enter the intersection after the signal turns red.
5. Steady Red With Green Arrow, Steady Yellow With Green Arrow, or Green Arrow Alone: This means you may, with caution, enter the intersection only to move in the direction indicated by the arrow. You must yield the right of way to pedestrians lawfully within a crosswalk and to other traffic lawfully using the intersection.
6. Flashing Red Signal: This means stop before the nearest crosswalk or limit line. If there is no such line, stop before entering the intersection. Proceed after yielding the right-of-way to any vehicle which has entered the intersection from another road or which is so close as to be an immediate hazard. This signal has the same meaning as a "stop" sign, and you should stop at the same place as for that type of sign.
7. Flashing Yellow Signal: This means you may proceed with caution.
8. When a Traffic Officer is Directing: Regardless of what the signal tells you to do, you should obey the officer's directions.

IV. SENSIBLE DRIVING

Good sense and good driving go hand in hand.

Rules that apply to our general conduct apply as well on the road. Yet every year, hundreds of people are killed and thousands of others are injured because they didn't use good sense. Being sensible and being alert go hand in hand. The first general rule of sensible driving is to keep alert, with your eyes on the road at all times. Here are a few other rules to help you drive sensibly. If you follow them, driving will be safer and easier for you.

A. SAFE DRIVING

<u>Night Driving</u>: The night hours between dusk and dawn are, by far, the most dangerous time to be on the highway. To protect yourself when it is dark out, you should follow these rules:

1. Your headlights must be turned on one half-hour after sunset until one half-hour b before sunrise.
2. Switch your headlights to low beam when an oncoming vehicle is within 500 feet, or when a vehicle you are overtaking is within 200 feet.
3. Drive more slowly. The distance you can see is shortened, even with properly adjusted headlights. Always be sure you can stop within the distance lighted by your headlight—350 feet or approximately 21 car lengths.
4. Be sure your taillight is working properly. It must be visible for 500 feet from the back of your car.
5. If you park your car at night, always be sure it is completely off the road. If you leave it facing traffic, keep your parking lights lighted.
6. Pedestrians who carry no lights never seem to realize how hard it is for you to see them after dark. Bad visibility carries no weight in court as an excuse for a pedestrian accident. Watch out for pedestrians.
7. Fix your eyes on the right-hand side of the road when passing an oncoming car at night. This will show you how far to the right you may go, and it also will help minimize the glare. There is always a second or two when you must drive blind past the oncoming car. Just before that brief period, slow down and try to get an impression of what is ahead, so you can drive from memory for that second or two when you are blinded.

<u>Alcohol and Gasoline</u>: No one knows for sure how many automobile accidents are caused each year by mixing drinking and driving. But a recent survey showed that in 62 percent of fatal accidents, alcohol was at least a factor.

It is dangerous to drink and drive. You may think you hold your drinks pretty well. But medical studies show that, under certain circumstances, one glass of beer or one cocktail is enough to impair your judgment. And when your judgment is impaired, you will take chances you would not normally take. When this happens, you are flirting with an accident.

How much can you safely drink and then drive? The amount varies, not only with the individual, but with other factors such as when he last ate.

The only safe rule is this: If you have had even as little as a single drink, then it is wise to let someone else do the driving. But under no circumstances should you permit yourself to drive if there is any possibility your judgment has suffered in the slightest as the result of drinking.

<u>Doors</u>: It is just plain good sense to be especially careful when getting out of your car. When you park by a curb, you may leave or enter your car from the left side only when no traffic is approaching. By the same token, when you see a parked car ahead always be prepared to handle the situation if an unthinking occupant should open his left door suddenly.

<u>Keys in Car</u>: When you leave your car unattended, you must stop the motor, lock the ignition, remove the key, and set the brakes. If you leave your keys in an unattended vehicle, you commit a traffic infraction.

<u>Litterbugs</u>: Not only is untidiness bad manners, it is also illegal and dangerous. Carelessly throwing refuse from your car can result in a fine (for first offense) of up to $50. Besides, the paper could blow into another car or against the windshield and confuse or temporarily blind the driver, causing an accident.

<u>Tailgating (Following Too Closely)</u>: You never can be absolutely sure what the car ahead will do. To give yourself plenty of space to stop in time, follow this simple rule: Allow at least one car length between your car and the one ahead for each ten miles of speed. At 20 miles an hour, allow two car lengths; at 60, allow at least six car lengths. You should also take into consideration the amount of traffic and especially the condition of the road surface. Also, you may not follow any fire apparatus on its way to a fire by closer than 200 feet in a city or 500 feet in rural areas.

<u>Coasting</u>: The motor of your car helps you keep the speed under control. But it can only do so when the car is "in gear." Thus, when you coast or drive with the car in neutral gear, you are losing needed control.

<u>Overcrowding</u>: The law forbids more than three persons in the front seat of your car. More specifically, it says that the front seat shall not be so crowded that the passengers obstruct the driver's view or interfere with his control over the mechanism. If your car is small, then sometimes even three in the front seat is too many.

<u>Horns</u>: Nobody likes a loud-mouth, and a driver who constantly toots his horn is the loud-mouth of the road. Horns are to be used when passing other cars, or as a warning, but not otherwise.

<u>Hitch-Hiking</u>: It may seem the neighborly thing to do if you pick up a hitch-hiker. But not only are you taking a chance on the character of the hitchhiker; you also are posing a traffic hazard by suddenly stopping to pick him up. The picking up of hitch-hikers is not recommended. Hitchhiking itself is against the law.

<u>Monoxide Gas</u>: The exhaust from your car is highly poisonous. If your car is not properly sealed, there is danger of the fumes seeping in and killing you. So always drive with a window open wide enough to allow proper ventilation, even in the coldest or wettest weather.

<u>Fatigue</u>: When you are tired, it is dangerous to drive. Sometimes the monotony of driving can tire you. If this is the case, simply pulling off to the side of the road and getting out to stretch and rest your eyes a few minutes will help you. At other times, it is better to pull off and sleep for an hour or two. Accident records are filled with cases of overtired drivers who thought they could stay awake another hour or two—and could not.

<u>Speeding</u>: Besides being illegal, speeding is one of the most dangerous of all traffic violations. A surprisingly high percentage of accidents, especially fatal accidents,

result from this offense. Maximum speed limit is 50 miles an hour unless otherwise posted. In addition, certain areas are designated for speeds below. Thus when you see a posted speed limit, you can be sure it is a realistic limit, and you should govern yourself accordingly. Furthermore, the legal speed limit is not necessarily the safe speed. Many factors, such as traffic volume, or bad weather, may call for lower speed.

Seat Belts: Research studies have proved that in case of an accident, you are much safer from injury or possible death if you are wearing a seat belt.

Children and Pets: It is extremely dangerous to allow pets or small children to ride in the front seat of a car, where they may distract the driver. Children should be encouraged to "sit back in the seat," where they are less likely to bump their heads in case of a sudden stop. Seat belts are especially helpful for children.

Winter Driving: You need special equipment, such as snow tires or reinforced tire chains for winter driving. Windows should be kept clear of snow and ice. If it is slippery, test your stopping distance where there is no traffic, to give yourself an idea of how much space you need to stop. Be particularly careful at curves, hills, and intersections. Pump your brakes one, two, or more times a second to stop on slippery roads, rather than simply pressing down on the brake pedal.

Other Bad Weather: Rain reduces your visibility and ability to stop quickly. High speeds when it is extremely windy can result in loss of control. The best rule to follow is to keep your speed down—you should never drive faster than weather and road conditions permit. In dense fog, you should reduce speed and use the low beam of your headlights.

At Intersections: If traffic ahead is blocked so that you cannot clear the intersection, stop before you enter the intersection.

Negotiating Curves: To guide your car on a curve in the highway, you should enter such curve at reduced speed, accelerating slightly as you round it.

Skidding: Should your car be thrown into a skid, you may regain a straight path by turning your front wheels in the direction of the skid. Never apply the brakes hard, but lift your foot from the accelerator.

Off the Pavement: Should your right wheels drop off the pavement, slow down immediately and turn your front wheels sharply to the left until all four are back on the pavement.

V. **OTHER ROAD CITIZENS**

   A. PEDESTRIANS

Crossing on Signal: Pedestrians may cross a road, being sure to stay within the crosswalk, on a green signal. They may not cross it facing a "wait" or "don't walk" signal, nor may they cross on the red or yellow signal or the red-green combined or dark period following a green signal unless facing a "walk" signal. On a green arrow, whether alone or accompanied by a steady red or yellow, the pedestrian may enter the road only if he can do so safely and without interfering with vehicle traffic.

Intersections Without Signal: When there are no traffic signals or if they are not operating, drivers must yield the right-of-way, slowing or stopping if necessary, for a pedestrian crossing within a crosswalk.

Crossing Between Intersections: A pedestrian crossing the road between intersections, except at a marked crosswalk, must yield the right-of-way to all vehicles on the road. Pedestrians crossing a road where a pedestrian tunnel or overhead crossing has been provided must also yield the right-of-way to vehicles.

Walking on the Road: It is unlawful for pedestrians to walk in the road where there are sidewalks. Where there are no sidewalks, a pedestrian must walk on the left side of the road or its shoulder facing the traffic, and move as far to the left as possible when a vehicle approaches. Two or more pedestrians should walk in single file and never abreast of each other.

Tipsy Pedestrians: Research has shown that many pedestrians killed by automobiles have been drinking. Such pedestrians do foolish things, and, what is worse, they often do them at night when the driver has less chance of seeing them. As a driver, you must realize that such pedestrians may be unreasonable, but since they have so little chance to survive a collision with your car, you must protect them.

Bus Stops: Remember that pedestrians leaving buses may be confused as to direction, so always watch out for them. And be sure to stop when overtaking or meeting a standing school bus which is taking on or discharging passengers or displaying flashlight lights.

Blind Pedestrians: You must be especially careful when encountering blind persons. The law requires drivers at or near intersections to grant the right-of-way to blind pedestrians. Under the so-called "White Cane Law" you must yield the right-of-way to pedestrians who are crossing or attempting to cross a highway and who are guided by seeing-eye dogs or who are carrying, in a raised position, a white or metallic cane, or a white cane with a red tip.

White Clothes: Pedestrians should bear in mind that part of the responsibility for their safety rests on themselves as well as the driver. At night a pedestrian should wear light-colored clothes so the driver can see him better.

VI. IN CASE OF ACCIDENT

No matter how carefully you drive, you may become involved in a motor vehicle accident. There are a number of things you should do, and some you MUST do, in this eventuality. In the interest of humanity, you are called upon to give whatever assistance you can to the injured. In the interest of preventing similar accidents in the future, you are required to make a report to the Department of Motor Vehicles on how the accident occurred, where, at what time of day, the condition of the weather and of the street or highway, and other pertinent data.

A. IF YOU ARE INVOLVED

Stop: Perhaps your car is damaged severely and cannot proceed, or maybe the harm is only slight. Nevertheless, you are to stop immediately.

At Night: If an accident occurs at night or on a heavily-travelled street or highway, or where your car cannot be readily seen by approaching vehicles, move it off the highway immediately if possible. Leave your parking lights on.

Injuries: First, see if anyone has been injured, and give whatever assistance you can. If the injuries are serious, do not attempt to move the person, but try to get medical help as quickly as possible.

Information: If you are not hurt, make your name and address, license and registration number and name of your insurance company known to the operator of the other car (and to any officer). At the same time, obtain the other operator's name, address, license number and name of his insurance company and write it down. In case of a pedestrian, get his full name and address, if possible.

Report to Police: Even if the other party on the accident is unable to take your name and address, report to the nearest police station as soon as you can. The police will show you how to make out your report of the accident on the forms which are provided by the Department of Motor Vehicle.

If You Are Hurt: If you are unable to make a report to the Department of Motor Vehicles within 48 hours, as the law requires, get some passenger, member of the family, a friend or your doctor to send the report in for you. Report forms are available at all police stations, courts, or branch offices of the Department.

Unattended Vehicles: You also must report any accident in which you collide with an unattended vehicle or other property. Find the owner and give him your name and address, or report to the nearest police station.

What Accidents to Report: Any accident which involves personal injury or death or property damage in excess of $1,000 must be reported to the Department of Motor Vehicles within 48 hours. Accident report blanks may be obtained at any police station, Department of Motor Vehicles office or Motor Vehicle section of a County Clerk's Office.

Animals: If your car hits and injures a horse, a dog, or cattle, you must stop and report the accident to the owner, is possible, or to a police official, and see that the animal gets necessary attention. Wild and domestic animals are entitled to humane treatment.

Penalties: Always remember this: If you fail to stop your car after an accident, if you fail to report and make yourself known to the other driver or a police official, or if you fail to fulfill any of the other requirements in this section, you may lose your license and face criminal court action for leaving the scene of an accident.

Conscience: On top of those penalties, your conscience will always bother you, if by your failure to observe the rules of conduct someone dies or suffers needlessly.

Submersion: If your car goes into deep water—do not panic. If it dips below the surface with the wheels down, the best escape technique is through the open windows before the water reaches window level. If it sinks too rapidly for you to escape while it is at the surface, climb into the rear seat. A pocket of air will form there and will give you time to plan your way out. You can open the nearest window or wait until the pressure of the water inside is equal to that outside and then open a door.

Moral Responsibility: Suppose you come upon the scene of an accident in which the car ahead of you has smashed into some object or has skidded and overturned. Do you:
1. Drive as closely as you can to the crash?
2. Try to haul people out of the wreckage?
3. Speed past and let someone else be the Good Samaritan?

Sounds ridiculous, doesn't it? But some people would, simply because they do not know any better or they do not want to get involved.

You owe it to yourself and to others to help all you can. For you might be in a position sometime of being the occupant of a car in an accident and will not be able to help yourself. So do the smart thing. Follow the common sense suggestions which are listed here; you may save a life or you may prevent further damage.

B. IF YOU ARE FIRST AT THE SCENE
<u>Stop</u>: Get your car off the road far enough away from the wreck to protect it from other traffic. Then as calmly as possible decide what to do.
<u>Warn Traffic</u>: Find some way or get some other person's help to warn or stop approaching traffic if necessary to prevent other crashes. Ask others to go for help, either to the nearest telephone or the nearest police officer. Warn traffic coming from both directions far enough from the scene so that cars nearing the accident will slow down in plenty of time.
<u>Turn Off Ignition</u>: As soon as possible, get to the wreck and turn off the ignition to prevent fire if it has not already started. If a fire does not start right away, the chances are it will not, and you can relax somewhat. If it has, however, get the people out as quickly as possible and as far away as possible in the event there is an explosion.
<u>Helping the Injured</u>: If there are injured persons in the car or lying on the ground nearby after being thrown out and there is no fire, don't move them. Make sure they are protected from traffic and covered with coats or blankets to keep them warm. Without trying to move them, loosen collar, ties, and belts to help them breathe easier. Unless you are skilled in first aid, however, do not try to treat their injuries before medical assistance arrives except to try to stop any bleeding. You may make their hurts worse.
<u>If Someone is Pinned</u>: If the wreck is overturned with someone underneath, don't try to lift the car unless you have enough strong persons to do it, and then not until you are sure no one will be crushed under the other side. Police, highway patrolmen and emergency truck operators are skilled in dealing with accidents. Unless you know what you are doing, leave it to them.
<u>Make Yourself Known</u>: After you have done what you can to assist the injured, give your name and address to the police. Since you may have seen the accident occur, your eyewitness account may be of help to them.
<u>If You Are Not There First</u>: Don't be curious. If you are not asked to stop and lend your assistance, move on so as not to cause a possible traffic jam and further accidents. Many drivers slow down or stop to rubberneck at the accident scene, thereby neglecting their driving.

VII. **SUMMARY OF BASIC DRIVER'S RULES**

  A. OBJECTIVES
   1. Be alert; concentrate on your driving whenever you operate a vehicle.

  B. SPEED
   2. You shall continuously maintain your vehicle under such control so as to be able to bring it to a complete stop within the assured clear distance ahead.
   3. You shall not operate a vehicle at a speed greater than is reasonable and proper having due regard to weather, visibility, traffic, intersections, width and character of roadway, type, condition and loading of the vehicle, your own alertness, and any existing condition affecting your ability to stop before collision.
   4. You shall not drive in any state, county, city, municipality, or area under the control of the Federal Government at a speed greater than that permitted by the

authorities in those areas. All personnel shall follow rules and regulations laid down by the Bureaus in which they are employed.
5. When meeting or overtaking a school bus, which has stopped to load or unload passengers, you shall stop and proceed only when the bus is in motion.
6. You shall approach a railroad crossing or drawbridge at such a speed as to permit stopping should danger of collision require and shall proceed only if the way is clear. (Exception: See Rule 39 for buses and trucks transporting personnel.)

C. RIGHT-OF-WAY
7. You shall give the right-of-way when required by signs, traffic lights or signals from authorized individuals, always coming to a full stop at a STOP sign.
8. You shall give the right-of-way to all vehicles on a main highway or thoroughfare which you intend to enter or cross.
9. You shall give the right-of-way to every pedestrian unless he clearly indicates that he is giving it to you.
10. At unmarked intersections you shall give the right-of-way to vehicles approaching from your right, and to those which entered the intersection before you.
11. You shall give the right-of-way to a vehicle making a left turn across your path if it has started to turn before you reach the intersection.
12. You shall give the right-of-way to emergency vehicles, such as police car, firetrucks, and ambulances.
13. You shall give the right-of-way to persons on bicycles.

D. OVERTAKING AND PASSING
14. You shall not attempt to pass another vehicle proceeding in the same direction on curves or hills unless you have at least 500 feet of unobscured vision.
15. Do not attempt to pass before checking your left side and rear view mirrors for danger.
16. When driving in heavy traffic, with several lanes moving in the same direction, you shall stay in your own lane and proceed at its pace, except when changing lanes in preparation for a turn.
17. You shall not recklessly move into the right lane from a lane which has stopped apparently for left turns.
18. You shall not pass at intersections.
19. You shall allow an overtaking vehicle to pass you safely.

E. SLOWING, STOPPING, TURNING, BACKING
20. You shall test the brakes of your vehicle before departing from your station.
21. Unless it is unavoidable, you shall not stop suddenly.
22. Maintain a reasonable distance, depending upon speed and driving conditions, between your vehicle and a vehicle ahead of you.
23. Make turns at intersections only from the proper lane.
24. Before baking you shall survey the area to ascertain that it is clear and suitable.

F. SIGNALS
   25. You shall always clearly indicate your intention to stop, change lanes or turn at intersections by signaling.

G. NIGHT DRIVING
   26. Always use extra caution when driving at night.
   27. Display your lights from one-half hour after sunset to one-half hour before sunrise and whenever else poor visibility demands them.

H. USE OF SEAT BELTS
   28. All front-seat passengers and all children must have seat belts fastened whenever the vehicle is in motion.

I. TRAFFIC AIDS: LIGHTS, SIGNS, AND MARKINGS
   29. You shall obey all applicable traffic signs and signals.

J. WEATHER AND ROADS
   30. Limit the operation of vehicles to a bare minimum in inclement weather.

K. HILLS
   31. You shall not drive downgrade with your gears in neutral or your clutch disengaged.

L. PARKING
   32. You shall park properly and safely at proper places.
   33. You shall secure your vehicle to avoid its movement while unoccupied or its use by an unauthorized person.
   34. You shall always check traffic flow before leaving a parking space to enter any thoroughfare.

M. USE OF VEHICLES
   35. You shall not operate a vehicle unless you have in your possession a personal motor vehicle operator's identification card.
   36. You shall not remove your vehicle from your station without proper authorization.
   37. You shall not permit unauthorized persons to ride in your vehicle.
   38. You shall not operate a vehicle when you are physically unfit from any cause.

N. BUSES, TRUCKS, AND EMERGENCY VEHICLES
   39. Upon approaching a railroad crossing when transporting personnel in a bus or truck, you shall bring your vehicle to a full stop not less than 10 feet nor more than 50 feet from the rails and shall not proceed until you have ascertained that the crossing is clear.
   40. When transporting personnel in the bed of a truck, you shall not exceed a speed of 30 miles per hour.
   41. Buses or other vehicles carrying eight or more passengers shall be operated only by persons who are at least 21 years of age.

42. You shall take all necessary precautions to prevent the injury of personnel transported in trucks or buses.
43. When transporting personnel, you shall not load beyond capacity.
44. You shall not load your vehicle in a manner which will obscure your view ahead of to either side or in any way interfere with the safe operation of your vehicle.
45. Every trailer shall be coupled with suitable safety chains or cables to the towing vehicle.

VIII. SUMMARY OF DRIVING SKILLS

A. WHAT ARE THE MOST IMPORTANT SKILLS IN DRIVING?
There are two basic skills that are the most important.

One is called *tracking*. By this is meant the physical ability to drive a car from point A to point B.

The other is called *detection*. And that is often the hardest part. Being able to sense what is happening around you and detecting potentially dangerous situations.

To be a really good driver, you must master both. And that requires using *tracking* and *detection* at one time. It is not easy.

B. WHICH ARE MORE IMPORTANT—PHYSICAL OR MENTAL DRIVING SKILLS?
You really cannot separate the two. How fast you *react to* something on the road is often dependent on *when* you realize an action must be taken. The more vigilant you are about the task of driving, the more likely you will be to detect and respond quickly to a potential problem.

C. IS THERE ONE DRIVING TECHNIQUE THAT IS BETTER THAN OTHERS?
Defensive driving is the best technique.

To be a good defensive driver you have to be alert. And the more alert you are, the better you drive. A chauffeur once gave a good tip about defensive driving. He said that he builds a *moving oval* of space around his car. As he drives, he tries to position himself so that he has space all around. That way, he can move right or left, forward or backward, to avoid trouble. Traffic conditions make this difficult to do all the time. But when he has the chance, he does it, because he stays on the defensive.

D. WHAT IS THE CORRECT POSITION FOR YOUR HANDS ON THE STEERING WHEEL?
Many people are taught that the 10 o'clock and 2 o'clock positions are best. But an authority says the 9 o'clock and 3 o'clock positions are better. You have more control and your arms will be less likely to tire.

E. THE SPEED LIMIT IS ALWAYS A SAFE SPEED, TRUE OR FALSE?
False. Speed limits are set for the best driving conditions. Slow down in heavy traffic, darkness and bad weather. But remember, if you are on a freeway, do not go too slowly. That can be very dangerous. Concentrate on staying within the speed limit and "going with the flow."

F. ARE THERE ANY TRICKS TO KEEPING YOUR MIND ALERT WHILE DRIVING?
One way is to keep your body alert. Sit up straight in the seat. Your car will tell you how it is responding. But you have to listen with your body as well as your ears. When you turn a corner too swiftly, you will feel it first in your bottom and your legs.

If there is a handling problem, you will notice it first in your hands and your arms.

You should be comfortable while driving, but not so comfortable that you are not prepared for the signals your car can give you.

G. ANY TIPS ON MAKING TURNS AT BUSY INTERSECTIONS?
Here is a tip on what *not* to do. Don't be in such a hurry to turn left that you turn your wheels before you start to make your move. Leaving your wheels straight is a defensive technique. Why? Because if you are struck from the rear and your wheels are turned left, you will be knocked into the path of oncoming traffic.

When you are making any turn, stay in the same lane. Do not swing wide into a different lane. Besides, taking more road than you need, you could really be inviting disaster.

H. WHAT IS A SAFE FOLLOWING DISTANCE?
The familiar answer is at least one car length for every 10 miles per hour. But there is a better answer: *at least a two-second interval.* To use it, simply select an object along the roadside ahead. When the car in front of you passes it, start counting "one-thousand-one, one-thousand two…" You should finish "one-thousand-two" as you reach the object. If you reach the object first, you are too close.

I. HOW SHOULD YOU SHAKE A TAILGATER?
Don't hit your brakes and try to scare him out of his wits. He may not react quickly enough and plow right into you. *Don't* let him intimidate you into driving too fast. Gradually slow down and give him every opportunity to pass. If he is really in a hurry, he will go around you when you slow down.

J. HOW SHOULD YOU REACT WHEN PEOPLE CUT IN FRONT OF YOU?
You are following at a safe distance and someone cuts in front of you. You back off to a safe distance and someone cuts in front of you. You back off to a safe distance and someone does it again. What next?

The answer is to back off again. If you get frustrated and start following too closely, you are only increasing your chances of a possible rear-end collision. Keep a level head. Never let emotion get the best of you.

K. SO WHAT DOES IT TAKE TO BE A SKILLFUL DRIVER?
The three C's of driving are:

Cooperation: Competition has no place on the road. Be friendly and courteous. Help other drivers. You would want them to help you.

Communication: Don't isolate yourself. Let other drivers know what you plan to do. Use your signals.

Concentration: Perhaps the most important thing of all. Keep your mind on your driving. Remember that driving is a task. Be vigilant in your efforts to stay alert. A skillful driver is a safe driver.

L. DRIVER PLEDGE

I will:
1. be courteous to other drivers and cooperate with them by driving friendly;
2. consider safety above all else;
3. feel responsible for all who ride with me;
4. remain calm and vigilant at the wheel;
5. keep an especially watchful eye for pedestrians;
6. try to help other drivers when they are in difficulty;
7. remember that the roads belong to two-wheeled vehicles as well as cars;
8. see that regular maintenance and safety inspections are performed on my car;
9. not drive if under the influence of drugs or alcohol; and
10. obey all traffic laws.

COMMON DRIVING ERRORS

CONTENTS

	Page
DRIVING ERRORS	1
DRIVING VIOLATIONS	3
VEHICLE ABUSE	4
DRIVER DISCOURTESIES	6

COMMON DRIVING ERRORS

DRIVING ERRORS

You can learn to recognize driving errors that lead to accidents before they happen. This appendix lists such errors under twelve categories.

1. Before Startup:
   a. Failure to properly evaluate personal, mental, and physical condition.
   b. Failure to signal when pulling away from curb.
   c. Failure to wait for a break in traffic before moving.

2. Speed Control:
   a. Too fast for traffic volume.
   b. Too fast for conditions (road surface, visibility, weather).
   c. Too fast for light conditions (e.g., dusk/darkness).
   d. Too fast for neighborhood or roadside environment.
   e. Too fast for street/highway layout and traffic control devices.
   f. Too slow for speed of traffic stream.

3. Improper Lane Usage:
   a. Failure to select proper lane.
   b. Failure to drive in center of lane.
   c. Abrupt lane changes.
   d. Failure to signal intent to change lanes.
   e. Weaving in and out of traffic lanes.

4. Passing Errors:
   a. Misjudging speed and nearness of oncoming vehicles.
   b. Failure to check side and rear before pulling out to pass.
   c. Overtaking and passing too slowly.
   d. Cutting in too quickly after passing.
   e. Failure to signal intention of passing to the driver who is being passed.
   f. Unnecessary passing.
   g. Racing another vehicle trying to pass the bus.
   h. Passing while in, or close to, an intersection.

5. Turning Errors:
   a. Turning from wrong lane.
   b. Failure to allow oncoming traffic to clear before turning left.
   c. Failure to block area to right of vehicle on right turns so no other vehicle can wedge in.
   d. Running over curb on right turns
   e. Abrupt turn on slippery road surface, leading to skid.
   f. Failure to signal intention to turn.

6. Stopping Errors:
   a. Failure to make smooth, gradual stop.
   b. Failure to signal stop.
   c. Failure to stop in time.
   d. Abrupt braking on slippery road surface, leading to skid.

7. Parking Errors:
   a. Parking in unsafe or illegal place.
   b. Parking with front or rear of vehicle protruding into traffic.
   c. Failure to secure properly unattended vehicle on grade, permitting roll.
   d. Failure to mark disabled vehicle properly.

8. Specific Signaling Errors:
   a. Failure to signal.
   b. Signal too late.
   c. Wrong signal.
   d. Failure to use horn.
   e. Excessive or improper use of horn.

9. Errors in Clearance Judgment:
   a. Following vehicle ahead too closely.
   b. Failure to check clearance to rear when backing.
   c. Failure to check right side when backing.
   d. Failure to check left side for clearance.
   e. Failure to check top clearance.
   f. Failure to yield space in any traffic encroachment.

10. Errors in Observation:
    a. Failure to observe object or pedestrian in vehicle path.
    b. Failure to observe traffic to the rear while moving.
    c. Failure to observe to left and right of vehicle at locations from which vehicle or pedestrians could enter vehicle path.
    d. Inadequate observation, leading to failure to see vehicle or pedestrian approaching.
    e. Observation made too late.
    f. Failure to anticipate parked vehicle pulling out.

11. Lack of Personal Control:
    a. Inattention—any cause.
    b. Distraction—any cause.
    c. Driving while drowsy.
    d. Reacting emotionally to driving situations.
    e. Driving under influence of alcohol or other drugs.
    f. Driving while ill.

12. Lack of Knowledge and Awareness of Equipment, Load, and Route:
    a. Failure to inspect equipment before, during, and after trip.
    b. Being unfamiliar with equipment.
    c. Being unfamiliar with route.

DRIVING VIOLATIONS

This appendix lists the most frequent driving errors that also are traffic violations.

1. Moving Errors:
    a. Speed in excess of legal limit.
    b. Speed too fast for conditions.
    c. Speed too slow for conditions.
    d. Following too closely.

2. Passing Errors:
    a. Passing at illegal place.
    b. Passing at unsafe place.
    c. Unnecessary passing.
    d. Exceeding legal speed to pass.

3. Intersection Violations:
    a. Failure to yield right-of-way.
    b. Running red light.
    c. Coasting through stop sign.
    d. Failure to reduce speed for intersection.
    e. Failure to yield to oncoming traffic when making left turn.
    f. Failure to yield right-of-way to pedestrians.

4. Improper Lane Usage:
    a. Failure to select proper lane.
    b. Turning from wrong lane.
    c. Sudden change of lane.
    d. Failure to signal lane change.

5. Parking and Stopping Errors:
    a. Illegal stopping on street or roadway.
    b. Obstructing traffic.
    c. Double parking.
    d. Failure to secure parked vehicle on hill.

VEHICLE ABUSE

Following is a list of driving practices that lead to undue wear and premature failure of a vehicle and its components.

1. Engine Abuse:
   a. Engaging starter too long at one time.
   b. Excessive acceleration of cold engine.
   c. Operating overheated engine.
   d. Operating engine with low oil pressure.
   e. Racing engine.
   f. Lugging engine.
   g. Failure to keep checking the instrument panel gages.

2. Clutching Errors:
   a. Slipping the clutch.
   b. Riding the clutch.
   c. Snapping the clutch.
   d. Depressing clutch pedal and drifting.
   e. Not double clutching when shifting gears.

3. Errors in Shifting Gears:
   a. Starting out in wrong gear.
   b. Rapid acceleration from stops.
   c. Scraping and jerking gears.
   d. Shifting into neutral and coasting downhill.
   e. Failure to double clutch, if necessary, when changing gears.
   f. Lugging-operating in improper gear.

4. Errors in Brake Use:
   a. Failure to release hand brake fully when starting to move.
   b. Abrupt stops.
   c. Delayed braking.
   d. Excessive brake applications.

5. Errors in Tire Care:
   a. Operating with flat or under-inflated tires.
   b. Driving over curbs or objects or into potholes.
   c. Scraping tires against curbs in parking.
   d. Letting air out of tires "for better traction."
   e. Unnecessary spinning of tires on ice and snow.
   f. Unnecessary skidding of tires in braking.

6. Tampering with Equipment:
   a. Overriding governors.
   b. Crimping fuel return line.
   c. Tampering with trip recorder.
   d. Abuse of driver compartment.

7. Lack of Maintenance Responsibility:
    a. Driving unit when it needs repair.
    b. Failure to report defects and repairs.
    c. Failure to inspect equipment before each trip.

DRIVER DISCOURTESIES

Listed below are discourtesies drivers commit that can tear down a fleet's good public image.

1. Errors in Speed Control:
   a. Exceeding the speed limit and passing motorists who are obeying the law.
   b. Speeding through towns, restricted speed zones, and residential areas.
   c. Driving unnecessarily slow and backing up traffic.

2. Errors in Following:
   a. Following passenger cars too closely.
   b. Tailgating another bus or truck.
   c. Following too closely at night with high beams.

3. Errors in Passing:
   a. Passing when unnecessary.
   b. Cutting in too sharply after passing.

4. Errors in Lane Use:
   a. Crowding center line.
   b. Taking up two lanes.
   c. Drifting across lane dividers.
   d. Weaving from one lane to another.
   e. Use of wrong lane for speed or proper traffic flow.

5. Errors That Obstruct Traffic:
   a. Blocking crosswalk.
   b. Double parking.
   c. Not providing opportunity for traffic buildup to pass.

6. Errors in Noise and Consideration:
   a. Unnecessary use of horn.
   b. Racing engine to hurry pedestrians across intersection.
   c. Splashing pedestrians in bad weather.

Basic Fundamentals of Automotive Vehicles

Contents

	PAGE
I. TYPES OF AUTOMOTIVE VEHICLES	1
II. WEIGHT DISTRIBUTION AND LOAD SECURING METHODS	1
III. AUTOMOTIVE VEHICLE OPERATION	5
IV. OPERATOR'S MAINTENANCE	23
V. LUBRICATION	27
VI. TIRES	31

Basic Fundamentals of Automotive Vehicles

This chapter provides general information on starting, operating, and maintaining automotive equipment for hauling materials, equipment, passengers, and fuels. It includes information on the capabilities, gross limits, and utilization of automotive equipment. Also covered are safety precautions to be observed when operating or working near automotive equipment, inflating and changing tires, and handling, loading, hauling, and offloading materials, equipment, and fuels. Knowledge of the information in this chapter and its application to the job will enable you to perform your duties more efficiently.

I. TYPES OF AUTOMOTIVE VEHICLES

PASSENGER CARRYING VEHICLES

The most common types of passenger carrying vehicles are automobiles, buses, carryalls, station wagons, and ambulances. These vehicles are used to transport light cargo and personnel.

HAULING VEHICLES

The most common standard trucks are classified by weight-carrying capacity and by body type. The weight-carrying capacity may be referred to as <u>light</u> trucks, from 1/2 to 2 tons; <u>medium</u> trucks, from 1 1/2 to 2 1/2 tons; and <u>heavy duty</u> trucks, from 2 1/2 to 5 tons.

A body-type classification may refer to the principal purpose for which the truck is used (hauling of cargo), or to the physical character of the particular body (stake, van, or dump).

TRUCK-TRACTOR AND SEMITRAILER

Besides standard trucks, industry uses many truck-tractors with semitrailers. Truck-tractors used to tow semitrailers may be gasoline or diesel engine powered, and range in capacity from 5 tons through 15 tons. Semitrailers are made in a variety of body types such as personnel carrying, fuel tank, cargo van, stake, bitumen tank, and low-bed (equipment hauling). Low-bed trailers of several lengths and widths up to 75-ton capacity are also used.

FUEL HANDLING VEHICLES

Fuel handling vehicles are classified as *fuel tank trucks* or *fuel tank semitrailers*. Each vehicle has distinguishing characteristics (model, size, and capacity). The purpose of fuel handling vehicles is to load, haul, and discharge fuel to other vehicles, aircraft, or fuel depots.

II. WEIGHT DISTRIBUTION AND LOAD SECURING METHODS

Distribution of cargo has definite bearing on the life of tires, axles, frame, and other parts of the vehicles. The fact that a truck or trailer is not loaded beyond its gross vehicle weight capacity does not mean that the individual tires and axles may not be overloaded by faulty distribution of the cargo.

As an aid to properly loading a truck or semitrailer, the center of the payload must be determined. In a truck, the position of the center of payload is the center of the body, or the point midway between the rear of the driver's cab and the tailgate. In a truck-tractor semitrailer unit, the position of the center of the payload is roughly the center of the semitrailer body, because the tractor's front wheels seldom carry any of the payload. When loading, it is important that the maximum capacity of the vehicle is not exceeded over any one of the axles and, if possible, that loads are distributed so that there is a less-than-maximum axle loading. No vehicle will be loaded over its rated capacity without direct authorization.

The trend of vehicle manufacturers is to rate trucks in terms of maximum gross vehicle weight instead of by tonnage capacities. This has resulted in poor utilization of trucks because of loading below rated capacities. It has also caused confusion, in many instances as to the maximum pounds of payload that may be transported in trucks rated in tonnage capacities.

The maximum permissible payload of a truck is determined by deducting the curb weight and weight of the driver (175 lbs.) from the manufacturer's gross vehicle weight rating. The maximum gross vehicle weight rating for a specified operating condition applies only when the tires and equipment on the truck are in accordance with the manufacturer's recommendations for the specified operating condition, which is referred to as *ideal, moderate,* or *severe,*

Ideal conditions mean that the truck is operated over improved, level roads, such as asphalt or concrete, at constant, relatively moderate speeds, with no adverse weather or road conditions. Under these conditions, recommended payload equals 100 percent of maximum permissible payload.

Moderate conditions mean that the truck is operated at high speeds over improved highways, such as asphalt or concrete, with or without long or steep grades, or at moderate speeds over semi-improved roads with gravel or equivalent surfacing, in gently rolling country with few steep grades and no adverse weather or road conditions. Under these conditions, recommended payload equals 80 percent of maximum permissible payload.

Severe conditions means that the vehicle is operated off the highway on rough or hilly terrain or over unimproved or pioneer access roads with deep ruts, holes, or steep grades; or where traffic has created deep holes or ruts in heavy snow covering normally good city streets or highways. Under these conditions, the recommended payload equals 64 percent of maximum permissible payload.

It is important that the payload weight be properly distributed over the body so that the percentage of weight carried by the front axle and that carried by the rear axle will be in the ratio for which the vehicle was designed.

A knowledge of the following terms will give you a better understanding of payload weight distribution for vehicles.

Gross Vehicle Weight (GVW) means the total weight of the loaded truck. It is the sum of the weights of the chassis, accessories, equipment attachments, cab, body, full complement of fuel, lubricants and coolant, payload, and driver.

Curb weight is the weight of the empty truck - without payload and driver - including fuel tank, cooling system, and crankcase filled. It also includes the weight of tools, spare wheel, and all other equipment specified as standard.

Dry chassis weight means the weight of the chassis complete with cowl, but not including weight of cab, body or fifth wheel, spare wheel, tire assembly with carrier, fuel, lubricants, coolant, tools, payload, operator, and frame reinforcement where required.

Payload allowance means the maximum weight of material that can be transported.

Check material for damage before and during the loading operation. Do not accept damaged material unless the damage is noted on the dispatch order or written acknowledgement of the damage is received from the supply department.

Physical dimensions, capacities, weight limitations, and load distribution of trucks and trailers vary greatly. These variations preclude the covering of all types of loads. Therefore, the methods and procedures described here must be considered typical.

There are conditions which can cause load movement while in transit. However, almost all load movement can be prevented by proper blocking and bracing. All loads must be balanced in the vehicle lengthwise and crosswise before the vehicle is operated. Precautions must be taken to prevent vertical movement because of sudden stops or travel over rough terrain as vertical movement can cause the breakdown of good blocking and bracing. If the load is not placed tightly or is out of alignment, the unbalanced loading will cause unequal pressures. The use of bulkheads, separation gates, dividers (lengthwise and crosswise), layer separations, runners, blocks, cleats, and strapping, properly fabricated and applied, will prevent most load movement.

The truck and trailer combination can be adapted to transport various types of materials such as fragile, bulky, compact, dense, and rough items, and high center of gravity items. In order to accommodate the variety of items you must plan the load, properly prepare the truck or trailer, and secure the load to the vehicle. This will prevent any possibility of the load shifting or falling off the vehicle, shifting and contacting other traffic, fouling underpasses, culverts, bridge abutments, and creating a hazard to pedestrians. Securing the load can be accomplished by staying the load with proper lines, or chains secured by tie-down or binders. Use appropriate gear such as paper, cloth, or other type filler to protect fragile items from damage by chafing (rubbing together).

If the truck or trailer is not enclosed or covered, use tarpaulins to cover the cargo and prevent exposure, damage, loss of cargo, or littering.

When transporting pipe, lumber, or other unusually long loads which extend beyond the truck body, attach a red flag to the end of the load and use a red light to mark the end of the load when traveling at night.

Before operating a truck or trailer loaded with unusually heavy, long, or odd-sized materials, ensure that the load weight and dimensions are within the prescribed state and local regulations. If oversize or overweight vehicles are required to be used for a particular job, obtain special permits prior to moving such loads or vehicles on public highways.

When transporting explosives or material interstate, adhere to all instructions, state and local laws, and I.C.C. regulations.

PRINCIPLES OF OPERATION OF PASSENGER CARRYING VEHICLES

You should have knowledge about how components are assembled to make up the automotive chassis consisting of the engine, frame, power train, wheels, steering and braking systems.

Passenger carrying vehicles which include automobiles, buses, carry-alls, station wagons, and ambulances are all similar in their principles of operation although some assemblies and components will be different in body styles, types, and sizes.

PRINCIPLES OF OPERATION OF HAULING VEHICLES

A typical <u>dump</u> truck is equipped with a dump body which has a struck capacity of 5 cubic yards, and is hinged to the rear of a subframe which is mounted directly on the truck chassis. The hoist assembly used to raise and lower the dump body is comprised of a pair of double-acting hydraulic cylinders, a positive-displacement gear-type hydraulic pump, a hydraulic oil reservoir, and connecting

high pressure-type hoses. The hydraulic pump is driven by a propeller shaft connected to the power-take-off. Operation of the hoist assembly is controlled by the dump body control lever located to the left of the driver's seat.

By disengaging the vehicle clutch and shifting the dump body control lever to either position other than <u>neutral,</u> the power-take-off and hoist pump engages. When moving the control lever to the <u>power-up</u> position and engaging the clutch, the dump body will raise (when the dump body reaches its limit of travel, it automatically stops). Upon moving the control lever to the <u>power-down</u> position, the dump body will lower. Moving the control lever to the <u>neutral</u> position and locking it will secure the dump body.

Another hauling vehicle used is the <u>truck-tractor</u> and <u>semitrailer</u> combination. This combination is unique in the manner in which the semitrailer and truck-tractor are attached to perform the hauling services for which they are intended. A large part of the weight of the semitrailer in this combination is supported by a connection, called the <u>fifth wheel,</u> the remaining weight is supported by the wheels of the semitrailer. The trailer braking system (usually air) is coupled to the towing vehicle by a flexible hose and a detachable coupling. The trailer braking system is usually designed so that it will keep the trailer in place when the couplings are disconnected. The trailer is also equipped with a landing gear which is a retractable support under the front end of the semitrailer. This gear is used to hold up the front end when it is uncoupled from the truck-tractor. When semitrailers are coupled and uncoupled, it is important that operation of the landing gear be coordinated with operation of the fifth wheel lock. If the landing gear is elevated before the fifth wheel connection is fully locked, the front end of the semitrailer will drop to the ground when the truck-tractor is driven away, with the possibility of damaging both the load and the semitrailer. Before the semitrailer is uncoupled, the brake couplings should be disconnected so that the semitrailer brakes are applied to prevent it from moving.

The method of connecting the truck-tractor to the semitrailer is by means of a fifth wheel. The upper fifth wheel plate is securely attached to the underside of the front end of the semi-trailer frame. Permanently attached to the center of the upper fifth wheel plate is a kingpin by which the truck-tractor pulls the semitrailer after the upper fifth wheel is attached to the truck-tractor lower fifth wheel. The kingpin is locked into position by a kingpin lock which is a ring on the lower fifth wheel that clamps around this kingpin. The kingpin lock is operated by a hand lever that extends to the side of the lower fifth wheel and can be released by pulling it out when the semitrailer is to become detached from the truck-tractor.

PRINCIPLES OF OPERATION OF FUEL HAULING VEHICLES

A typical <u>fuel tank</u> truck is equipped with a tank body divided into compartments. Each compartment has a manhole and filler cover assembly, bottom sump or well, discharge valves with screen assemblies and drainpipe. The drainpipes end in a manifold in the equipment compartment. The compartment also houses a delivery pump, a discharge valve control assembly, a pump delivery line gate valve, automatic dump valve drain tube valves, a gravity line gate valve, a filter separator, a pressure gate, a meter, a water separate chamber, and a grounding cable.

The delivery pump is powered by the transfer power takeoff, which is controlled by the transfer power shifting lever located in the driver's compartment. The lever is moved backward to the <u>engaged</u> position to engage the power takeoff which causes the pump to operate. The lever is moved forward to the <u>disengaged</u> position to disengage the power takeoff and stop the pump.

The discharge valve control operating levers control the discharge valves located at the bottom of each tank compartment. Pulling back on a lever opens a discharge valve and permits the flow of fuel into the piping system. Squeezing the trip rod operating handle mounted on the lever, and moving the lever forward, locks the compartment valve and shuts off the flow of fuel.

In an emergency, the discharge valve control remote control lever, located on the left side of the discharge valve control operating lever bank, provides a means of locking all discharge valves. Pulling the handle causes a release lever to trip the operating levers and locks the valves.

III. AUTOMOTIVE VEHICLE OPERATION

The sole source of complete and authentic information on operating a given automotive vehicle is the operator's manual issued by the manufacturer.

The information given in this section describes the prestart checks, starting checks, and operating procedures which are typical of automotive vehicles used.

PRESTART CHECKS

Before operating any vehicle, be sure that it is ready for the run. A prestart check should begin as you approach your vehicle. Take a look at it. Does its overall appearance seem normal? Oftentimes you will be able to tell from this first look if your vehicle has a broken spring or other exterior defects.

As you continue with the prestart check, move around to the front of your vehicle and raise the cap. If the coolant level is not visible, add coolant. Continual lowering of the level of coolant indicates a possible leak in the cooling system. In freezing weather, test the antifreeze solution in the radiator with a hydrometer. If necessary, add enough antifreeze to the coolant to prevent freezing at predicted minimum temperatures. Be sure to report a leaking cooling system on the Operator's Trouble Report so that corrective action can be taken by the maintenance shop.

Next check the level of the lubricating oil in the crankcase. It should be at or near the <u>full</u> mark on the dipstick. If it is not, add sufficient oil to raise the level to full. If the oil is dirty and gritty when rubbed between the fingertips, it will have to be changed.

Fan belts should be checked for defects in the belt, and excessive looseness or tightness. When found to be defective, the belts must be replaced. When found to be too loose or too tight, adjust according to the manufacturer's specifications.

Battery water level must be checked. If the level is not visible, add battery water to the level required. Check for loose battery wire connections, and tighten if required. Have worn or frayed battery wires replaced by the maintenance shop.

Close the hood, making sure that it latches properly.

Check the fuel tank. Most fuel tank gages register when the ignition switch is turned on. If the fuel gage is not working properly, and you have no way of knowing how much fuel is in the tank, fill it up. Running out of fuel could be very inconvenient and embarassing. Be sure to report improper operation of the fuel gage on the Operator's Trouble Report, so that corrective action can be taken by the maintenance shop.

Leaks found during your checks can often be corrected by tightening bolts, filler plugs, and line connections. If these steps fail to stop a leak, report the trouble for corrective action by the maintenance shop.

As you check the wheels and tires, be sure the tire pressure is as recommended (usually stenciled on each fender of the vehicle) by using either a tire gage or a tire air-hose that is equipped with a gage. Be particularly alert for uneven tread wear; this condition may indicate misalignment, need for balancing, or improper inflation. You may replace the tire at the tire shop, but balancing or alignment will be handled by the maintenance shop. When inspecting the wheels, see that the wheel flange bolts are in place and properly secured.

As you continue your prestart checks, examine the vehicle body for missing components, dents, doors that close improperly, and door windows and windshield glass that are cracked or broken. Next look under the vehicle to check the drive shaft, rear end, and rear axles for leaks or other obvious defects. Any discrepancies must be reported on the Operator's Trouble Report, so that corrective action can be taken by the maintenance shop.

When you have completed the external portion of the prestart checks, get into the cab and check the lights by turning on the light switch and observing whether the headlights are burning on both high and low beam. Have someone observe whether the stoplights on the rear of the vehicle go on when you apply the brakes. As you inspect the lights, wipe the glass lenses with a cloth. A film of mud or dust can cut light beams considerably. If the vehicle has special lights, such as turn signals, fog lights, and spotlights, they, too, must be in good working condition. Test the horn, check seat belts, and inspect the rear view mirror for damage. Before moving on, check the condition of the windshield wiper blades. In addition, check the vehicle's brakes, making sure that the brake lines are not broken or leaking, and that the parking brake cable and assembly are in working order. If any item needs to be adjusted, repaired, or replaced, note the trouble on the Operator's Trouble Report, so that corrective action can be performed by the maintenance shop.

A prestart check will be slightly different for each type vehicle, but the basic principles apply to all. At first, these checks may seem like a long and useless procedure. Once you have established a routine, however, you will find that the complete check requires only a few minutes. Many times this check will save you hours of trouble in the field or on the road.

STARTING CHECKS BEFORE OPERATION

After starting the engine, but before putting the vehicle or equipment into motion, make a few additional checks. First, and most important, make certain that you get an oil pressure indication. This indication may be below operating range at first, but be certain that it is registering. If your equipment has an oil pressure low warning light, make certain the light does not remain on more than several seconds after the engine is started. If the light does not go out after several seconds of engine operation, stop the engine and call a mechanic. Occasionally, a defective system causes the light to stay on, but in either case you will need the mechanic.

Your vehicle or equipment ammeter should also register a positive charge as the engine starts to run. This may be indicated by an ammeter which begins to register in a positive direction or by a red light which goes out when the charging begins. You should also check the temperature indicator, which should start to move upward on its scales as the engine warms up. In addition, check the windshield wipers to see if they are operating properly.

DURING OPERATIONS CHECKS

When a vehicle or piece of equipment is not operating properly, there are various symptoms by which the malfunction can be identified. You should be able to recognize these symptoms immediately and stop the machine before damage results. We have already mentioned the starting checks for oil pressure and the electrical system. Now let's look at some of the troubles that may occur during operation.

Temperature. The operating temperature of your piece of equipment is a measure of its mechanical condition. An engine that is running too hot or too cold is not functioning properly, and the cause of the high or low temperature should be determined immediately. If there is trouble in the cooling system, the engine, in most cases, will overheat.

Before you run your piece of equipment into the repair shop or call a mechanic, make a few checks to see if you can locate the trouble. First, check the radiator. If the water is low, refill. In addition, check to see if there are leaves or other matter clogging air passages of the radiator grill. Check the oil level. An insufficient amount of oil can cause overheating. Loose, slipping water pump belts and fan belts will cause overheating; check and tighten them if they are slipping.

If you eliminate these possible causes of overheating, and the temperature is still not normal, it is time to call a mechanic.

Oil Pressure. As mentioned earlier, you should make certain that oil pressure registers when the engine is started. High pressure readings may be observed while the engine is warming up in cold weather, before the oil has reached operating temperature. After a brief warmup period, the gage indicator should return to normal. Do not forget, however, to keep constant check on oil pressure throughout the day. If the pressure should drop, stop the engine and notify a mechanic.

There are a number of things that can cause low oil pressure. Diluted lubricating oil will cause a drop in pressure. If the oil is at the proper level, but is thin and lacks body, it may have been diluted with fuel leaking past the piston rings. The crankcase should be drained and refilled with the proper grade of oil. If frequent oil dilution or low oil pressure continues after changing the oil, your engine needs further services of a mechanic. As mentioned before, on rare occasions the trouble will be in the pressure gage rather than in the engine proper.

Electrical System. If your piece of equipment has a generator and battery, the ammeter indicates the condition of the electrical system. If the ammeter shows a discharge when the engine is running and all electrical accessories such as lights have been turned off, there is something wrong with the system; call a mechanic. Some vehicles have a warning light instead of an ammeter; if this light comes on and stays on during engine operation (except when the engine is idling), this too is an indication of trouble in the electrical system.

Smoking. Whenever you are operating motorized equipment and you see smoke coming from the exhaust pipe, there is trouble of some sort. The most common causes of smoking in a gasoline engine are worn pistons, rings, or cylinders, and faulty fuel mixtures. Smoking caused by worn engine parts is usually coupled with high oil consumption and calls for a major overhaul.

There are a number of mechanical troubles that will cause a diesel to smoke. If the engine is running too cool, the exhaust will form a cloud of white smoke. If the radiator is equipped with adjustable shutters, close them until the engine reaches the proper operating temperature. If the engine does not have shutters, place a partial covering over the radiator to bring the temperature up. Another cause of smoky exhaust is a clogged air cleaner. Follow the maintenance instructions printed on the air cleaner.

If the engine is allowed to idle for considerable periods, there will be more fuel injected into the cylinder than will burn, and consequently it will smoke. Do not idle the engine for long periods.

If the engine is subjected to loads that cause it to slow or lug down, it will begin to smoke. The remedy is to keep the engine revved up and to use the proper gear to handle the load. If you eliminate these causes of smoking and the engine still smokes, it is probably due to injectors, valves, fuel pumps, or worn piston rings; any of these conditions means a repair job for the mechanics.

Wheel Trouble. If you are operating automotive equipment, your hands on the steering wheel will tell you if the vehicle pulls to the right or to the left. You will feel vibrations caused by unbalanced wheels. When you apply the brakes, you will be able to feel whether the wheel is pulled to the right or to the left; thus you will know whether the front wheel brakes are operating evenly.

When you feel the vehicle pull to one side, stop and check the tires. If the tires are evenly inflated and the vehicle still pulls to one side, you should have the wheel alignment and the wheels checked by a mechanic. Your hands on the wheel will also tell you if the vehicle turns hard and whether the play in the steering wheel is excessive.

Transmission and Differential. Transmission difficulties may be characterized by shifting difficulty, gears jamming, and by unusual noises from the area where the transmission is located. This is true of a vehicle having either a manual or an automatic transmission. About the only thing that an equipment operator can do is to check the level of lubricant; if the transmission is low on lubricant, fill it to the proper level.

Differential trouble can often be recognized by noise from the differential area. However, noise from defective universal joints, rear wheel bearings, tires, or mufflers are sometimes mistaken for differential trouble. Stop the vehicle if noise occurs. For the purpose of operational maintenance with respect to differentials, an equipment operator has the responsibility of seeing that lubricant is at the proper level and bringing it up to the proper level if it is low. If there is differential trouble and you find that the level is not low, you should turn the job of locating and correcting the trouble over to a mechanic.

Brake Troubles. If your equipment is fitted with airbrakes, be aware of the air pressure indicator reading at all times. The reading may be too high; a high reading would probably indicate a faulty gage, a governor out of adjustment, or a defective governor. The most usual trouble with airbrakes is too little pressure. Low pressure can indicate a number of things, but most commonly it indicates a defective air safety valve, a governor out of adjustment, or an excessively worn compressor.

The air pressure gage is only one of the possible means by which you will discover trouble. Some of the other airbrake troubles are that they release too slowly, grab, or brake unevenly.

On hydraulic brakes, a soft, spongy pedal indicates either improper adjustment of air in the system. A pedal that goes to, or nearly to, the floorboard calls for immediate attention by a mechanic. Stops that require excessive pressure on the pedal, and brakes that are overly sensitive and grab when only slight pressure is applied to the pedal are other troubles that mean work for the mechanic.

Be sure that your brakes are in the best possible condition; your life may depend on them.

Clutches. If the clutch does not completely disengage when the pedal is entirely depressed, or if the clutch takes hold too near the floorboard, you should report the condition to a mechanic.

Vibration. On most of the equipment you operate, you will feel a certain amount of vibration; an unusual amount of vibration should not have to shake you out of your seat to make you realize that something is wrong. Unbalanced wheels, a cylinder that is not firing, a bent drive shaft, and other mechanical defects will cause excessive vibration.

After operating a piece of equipment for a period of time, you should be so aware of its characteristic sounds and its feel that you will be able to detect the slightest variation from normal operation. You may not be able to diagnose the mechanical symptoms, but you should be able to recognize trouble when it starts.

OPERATING PASSENGER CARRYING AND HAULING VEHICLES

After completing all prestarting and starting checks, and ensuring everything is in order, place the transmission in <u>neutral</u> or <u>park</u> and start the engine. Before you pull onto the road, be sure that it is clear enough for you to do so safely.

If your vehicle has an automatic transmission, set the transmission lever at D (Drive) or push in the D button. Release the emergency brake and speed up the engine by depressing the accelerator about one quarter of the way toward the floorboard. The vehicle should accelerate in <u>Low</u> smoothly. At a speed of about 18 to 25 mph under normal acceleration, the transmission should shift automatically into Drive. On some vehicles you must release the accelerator momentarily to let the transmission shift into Drive. A faint click in the transmission indicates the shift to the higher gear.

With a standard transmission, depress the clutch pedal, shift into first (low) gear, release the emergency brake, and engage the clutch slowly and smoothly while speeding up the engine a bit with the accelerator. Let the vehicle get up to about 10 to 15 mph before shifting into second gear, and to about 20 to 25 mph before shifting into third or high gear. Depress the clutch pedal before each shift, and release it smoothly after shifting.

On many vehicles with standard transmission, the gear shift lever is mounted on the steering column. Refer to the vehicle instruction manual for gear shifting directions.

<u>Up and Down Grade.</u> In starting a vehicle with a standard transmission up a grade from a stationary position, keep the emergency brake on to prevent the vehicle from rolling backward. Push in the clutch, shift into low, then ease off on the clutch pedal. As the clutch begins to take hold, release the emergency brake slowly, <u>at the same time,</u> increasing the speed of the engine. If these operations are performed carefully, the vehicle should start smoothly. Shift the vehicle into second only when it has reached enough speed to continue upgrade without laboring or jerking. You may not be able to shift from second to high until the end of the grade. If the grade is very steep, you may have to use low gear all the way up.

Downgrade always use the same gear that would be used going upgrade. Depress the clutch, shift into neutral, accelerate the engine to a speed that will pull the vehicle in a lower gear, then shift into the lower gear. If the procedure is efficiently carried out, the shift will be virtually noiseless.

UNDER NO CIRCUMSTANCES SHOULD THE VEHICLE COAST DOWNGRADE IN NEUTRAL. A vehicle out of gear is out of control except, possibly, when the brakes are applied. Even then the vehicle may pick up speed in excess of its braking ability, and you risk not only burning up the brakes, but having a serious accident as well.

<u>Low Range and Double-Clutching.</u> Heavy trucks may be equipped also with a two-speed rear axle and have what is known as a <u>low range.</u> By shifting to this low range, you tap the extra engine power that is needed to start an extremely heavy load, in rough driving, and in steep climbing. Under normal driving conditions, you would use the normal range.

No matter what kind of load the truck is carrying, start out in low gear, not in second. Together, the low range and low gear give maximum starting power. Take your time and accelerate smoothly in each gear before shifting to the next higher gear. Under some road or load conditions, the series of shifts from low to high may require as much as a mile of travel.

The transmissions of some trucks and buses are constructed in a form which makes it necessary to <u>double-clutch</u> to prevent the clashing and grinding of gears when shifting. Double-clutching adjusts engine speed to vehicle speed in a particular gear.

Double-clutching requires some practice. If you can possibly arrange to do so, take a truck around a given area with a supervisor or other experienced equipment operator to instruct you.

```
DOUBLE-CLUTCHING FROM A LOWER
       TO A HIGHER GEAR

• Push in clutch pedal
• Take foot off gas pedal
• Shift into neutral
• Let out clutch pedal
• Wait momentarily
• Push in clutch pedal again
• Shift to higher gear
• Let out clutch pedal
• Depress gas pedal
```

```
DOUBLE-CLUTCHING FROM A HIGHER
        TO A LOWER GEAR

• Push in clutch pedal
• Take foot off gas pedal
• Shift into neutral
• Let out clutch pedal
• Accelerate engine
• Push in clutch pedal again
• Shift to lower gear
• Let out clutch pedal
• Depress gas pedal
```

<u>Steering.</u> Proper steering is a matter of keeping your hands on the wheel, your eyes on the road, and your mind on safe driving. It also means keeping the vehicle on your side of the road, avoiding holes and obstructions, and passing other vehicles safely.

If your vehicle steers hard, pulls to the right or left, or the front wheels shimmy, try to find the cause of the trouble at once. It may be due to nothing more than underinflated tires, or it may be caused by the wheels being out of balance or alignment. It may also mean that some part of the steering mechanism needs adjusting, or repair.

If not accustomed to power steering, you may have difficulty at first in guiding this type of vehicle, because its steering mechanism responds more readily than one with conventional steering. Under power steering, a mere finger nudge of the steering wheel will turn the vehicle from its path.

<u>Backing.</u> Not all driving is forward. You will also have to back into loading platforms and parking spaces and into position lor shovel loading and other jobs on construction projects. Backing must be done with skill and caution. If the rear view of your vehicle is restricted, have someone direct you. Otherwise, get out frequently to check whether the way is clear. NOTE: The operator is responsible for all backing accidents.

<u>Curves.</u> Speeding under any conditions is dangerous and unsafe, but speeding on curves is extremely dangerous for at least four reasons: it increases the hazard of skidding; it heightens the _ possibility of load shifting; it wears tires away very fast; and the vehicle may run off the road or overturn.

It is not easy to state at what speed you can safely round a curve. The maximum safe speed depends on the arc of the curve, the width of the road, and the condition of its surface. Many curves are posted with safe speed limit signs, but on many, YOU still must judge how fast to take them.

In approaching a curve, SLOW DOWN as soon as it comes into view, then accelerate enough to keep the vehicle pulling steadily. If the road ahead curves frequently, maintain a speed moderate enough to keep the vehicle on an even keel, using the highest gear possible. Avoid using the brakes. NEVER try to pass another vehicle on a curve. Stay on your own side of the center line.

Skids. To avoid skids, watch for obstructions, pavement breaks, holes, shoulder edges, and loose gravel that might grab your wheels. Beware of wet roads, roads strewn with leaves, roads full of mud or slush, and railroad and trolley tracks.

To prevent going into a skid, cut down your speed, and increase the distance between your vehicle and the one ahead. Do not accelerate too fast or the wheels may spin; drive in as high a gear as possible. The higher the gear, the less the tendency to skid. Should you get into a skid, however, turn the wheels IN THE DIRECTION OF THE SKID, stay in gear with the clutch engaged, and accelerate slightly to help straighten the course of the vehicle. DO NOT APPLY THE BRAKES; you will only increase the skid by locking the wheels. If any slowing is necessary, it should be done in a lower gear.

Off and On The Shoulder. Getting off and on the shoulder is a common occurrence on narrow roads and in congested traffic, and it usually is not difficult to get back on the road. However, if the shoulder is lower than the road, first change to a lower gear without braking. Second, instead of scrapping or tearing away the side walls of your tires by trying to creep back upon the road gradually, proceed slowly until you are able to get back by making a sharp angle turn to the left.

OPERATING TRUCK TRACTOR AND SEMITRAILER

Before setting out with a truck tractor and semitrailer, you must know the procedures for coupling and uncoupling the truck tractor from the semitrailer. To couple the truck tractor to the semitrailer, proceed as follows:

1. Place wheel chocks in front of and behind the trailer wheels.

2. Make sure the fifth wheel lock is open; then back the tractor close enough to the trailer to permit coupling of the brake lines,

3. Connect the brake hoses in the proper order by first connecting the truck tractor <u>service</u> air line hose to the trailer, followed by the <u>emergency</u> air line hose.

4. Open the cutout valve to allow pressure to build up in the reserve tank on the trailer.

5. Apply pressure to the trailer brakes, if they are operated independently. If the trailer brakes are not operated independently, proceed as described below.

    a. For vacuum-operated brakes, turn off the service line valve and disconnect the hose; this should automatically apply pressure to the trailer brakes.

    b. For air-operated brakes, turn off the emergency line valve and disconnect the hose; this should automatically apply pressure to the trailer brakes.

6. Back the tractor under the trailer until the fifth wheel engages the trailer kingpin and locks. If the tractor is not in line to engage the trailer kingpin and must be repositioned, uncouple the airhose before moving the tractor to avoid breaking the hose.

7. When the fifth wheel and the kingpin are locked, test security of the hookup. Remove the chocks, place the tractor in first gear, engage the clutch, and move the tractor forward slightly while applying pressure to the brakes.

8. If the trailer is properly connected, stop the tractor and set the hand brake; double check all couplings, reconnect the air brake hose, and open the air valve.

9. Connect the trailer electrical power line; check for proper operation of lights and, where applicable, heating or refrigeration equipment.

10. Raise the trailer parking legs, and release the trailer parking brake.

11. Before moving the tractor, check the brakes for proper functioning and for adequate air pressure; minimum operating air pressure is 60 pounds.

To uncouple a truck tractor from a semitrailer, proceed as follows:

1. Set the tractor hand brake.

2. Apply pressure to the trailer brakes by disconnecting the hose lines, as described above, step 5.

3. Disconnect the trailer electrical power lines and secure them to the tractor.

4. Place wheel chocks in front of and behind the trailer wheels and set the trailer parking brake.

5. Lower trailer parking legs; be sure the ground is firm enough to prevent the parking legs from sinking.

6. Place the fifth wheel hook lock handle in the release position; move the tractor foward slightly, leaving the trailer kingpin partly in the fifth wheel slot.

7. Recheck the trailer supports; if trailer is secure, move the tractor away from the trailer.

Safe Operation. In driving a tractor-trailer, watch for obstructions. Since a trailer body is often considerably higher than a truck body, you must allow for this height and watch out for viaducts, tree limbs, extended roofs OVER loading docks, and other obstructions. Also watch weight limitations on bridges. A tractor-trailer usually is longer than a truck; therefore, you must drive it carefully to avoid cutting in on other motorists.

Braking, Stopping, and Parking. With independently operated trailer brakes, apply the trailer brakes FIRST, gradually and smoothly, to avoid locking the wheels and skidding. As speed is reduced, apply the truck or tractor brakes to spread the braking load on all wheels. With synchronized brakes, both tractor and trailer brakes are operated by one foot pedal like the brakes on automobiles.

In making emergency stops, be sure the trailer brakes are applied either first or simultaneously with - never after - the tractor brakes. Attempting to stop without using the trailer brakes will cause the trailer load to push the tractor forward, and possibly push it into whatever you are trying to avoid.

In the event of any stop where you leave your cab, set your parking brake. This applies to all automotive equipment. If you have operated tractor-trailer units, you know that you can hold the unit on a grade by setting the trailer brake. Holding your rig on the grade by setting the trailer brake is all right AS LONG AS YOU ARE IN THE CAB, but DON'T set the trailer brake and LEAVE the cab. The engine on your rig may die and cause the air pressure to drop off. If this happens, your trailer brakes will release, and you will have a runaway rig.

Turning and Backing. In turning a tractor-trailer, remember that the outside turning circle of the complete unit is the same as that of the tractor, and that the trailer wheels cut inside the path of the tractor.

At first, it might seem that backing would be a difficult operation. Actually, the hinged-in-the-middle feature of tractor-trailer units makes them easier to handle in cramped quarters than conventional trucks.

If you wish to back your automobile or truck to the right, you would naturally turn the steering wheel to the right. To back your semitrailer to the right, you turn your steering wheel to the left. This action pushes the front of the semitrailer to the left and steers the semitrailer wheels to the right.

If you have to make a right-hand back into an alley (sometimes called a blind back), drive the unit past the alley entrance, keeping it far enough from the curb so that the tractor can head slightly to the right as you come to a stop.

Before you start to back, check behind the trailer from both sides of the cab to be sure of your distance, and that traffic is clear. Turn the steering wheel to the LEFT to push the semitrailer around and back it to the right. As you continue to back slowly, keep the tractor wheels turned to the left and continue to check clearances from the right-hand door of the cab. As the trailer swings into the alley (with clearance on all sides), turn the steering wheel to the RIGHT and continue to back the semitrailer into the alley.

As the unit gets into line, straighten the front wheels and back down the alley, watching at all times to see that the semitrailer does not veer to either side. If the semitrailer angles to the left wall, adjust it to the right by turning your steering wheel to the left. If the semitrailer veers to the right, adjust it to the left by turning your steering wheel to the right.

A left-hand back is easier, because you can see the trailer from the driver's side of the cab. Of course, the direction you turn the steering wheel is just the opposite to a right-hand back.

Remember that to back the semitrailer to the right you turn the steering wheel to the left; and to back the semitrailer to the left, you turn the steering wheel to the right.

A skidding tractor-trailer unit is handled in a slightly different manner than a conventional vehicle. Turn your wheels immediately in the direction of the skid, accelerate slightly and (ONLY if the tractor is equipped with independent controlled brakes), apply the trailer brakes off and on gently so that the wheels will not lock. The trailer will then act as a drag and tend to pull both units back in line.

If the trailer starts to skid, handle it like a conventional vehicle, that is, do not apply brakes and turn in direction of skid.

BUSES

When operating buses to transport personnel, you will have responsibilities in addition to those concerning the operation of trucks and trailers.

Whether you operate a small shuttle bus on the base or a large passenger bus through a community from installation to installation, you are expected to observe a schedule of arrivals and departures, and to account for your runs.

Operation. The following rules for the operation of buses are supplementary to those applying to all motor vehicles:

1. Only operators with satisfactory records of safe driving will be assigned to drive buses.

2. Operators must be trained to stop, start, and operate buses smoothly and without jerks or sudden changes in acceleration.

3. Operators must not put vehicle in motion with the doors open,

4. Operators must not close the doors of a bus until passengers are completely clear of the bus when discharging, or fully inside and off the steps when entering the bus.

5. When making a turn or upon approaching a sharp curve, operators must reduce speed and use care to avoid injuring passengers.

6. The bus operator must give his attention to the road when driving and will not carry on unnecessary conversation with the passengers while the vehicle is in motion.

7. Operators of fare-charging buses will not make change while the bus is in motion.

Regulations. The driver of a school bus is required to exercise all precautions listed above in addition to the following special precautions:

1. Speed. No school bus will be driven at a speed greater than that authorized by the laws of the state in which the vehicle is being operated. When children are on the bus, the speed must be not more than 45 miles per hour.

2. Orderly Conduct. Passengers will be under the authority of and directly responsible to the operator of the bus, and the operator will be held responsible for the orderly conduct of the passengers.

3. Regular Stops . Pick up or discharge of any passenger except at regular stops designated is prohibited.

4. Railroad Crossings. Before crossing any railroad track or tracks, you must stop the bus within 50 feet but not less than 15 feet from the nearest rail of such railroad; while stopped, listen and look in both directions along the track for any approaching train; do not proceed until such precautions have been taken and until you have ascertained that the course is clear.

5. Crossing Street. Whenever a school bus stops to discharge passengers who must cross the street or highway in order to reach their destination, such passengers must cross in front of the bus, except when laws regulating local traffic prohibit this. In case of separated lanes with a median strip, the rule applies to both roadways. The bus must not be started until passengers desiring to cross have done so.

6. Escorting Children. The operator of a school bus must not permit pupils to cross a street or highway until they can do so safely; and he will, if necessary, secure the bus, dismount, and act as their escort.

The following precautions apply to operation of semitrailer buses:

1. Passengers

    a.   Standing in moving vehicles is prohibited except where handholds or straps are provided for each standee.

    b.   No passenger will be permitted to ride on running boards or with arms or legs extended outside the vehicle, or seated on fenders, top of cab, cab shields, or in door wells.

c. No passenger will be permitted to get on or off while the vehicle is in motion.

2. <u>Exit-Entrance</u>

a. Exit-entrance on semitrailer buses without doors should be equipped with a heavy gage safety chain across the opening 36 inches above floor level. Chains should be attached by a secure latching arrangement which will permit easy latching and unlatching.

b. The following signs must be posted at or near the inside of the exit and entrance of semitrailer buses not equipped with doors:

SITTING OR STANDING ON STEPS OR IN DOOR WELLS IS PROHIBITED

SAFETY CHAIN MUST BE LATCHED WHILE BUS IS IN MOTION

DUMP TRUCK OPERATION

During dumping operations, the truck should be on level ground or inclined uphill with front of truck facing downward. When the truck is in position, release the lower latches of the tailgate with the hand lever at the front left corner of the body. Now engage the power control with the dump body control lever, located in the cab. With the control lever at the farthest forward position, accelerate the engine moderately; do not race it. Hydraulic pressure will begin to hoist the dump body.

As the body rises, the load will slide backward under the open tailgate. If the load piles up and blocks the tailgate, place the truck in low gear and move it forward until there is more space to dump the remainder of the load. Do not change the position of the body control lever. If the load does not slide out easily, have someone dislodge it with a long hand shovel (taking care not to stand in the immediate dumping area). When dumping a load containing rocks or other large solids, the tailgate should be latched at the bottom, but unfastened at the top so that the tailgate can drop down and the load can drop. To spread a load over a large area, shift the truck into low gear and drive it slowly forward while dumping.

You can hold the body in any position by returning the control lever to position C. When dumping is completed, lower the body by returning the control lever to position A. Then close the tailgate latches.

TANK TRUCK OPERATION

Tank trucks are used to haul and dispense fuels or other types of liquids. A tank truck is equipped with a stainless steel, 1,200-gallon tank body, which is divided into two 600-gallon compartments. The fuel delivery system is equipped with an upright filter/separator and meter. Since there are only two tank compartments, the discharge valve control has two operating levers. There is a speed control linkage assembly which controls speed of the engine, power takeoff, and delivery pump.

The filter/separator is equipped with three filter elements, three go-no-go fuses, a pressure gage, and an automatic dump (drain) valve. The primary function of the filter element is to collect solid contaminants and separate water from the fuel.

The go-no-go fuses shut off the fuel flow if water or solid contaminants exceed a safe level; the shutoff of flow indicates that the filters are not operating properly. The malfunction must be located and corrected, and the fuses must be replaced before operation is continued.

The pressure gage reflects the condition of each of the filter elements and go-no-go fuses. When the pressure differential between the inlet pressure and the outlet pressure (gage handle in position 1) exceeds 20 psi, or when pressure differential between the inlet pressure and the internal pressure (gage handle in position 2) exceeds 15 psi, filter elements must be replaced. When pressure differential between outlet pressure and internal pressure (gage handle in position 3) exceeds 15 psi, replace the go-no-go fuses.

The automatic dump (drain) valve is float-operated. The float sinks in fuel but rises in water. When water is present in the valve housing, the float rises, the valve opens, and the water drains away through the valve drain tube. Open the automatic dump (drain) valve during fueling operations. Check pressure differential every day that equipment is in use; check it while the pump is operating, and record the readings.

When operating the fuel tank truck for discharging of fuels, follow instructions prescribed in the manufacturer's operating manual or the directions on the inside of the equipment compartment door. The general instructions which follow are typical.

Close the meter drain valve, delivery pump drain cock, and filter/separator drain valve. Open the automatic dump (drain) valve. Enter the driver's compartment and start the engine; depress the clutch, and put the transfer shift lever in neutral; place the transfer power takeoff shift lever in the engaged position; then place the transmission gearshift lever in fourth gear position, and release the clutch.

> CAUTION: Allowing the engine to run with transmission engaged and the transfer shift lever in neutral without the transfer power takeoff in the engaged position will cause bearing failure in the transfer case. Be sure to shift the transmission gearshift lever to neutral when not operating the power takeoff.

After the vehicle has been made ready, return to the fuel handling control compartment and set the remote hand throttle to allow the engine to operate at 700 rpm when the fuel dispensing pump is engaged. Move the discharge valve control operating lever of the tank compartment to be discharged to the open position; and be sure, before pumping operations begin, to attach the grounding wire to the vehicle being serviced. Open the pump delivery line hose and squeeze the nozzle operating lever and discharge the fuel. After discharging the fuel, close the pump delivery line gate valve, and move the discharge valve control operating lever to the closed position. Close the automatic dump valve drain tube valve and turn the hand throttle to the closed position. Return to the driver's compartment; depress

the clutch and place the transmission gearshift lever in neutral; then place the transfer power takeoff shifting lever to disengaged, and stop the engine.

When changing from one type of fuel to another, drain and flush the fuel compartment, pump filter/separator, service lines, manifold, meter, gage, and dispensing hoses and nozzles.

Remember, all pumping mechanisms are not controlled and operated in the same manner. You will find that each make or model will operate differently. If you are in doubt as to the proper pump operation and maintenance procedures, study the caution and instruction plates located near the pump and control mechanisms.

Drivers of fuel tank trucks must observe safe driving practices as listed below.

Drive defensively, and make allowances for other drivers.

Make turns only from proper lanes, and signal intent to other drivers. Never leave the proper lane except when necessary and then only when safe to do so.

Avoid excessive speeds at all times and especially on rough terrain, in gravel, and on curves. Be alert for passing or approaching traffic.

Drive downgrade in the same gear that would be used to drive upgrade.

Move completely off the road, if possible, when necessary to park. Set brakes, and chock wheels if stopping on a grade. Set flags during day and set flares or reflectors at night.

Stop at all railroad crossings, and be especially watchful in the case of multiple tracks.

Keep vehicle moving to prevent accumulations of vapor if a small leak develops in route. Arrange to discharge load at nearest point.

Ask for assistance if a large amount of fuel is escaping, such as might be the case if the vehicle is damaged. Immediately secure the engine, cordon the area, and obtain firefighting and security support.

Reduce refueling stops to a minimum under load. Stop the engine while refueling the prime mover.

Avoid driving past a fire or near the route until it is safe to do so.

Never smoke on or about tank vehicles used for hauling flammable liquids. Carry no matches on such vehicles.

Examine tires occasionally on long hauls for tire pressure and for damage that could cause an accident.

HAND SIGNALS

When you plan to turn, slow down, or stop, you must let the drivers approaching you and the drivers following you know well in advance what you intend to do.

The hand signals for these maneuvers are shown below. Instead of hand signals, mechanical directional signals may be used if your vehicle is so equipped. When operating vehicles in congested areas such as construction sites, docking areas, and pick-up and delivery areas, the hand signals depicted should be used.

① RIGHT TURN   ② STOP   ③ LEFT TURN

HAZARDOUS CONDITIONS

Speed should always be reduced for night-time driving. Too many drivers try to drive just as fast at night as they do in the daytime.

Night driving is two to three times more dangerous than day driving. Fatigue and sharply reduced vision are the primary causes for increased danger. The steady hum of the motor and the darkness on the road ahead tend to lull us to sleep at the wheel. Wide-awake driving is necessary at all times and especially at night, since we can see objects only a limited distance ahead. After-dark driving requires different skills and extra care for safe driving.

Listed below are requirements and practices applicable to night driving which should be carefully observed:

1. When you meet a vehicle at night, you must lower your headlight beams when within 500 feet of the approaching vehicle.

2. Lower your headlight beams when following another vehicle within 200 feet.

3. Lower your headlight beams when you are driving on well-lighted streets.

4. Use your lower headlight beams when driving in a fog, and reduce your speed. Driving with your high beams in a fog is like shining your lights on a mirror — light is reflected back into your eyes and blinds you.

5. Avoid looking directly into the lights of vehicles that you are meeting. Instead, watch the right-hand edge of the road.

6. Keep your headlights properly adjusted so that the lower beams are not aimed upward into the approaching driver's eyes.

7. Keep your windshield clean.

8. Slow down when facing the glare from approaching headlights.

9. Be sure you can stop whenever necessary within the vision distance of your vehicle's headlights, and watch continually and carefully for pedestrians along the roadside.

10. Use your headlights during the period from one-half hour after sunset to one-half hour before sunrise, and whenever visibility is reduced.

When overtaking and passing other vehicles on the road, observe the common rules of passing. Use extreme caution whenever passing a vehicle as the view immediately beyond the other vehicle is blocked on that side. The greater the speed of the vehicle ahead, the more road space and time will be required to overtake and pass the vehicle.

Listed below are restrictions for overtaking and passing:

1. Do not pass to the right of another vehicle, except on multiple-lane divided highways (more than two lanes of traffic moving in one direction) and only then if such passing is permitted; use extreme caution in such instances.

2. Do not pass at an intersection or railroad crossing.

3. Do not pass on a hill or curve, except on multiple-lane, divided highways.

4. Do not pass a vehicle that is signaling to turn or to move into your lane of traffic, or one that has started to overtake and pass another vehicle.

5. Do not pass when the center line of the road is solid on your side.

6. Do not pass where the highway is divided by two solid lines.

7. Do not pass when the single center line is solid.

Rain, snow, ice, or fog affect visibility, stopping distance, maneuverability, and vehicle control. Follow these suggestions for driving under such conditions:

1. Adjust the speed of the vehicle to existing conditions.

2. For normal conditions, allow at least one car length between vehicles for every 10 mph that you are traveling. Increase the normal safe distance between vehicles to allow for wet conditions.

3. Use tire chains or snow tires on ice or snow; however, they are only an aid to increase traction and will not eliminate the necessity for added caution.

4. Slow down when approaching bridges, overpasses, and shady areas in the road; surfaces in such areas often freeze before regular roadway surfaces and remain frozen longer.

5. Keep the outside of the windshield and windows clear of snow, ice, and frost at all times, and use the vehicle defroster to improve visibility; use extreme caution when driving in fog.

6. Apply brakes with a light pumping action to prevent skidding and use engine compression to help control the vehicle.

7. Signal well in advance to warn others of an intended stop or turn.

Superhighways, designed for high speed driving, require drivers to be more skillful and alert to avoid accidents. When entering expressways, yield to all traffic. While traveling, allow necessary distance between vehicles for safe stopping; avoid highway hypnosis by making rest stops and opening vents or windows; and never exceed the posted speed. During emergencies, get the vehicle off the roadway; use flasher lights or flares behind the vehicle to warn other motorists; and look behind for oncoming or passing traffic before opening vehicle doors. When leaving expressways, get in the proper lane well before the turn-off, and use turn signals to warn other drivers.

When driving through water, reduce speed to prevent brake drums, engine, and ignition from getting wet. Test the brakes for effectiveness immediately after leaving the water. If water has entered the brake drums and wet the linings, drive at a very slow speed while gently applying sufficient pressure on the brake pedal to cause a slight drag, thereby squeezing the brake linings against the drums and forcing the water out of the linings.

Snow and Ice. Snow and ice severely limit the traction of any vehicle. To increase traction, put chains on all driving wheels. When moving over fresh snow, maintain a slow, steady speed. Rapid acceleration is likely to cause skidding, or cause the wheels to dig in. If your vehicle becomes stuck in a hole in the snow, rocking it back and forth by shifting from forward to reverse may enable you to start again. Brakes, when used, should be applied lightly and released quickly if skidding begins. If you are driving hauling equipment that includes a trailer, apply only the trailer brakes, or at least apply them first.

Hard packed snow or ice is even more dangerous to drive on than newly fallen snow. Snow tires are not much help on ice, as they add little or no traction and give you a false feeling of security. Deflating the tires a bit will assist in preventing skidding.

Mud, Sand, and Swamps. When approaching a stretch of sticky soil or of muddy or swampy ground, put chains on the rear wheels to save yourself a lot of distress. If chains are not available, and the going looks rough, go into the necessary low gear. Engage the front-wheel drive, if the vehicle has one. Size up the road ahead so that once you start you can keep going. As far as possible, avoid ruts, holes, and edges that may cause side slips and swaying loads. Speed should be maintained, but do not spin the wheels. If the wheels start to lose traction, decrease speed but stay in the same gear. If the vehicle should become hopelessly bogged down, do not spin the wheels and burn up the tires, and do not overtax the equipment. Instead disengage the clutch at once, and get out and look the situation over. How to get out of bad situations depends on circumstances.

You may be able to back out and select a better way through. If you have wheel mats, use them. You may be able to jack up one wheel and place brush, boards, rocks, or similar material under it, enabling you to pull out. You may be able to dig your way out by digging a ditch in the direction that the wheels are expected to move. When the wheels are in deep ruts, ditches dug at an angle to the ruts may be necessary to assist the wheels back to a straddle position over the rut.

Of course, if a suitable tow truck is available, use it to get out of trouble. If your piece of equipment is equipped with a winch, use it to pull yourself out.

If the truck has dual wheels, use two tow ropes and six strong stakes. Drive two stakes into the ground the same distance apart as the wheels. Drive these stakes in front of the truck, if the best route out is forward, and behind if the best route out is backward. Use the other four stakes as anchors. The loop ends of the tow ropes are secured to the wheels by passing them between the duals, out through the spokes, and over the hub. The ropes are then attached to the anchor stakes. When this is done, the vehicle can move out on its own power by allowing the tow ropes to wind up between the dual wheels.

If stuck in sand, chicken wire on heavy burlap or canvas tarpaulins staked to the surface will aid greatly in supporting the load of the truck - and usually will get you out. In some cases, sand is somewhat encrusted below the surface and the vehicle will continue to creep forward even though the wheels spin. As long as the vehicle continues to move, the wheels may be kept spinning slowly, allowing your vehicle to dig its way out. Do not allow the vehicle to develop a differential jump; should this occur, STOP VEHICLE and try another solution. You may have to let some of the air out of your tires to pull through a stretch of sand but, as a general rule, it is bad practice to run on underinflated tires. In going through sand, as in going through other tough spots, it is essential to maintain momentum and keep going. Changing of gears must be avoided by selecting the proper gear before entering the sand.

<u>Fording.</u> Before you start through water, whether fording or crossing a stretch of flooded highway, be sure that the water is not so deep that it will drown out your motor. Also make sure that the surface under the water will support your vehicle. As a rule, nothing is gained by attempting to use momentum in crossing streams or other water. Cross slowly in a low gear. If there is any danger of water surging or splashing into the fan, disconnect it before crossing. After crossing the stream, apply the brakes intermittently until dry, enough to hold. At the first opportunity, wheels, crank-case, universal joint, differential, transmission, and other parts submerged should be checked to determine that no water has entered.

SECURING

When returning to the equipment pool area at the end of the day's run, top off fuel tanks, check oil and coolant levels, and position vehicle in a safe manner. Let engine idle, check instrument readings, secure footbrake or handbrake, place transmission in neutral, secure engine by turning off ignition switch, complete daily trip ticket, roll up windows, secure doors, block vehicle if required, drain air tanks (if so equipped), and turn in required reports to the dispatcher,

IV. OPERATOR'S MAINTENANCE

Every equipment operator is required to perform certain daily maintenance services on his vehicle as a matter of routine. The faithful performance of these services does much to prolong the life of the vehicle, to avoid major repairs and overhaul, and to assure the equipment operator that his vehicle will perform consistently and dependably. *Operator's maintenance* is the term that describes the required inspection, service, lubrication, and adjustments performed by an operator to keep power tools and equipment in a safe operable condition, in order to prevent personnel injuries, mechanical malfunctions, and curtailment of production or progress.

FAN BELTS

Worn or loose fan belts are often the cause of engine overheating, especially when the engine is operating in low or second gear. Excessive looseness or tightness can be determined by applying the manufacturer's specified pressure to the belt at a point midway between the fan and the generator pulleys and determining that the deflection is within the range specified for the vehicle.

If it.is necessary to adjust the fan belt, first look at the type of device used to provide the fan takeup and follow the manufacturer's adjusting procedures.

IGNITION AND ELECTRICAL SYSTEMS

Ignition troubles are often a major cause of improper engine performance. When an ignition tuneup is required, it includes checking the battery, cleaning and inspecting all wires and terminals, cleaning or replacing and adjusting spark plugs, checking ignition timing, and adjusting breaker points. These are important jobs in an ignition tuneup, but you are only required to check the battery and clean and inspect all wires and terminals. An experienced mechanic using proper equipment will adjust and check timing and ignition breaker points, and clean or replace and adjust spark plugs to the manufacturer's specifications.

BATTERY AND BATTERY CONNECTIONS

The storage battery supplies power for all electrical accessories. The condition of the battery is the first concern in accessory maintenance. Check the battery periodically for water, and see that the battery terminals are tight and free from corrosion. If the battery fails to supply sufficient power to turn the starter or to operate other electrical units on a vehicle, report this malfunction to the maintenance section for corrective action.

Most electrical troubles can be traced to poor ground connections, loose wire connections, and worn or frayed wires that cause short circuits, rather than to a defective battery.

Tightening a loose wire connection is a simple operation; a worn, frayed, or broken wire should be taped to make temporary repairs ONLY. The vehicle should be taken to the shop where a mechanic will replace the wire with a new one.

COOLING SYSTEM

You will need to drain the coolant from the cooling system occasionally to remove sediment and rust scales and for periodic radiator flushing. Be sure all the coolant is removed. The manufacturer's maintenance manuals will show you the locations of drain cocks and plugs, which are usually found in the lowest points of the systems.

When refilling a cooling system that has been drained, allow water to pass through the engine and out the drain openings before closing them. When the water is clear and flows freely from the openings, close them securely and fill the cooling system slowly. Never add water faster than it can circulate through the various branches of the system, since water overflowing from the cap may give a false indication of a full system. Do not add water to the cooling system of an overheated engine; allow the engine to cool first. If you must add water before you are sure the engine is cool, run the engine and add water very slowly. Cold water in an overheated engine may crank a cylinder block or cause other serious damage to engine parts.

WHEELS AND TIRES

You should become familiar with the recommendations of tire manufacturers on the proper use and care of tires on vehicles. Probably one of the most common mistakes is incorrect tire pressure. To keep vehicles operating continuously and efficiently, you must follow the procedures recommended by the manufacturer for inspecting and inflating tires. To get the maximum life from a tire, you must maintain proper tire pressure to match the load the vehicle will carry at its actual operating speed. You must make periodic pressure checks on cold tires (before running equipment), and make visual inspection of tires for tread cuts, sidewall snags, and wear. Check wheel rims for splits, metal fatigue, and out-of-round condition.

When tires are to be removed, take the equipment to the tire shop, where special tools and personnel are available to replace or repair the tires. You will be required to help the tire repair personnel to disassemble and repair the tire. Detailed procedures on this will be given later in the chapter.

BRAKE SYSTEMS

When inspecting hydraulic brakes, ensure that the proper level of hydraulic fluid is maintained in the master cylinder reservoir, and check the system for leaks and worn parts. Be sure to add the kind of hydraulic fluid recommended by the manufacturer, because some brake systems are made with natural rubber seals and others with synthetic seals. Unless the recommended fluid is used, the seals will deteriorate quickly and the hydraulic brakes will not operate.

Dust and dirt that accumulates around the filler plug opening can also affect brake operation. A small particle of dust or dirt that may find its way into the operating mechanism can close a vent or prevent a valve from seating properly. See that all dust and dirt are removed before you uncover the master cylinder and add fluid. Add enough fluid so that the level reaches just below the filler plug opening. After filling the reservoir, see that the vent at the top of the reservoir is open and the filler plug is tight.

Leaks and loose joints in the brake system not only allow fluid to escape but also permit air to enter. Air in the hydraulic system can be felt by the soft, springy action of the brake pedal, and must be removed by bleeding to obtain a solid pedal. When bleeding becomes necessary, take the vehicle to the maintenance shop, where special tools and personnel are available to correct the situation.

When inspecting and servicing airbrake systems, the most common problem you will find is leaking air lines. The air line hoses and couplings should be checked for leaks and wear, particularly those connecting a truck and trailer. Replace worn hoses and tighten hose connections and couplings. The cutout cocks provided at the tractor hose connections are often responsible for air loss. These tapered valves should be checked often and kept tightly closed. When no trailer is being towed, they often jar open. Be sure these valves are closed tightly, but are free to open when trailer brakes are required. A little penetrating oil will free a binding cutout cock.

The drain cock at each air reservoir should work freely. Reservoirs should be drained daily to remove water that accumulates from condensation.

BODY AND FRAME

The mobility of trailers results in frequent shipment of vehicles, with consequent likelihood of damage to the body and frame during shipment. Of course, accidents are another cause of body and frame damage.

During the operator's maintenance, he will inspect the body and frame of the vehicle. He will look for damaged portions of the body and report the damage so that repairs can be made by the body shop personnel. These body repairs include straightening body panels, replacing body parts, and repainting.

If damage to the frame is detected by your inspection, this will also be reported and the body shop personnel allowed to repair the damage, if they are equipped to do so. If they do not have the equipment, the vehicle must be sent to a larger repair facility equipped with frame straightening machines.

LUBRICATING OIL SYSTEM

Check the oil level and, if necessary, add additional oil for a _full_ gage or dipstick reading. Do not overfill.

If the oil feels gritty to the fingers or has no body, it has lost its effective lubricating qualities and must be changed.

Oil changes should also be made in accordance with the manufacturers' lubrication and maintenance schedules. On most of your equipment, the grade and quantity of the oil to be used will be found on the lubricating charts.

Drain the oil only after the engine has run and is warmed up. This warmup period will thin the oil and stir up the sludge and foreign matter in the oil pan. After replacing with new oil, recheck the oil level to be certain that the oil column reaches the _full_ mark on the dipstick. Then run the engine for a few minutes to ensure no leaks exist, particularly around the oil filter and the oil drain plug. Get into the habit of looking at the ground or pavement over which the vehicle has been parked, for any oil spots that may indicate leakage.

Changing oil filter elements periodically will be part of your job. Usually the filter elements are changed at the same time the oil is changed in the crankcase. On new engines, it may be changed (1) after the first 500 miles; (2) according to the manufacturer's instructions; or (3) according to shop policy. The filter element should be replaced with the type recommended by the manufacturer. Be sure to remove the old gasket and see that the new gasket under the cover or in the crankcase is properly fitted, and that there are no oil leaks. Always check these points immediately after starting the engine.

FUEL SYSTEM

The fuel system consists of the fuel tank, fuel pump, carburetor, intake manifold, and fuel lines or tubes connecting the tank, pump, and carburetor.

Fuel tanks give little or no trouble, and as a rule require no servicing other than an occasional draining and cleaning. If, during inspection, you should find the fuel tank either punctured or leaking, report the trouble, leaving the repairs or replacement to the repair shop where there are proper servicing facilities. All fuel leaks will be considered cause for immediate shutdown.

If the presence of gasoline in the crankcase is observed, it is a good indication of a diaphragm leaking within the fuel pump. Usually, the mechanics will replace the pump or repair it using a repair kit for this purpose.

Inspect the fuel lines and connections, observing that the lines are placed away from the exhaust pipes, mufflers, and manifolds so that excessive heat will not cause vaporlock. Make sure fuel lines are attached to the frame, engine, and other units so that the effects of the vibration will be minimized. Fuel lines should be free of contact with sharp edges which might cause wear. In places of excessive movement, as between the vehicle frame and rubber-mounted engine, short lengths of gasoline-resistant flexible tubing are used. Occasionally, road vibration may loosen and break lines, and they can become pinched or flattened by flying rocks. Such damage could interfere with the flow of fuel.

A certain amount of scale forms within the fuel lines and sometimes causes a stoppage.

When, in the course of your daily maintenance services of the fuel system, you observe operational troubles with the carburetor, report the troubles, leaving the adjustments, repairs, or replacement of the carburetor with the maintenance personnel equipped to handle these troubles.

V. LUBRICATION

As you may recall, lubricants act as cooling agents, sealing agents, cleaning agents, and reduce friction and wear. This section discusses the procedures of lubrication.

Periodic lubrication prolongs the usefulness of a vehicle. Proper lubrication is more than merely placing a grease gun on a fitting and pulling the trigger. It means selecting the correct lubricants and applying them in a sufficient amount and in the proper places. The experienced equipment operator uses neither too much nor too little lubricant.

Lubrication, then, is a thorough job of oiling and greasing. The lube rack will likely carry several approved standard lubricants. This standardization of lubricants eliminates the variation and confusion in manufacturer's brand names and quality designations, and makes readily available a few standard lubricants.

Familiarize yourself with the lubrication chart of the vehicle with which you are working. These charts show what to lubricate, and where.

Of course, you must learn to use grease guns properly, as well as other dispensers of oils and grease.

Remember that grease on the outside of a fitting does not lubricate, and oil or grease in puddles or gobs around the grease rack can cause serious injury. So look for and remove spilled oil or grease that drops from chassis parts. Better yet, while lubricating a piece of equipment, remove all excessive grease from the fittings and wipe up lubricants that fall to the floor.

DISPENSING LUBRICANTS

Grease guns and dispensers operate either by hand or are air operated. You have probably used the hand-operated muzzle-loader type of grease gun. This grease gun can be taken apart to load it with grease. It is generally used in places hard to reach with a pressure gun, or in lubricating water pumps and other accessories requiring a special lubricant. Lubricants used for most chassis parts, however, are forced through the fittings by guns operated by air pressure.

Crankcase oil is generally dispensed with measured containers or with a hand- or air-operated pumping system. Hand- or air-operated systems normally have meters that register the amount of oil dispensed, Gear box lubricants are generally dispensed by some type of hand-or air-operated pumping system. Be sure you use the right lubricant dispensers. To prevent mistakes, each dispenser is marked to show the grade and type of lubricant it contains.

Before using the lubrication gun, all fittings which are to be lubricated MUST be properly cleaned to avoid forcing dirt into the bearing.

The proper technique for using the lubrication gun is essential. Improper use of the gun can damage the hydraulic coupler jaws and can also damage the fitting. Damaged coupler jaws will prevent proper sealing with fittings. To prevent damage, press the coupler straight onto the clean fitting.

CAUTION: Care must be exercised when using a high pressure lube gun on certain lube points. Excessive pressure can damage or *blow off* the grease seals and/or dust caps. To prevent this damage, apply grease by one or two quick pulls on the trigger; this prevents excess pressure building up in the seals.

After a vehicle is lubricated, clean and fill the grease guns. Then check them to see if they are working properly. Next see that they and other lubricating equipment are stowed in their proper places. Take an inventory of your tools to be sure they are not carried away on the vehicle frame or running board.

CHASSIS LUBRICATION

Most chassis lubrication fittings are located on the front suspension and steering mechanisms. The importance of proper chassis lubrication cannot be overstressed. This lubrication should always be performed in accordance with the manufacturer's lubrication charts.

Frozen fittings will not readily accept lubricants because the friction surface containing the fitting has dry and dirty working surfaces. Some relative motion in the connection is needed to permit

the lubricant to enter the frozen fitting. Vertical rocking of the vehicle is the usual method of providing this relative motion in the coupling. In some extreme cases, it may be necessary to disassemble the unit being greased in order to properly lubricate it. NEVER pass up a frozen fitting.

BODY LUBRICATION

To lubricate the hood, apply a few drops of oil on the fastener-and-release mechanism, coat the fastener pins and hooks with a light application of dry stick lubricant, and close the hood.

Car doors and trunk lids are lubricated by applying a drop or two of oil to the door latch and trunk lid mechanisms. Also apply a few drops of oil to the hinges and swing the door back and forth or raise and lower the lid to spread the lubricant over the contacting surfaces; wipe off any excess lubricant.

The door striker assembly is lubricated by applying a light coating of dry stick lubricant to all sliding surfaces and a few drops of oil to all bearing surfaces. Apply a drop or two of oil around the edge of the cylinder face and to the outer surface of pushbutton latches and press the pushbuttons several times to distribute the lubricant. Wipe off any excess oil and lubricants.

Never use oil to lubricate locks since it collects dust and lint. Inject graphite directly into the keyhole and work the lock several times to distribute the graphite in the tumbler mechanism.

A dry stick lubricant is best used for sliding weather-stripping surfaces of ashtrays, hinged visors, glove compartments, and other hinged units within the vehicle. Hinged surfaces outside of the vehicle may be lubricated lightly with oil. Always remember that the few minutes it requires to oil these various items will, in most cases, eliminate their failure.

Generator Service. Periodic lubrication service is required by most generators. A few generators have sealed bearings which require no lubrication. The generator should be lubricated only at those intervals specified by the manufacturer's lubrication chart.

Distributor Service. The distributor requires service lubrication at three points - the shaft bearing, the centrifugal spark advance mechanism, and the cam. The shaft bearing is lubricated through either an oil cup, grease fitting, or grease cup. Some distributors are equipped with a removable access plug to the shaft bearing reservoir.

The automatic spark centrifugal advance mechanism may be lubricated through a small, round felt wick located at the top of the distributor shaft. Apply two or three drops of motor oil to the

felt wick. With your fingertip, apply a light film of high temperature type grease to the cam. CAUTION: Excess lubricant on the cam may be thrown over to the points and cause ignition failure.

Steering Gear Service. The fluid level in the gear housing should be checked at every chassis lubrication. You should clean around the fill plug on top of the steering gear housing before removing the fill plug. Do not disturb the adjusting screw locknut adjacent to the fill plug. Check the lubricant level and add lubricant, if necessary, to bring the lubricant level to the bottom of the fill plug hole. You then replace the fill plug.

Three points require lubrication in power steering systems. The gear housing is serviced as above on the linkage type of power steering. As you may recall, the linkage type of power steering system has the power cylinder and control valve connected to the steering linkage and a steering gear of conventional design. Additional lubrication fittings under the car may be found on the power cylinder or the power cylinder attachment points in the linkage type. The fluid reservoir is serviced at each chassis lubrication by cleaning the area, removing the dipstick or reservoir cover, checking the oil level, and replacing the dipstick or cover after adding oil if necessary. Power systems can become inoperative due to dirt in the system, so use care to prevent dirt from entering the reservoir during service operations.

<u>Brake Service.</u> The fluid level in the hydraulic brake master cylinder should be checked at every chassis lubrication. The fluid level must be visually checked at the reservoir. Pumping the brake pedal does not constitute a complete check. Service the master cylinder by cleaning the area around the fill plug, removing the fill plug, checking the fluid level and refilling the master cylinder reservoir to within half an inch below the fill hole, and replacing the gasket and fill plug. Always use the hydraulic fluid recommended by the manufacturer's lubrication chart. The use of inferior brake fluid or one which contains mineral oil will result in deterioration of the rubber seal, making it necessary to completely overhaul the brake system and flush all brake lines.

FAN BELT ADJUSTMENTS

There are many types of fan belts and many procedures used for adjusting them. It is beyond the scope of this manual to present information on all types of fan belts. Therefore, the following information presented should familiarize you with fan belt adjustments in general.

Check the fan belt (sometimes called a drive belt) tension by applying the manufacturer's specified pressure to the belt at a point midway between the fan and the generator pulley. Belt deflection at this point should be as specified. If belt deflection is found to be more or less than specified, adjust tension as follows:

1. Loosen generator-to-adjusting-arm capscrew.

2. Insert end of pry bar between crankcase and generator so that the lower end of the bar will bear against crankcase.

3. Pull upper end of pry bar away from engine with a pull of approximately 50 pounds, and keep handle in this position; then tighten the generator-to-adjustment-arm capscrew. This procedure will place belts under proper tension and allow for specified belt deflection.

HANDBRAKE ADJUSTMENT

In most automotive vehicles, the handbrake has its own hookup. Either external-contracting brake bands are located on the drive shaft or some type of mechanical linkage operates the rear wheel brakes.

Handbrake controls consist of a handbrake lever connected by linkage to the brake shoe lever at the rear of the transfer case. The handbrake is properly adjusted when it will hold the vehicle on an incline with the handbrake lever moved one-third of the way in reverse, or if application of the brake at a speed of 10 mph stops the vehicle within a reasonable distance.

To increase braking action of the handbrake, turn the knurled end of the handbrake lever clockwise. To decrease braking action (to prevent dragging of the brake shoes), turn the knurled end counterclockwise. If braking action cannot be increased sufficiently by turning the knurled end clockwise, turn the knurled end counterclockwise, adjust linkage tension at the brake shoe lever, and then turn the knurled end clockwise until the correct brake adjustment is obtained. To adjust linkage at brake shoe lever, hold adjusting nut on transfer end of linkage, loosen locknut, turn adjusting nut clockwise on linkage, and tighten locknut.

VI. TIRES

Pneumatic tires and inner tubes are designed to provide traction and cushion the shocks of the road or terrain. Traction is provided by the natural friction of the rubber upon contact with the road or terrain, aided by the tread design of the tire. Cushioning is provided largely by the air within the tube, or the tire itself if of tubeless design. Both tires and tube are flexible enough to *give* when a bump or chuck hole is struck, and they are able to resume their former shape immediately.

CHANGING A TIRE

A word of CAUTION before you lift a vehicle with a jack to change a tire: If you are to jack either of the rear wheels, place a block or stone in front of both front wheels to keep the vehicle from rolling forward and off the jackj if you jack either of the front wheels, place the block or stone behind both rear wheels.

To remove the wheel, remove the hubcap, which snaps into spring clips. Then remove the five or six hub bolts or nuts that fasten the wheel to the wheel hub. Wheels on the right side are fastened with right-hand thread bolts or nuts, and those on the left side with left-hand thread bolts or nuts to eliminate the tendency to loosen with wheel rotation. In raising the wheel from the ground, be careful not to push the vehicle off the jack. The spare wheel and tire should be placed on the vehicle immediately.

Removing dual disk wheels to change tires on heavy vehicles is not too difficult. Generally, both disks are fastened together by two nuts on each hub bolt - one nut for each wheel. Either single or dual wheels can be securely mounted on the same hub with this arrangement. Outer nuts must be loosened first, freeing the outer wheel disk from the hub. Loosening the outer nuts, which thread over the inner nuts, unfastens the outer wheel disk. In removing dual disk wheels, you will find left-hand threads on both inner and outer nuts on the left wheels and right-hand threads on those of the right wheels. Reverse the procedure to mount and tighten the wheels.

On trucks having spoke wheels, the tire and tube are removed with the rim. After removing the clamps which secure the rim on the spoke spider, the rim with the tire and tube can be lifted off. If the spoke wheel has two rims and tires, the second rim and tire can be lifted off after the spacer separating the rims is removed. In replacing the tires, the inner rim should be placed so that the valve stem can be reached easily for periodic inflation.

A tire demounter should be used to remove a tire from the rim.

In mounting a tubed tire, inflate the tube until it is almost round. Put the inside bead of the tire on the rim and insert the tube into the tire with the valve at the red (balance) mark on the tire. Guide the valve stem through the valve hole. Be sure the valve stem is pointed in the right direction if you are mounting the tire for use on dual wheels. And if it is a rubber stem, see that the stem enters the hole without bending.

The first bead will slide in rather easily, but the second bead may offer a little trouble. Use the tire irons, and work both ways from the stem to slide both tire beads in the rim walls. DO NOT PINCH THE TUBE. Use a rubber mallet (NOT a hammer) to strike the center of the treald around the tire to help seat the second bead and the tube properly. On other than drop center rims, see that the lock rings are securely fastened.

Inflate the tire slowly alter mounting it on the rim. See that the tire beads fit snugly against the rim flanges, and that lock rings are turned face down and remain in the locked position. Serious accidents can result from failure to observe these precautions. Too much pressure applied at once can cause a lock ring to fly off the rim or the tire itself to be blown off and seriously injure personnel. Inflate tires inside a steel tire cage. This will confine the tire enough to keep it from striking you in case either it or the ring bursts its fittings.

TUBELESS TIRES

Most of the lighter and heavier vehicles now are equipped with tubeless tires. Instead of being sealed in an inner tube, the air in these tires is sealed in a space between the outer casing and the rim. Both this space and the point of contact of the tire against the rim must be airtight. The rim, on which the valve for inflating the tire is mounted, becomes a part of the air retaining chamber. When using tire irons, exercise care not to tear or otherwise injure the sealing ribs or beads on the tire being repaired.

Before replacing a tubeless tire, examine the rim carefully for dents, roughness, and rust, any of which may impair or break the air seal. Straighten out any dents with a hammer, and use steel wool to clean the bead seat area of any rust or grit. If the rim is badly bent or out of round, a new wheel should be installed on the vehicle.

Removing and remounting a tubeless tire are similar to the operations for tubed tires. If the tire seal is broken or defective, it will be necessary to use a tube inside the tire. Otherwise, the tire will lose air, and you will have to inflate it frequently. Some tubeless passenger car tires must be removed from the rear of the rim to prevent stretching the bead wires too far and causing them to break. If in doubt about any other details of changing tubeless tires, follow the tire manufacturer's instructions, or consult with your supervising petty officer.

ROTATING TIRES

Rotating tires is recommended by the manufacturer. If several tires show more wear than others, or if the mileage is approaching another mile interval, you will rotate all the vehicle's tires in the following manner:

1. On automobiles having a spare tire, the left front tire should be moved to the left rear, the right front to the spare, the two rears to the opposite front wheels, and the spare to the right rear.

2. On automobiles having no spare, move the front tires to the rear on the same side, and move the rear to the opposite front wheels.

3. On vehicles having six tires (dual tires on rear), new tires should normally be mounted on the front wheels for one-third of their life, then moved to the outside rear wheels for another third, and finally shifted to the rear inside wheels. A few service conditions which demand maximum traction on rear wheels may require that new tires, or tires with relatively good treads, be mounted on the rear wheels.

CAUSES OF TIRE WEAR

Pneumatic tires have been installed on many items of equipment to increase mobility and efficiency. However, unless tires are properly cared for, much of this efficiency and mobility is lost to the user.

Probably the greatest factor in prolonging the life of pneumatic tires is proper inflation. Correct tire pressure cannot be checked by kicking the tire. It requires the use of a pressure gage. Tire pressure checks should be made prior to the vehicle being moved. This can be accomplished during the *Before Operation Services.* (Don't forget to check the spare tire.) If the pressure is neglected, the results can be costly. Tire pressure should be stenciled on the dash or fenders.

Abnormal wear from improper tire inflation can be divided into four categories. These are: overinflation, overinflation-impact injury, underinflation, and underinflation injury. Let's look at each of these in detail, and learn how to get maximum life from our tires.

<u>Overinflation</u> stretches the tire and permits only the center section of the tread to come in contact with the road. Since the wear is concentrated on the central part of the tread, the indication of overinflation is wear in the center of the tread. An overinflated tire has no give and is constantly subjected to hard jolts, causing the drive wheels to bounce and spin, literally abrashing the rubber. There is also less tire to road surface contact with an overinflated tire, and this causes a safety hazard in both braking and sliding.

An overinflated tire is more susceptible to impact injury because the cords are stretched tight. In this condition, the tire will not give or flex and distribute the shock over a great area of the ply cords.

The external indication of an underinflated tire is more wear on the edges than in the center of the tread. <u>Underinflation</u> causes excessive movement and scuffing between the tire and the road, which in turn results in faster tread wear. There may be occasions when chains are not available and tire pressures must be lowered to get better traction in sand, ice, mud, and snow. When this occurs, prescribed pressures for these conditions should be maintained to prevent tire damage.

The excessive flexing and movement of the ply cords cause a tire to get hot resulting in separation of cords and rubber. When the cords are separated from the body, the tire is permanently damaged and must be replaced. This replacement is a direct result of operator neglect and not fair wear and tear. While the tire must be removed from the wheel to properly identify this condition, in many instances radial cracks will appear on the outer wall of the tire which will serve as a warning that the tire has been operated underinflated.

All uneven tire wear is not caused by improper inflation. Wear of this type can be caused by wheels out of line or improperly balanced, excessive toe-in or toe-out, or improper camber. Uneven tire wear can also be caused by operating a vehicle with the front wheel drive engaged on dry hard surfaced roads. When uneven tire wear occurs, the mechanical defects must be corrected immediately and the tires rotated.

The proper selection and mounting of tires for dual assemblies is extremely important. Mismatched tires cause uneven distribution of the load which defeats the purpose of the duals. In this case, the larger tire carries the greater load, subjecting it to excessive wear and early failure. Also, the smaller tire wears more rapidly than normal. It scuffs along without sufficient road traction causing excessive wear. Since you are not always able to match sizes of tires exactly, except with new tires, certain tolerances are allowed. The larger of the two duals should always be mounted on the outside so that they will conform to the *crown* of the road and shoulder the load more evenly.

Directional bar tread is commonly used on road graders and other earthmoving equipment. The bars and open center pattern are designed to permit each bar to dig in deep, take a firm hold, and give maximum traction in soft, muddy, or slippery surfaces. Since this is a directional tread tire, it must be mounted on live axles so the point of the *V* comes in contact with the ground first. When the directional tire is mounted in this manner, it is *self-cleaning.* It forces the dirt and mud out to the side. When the directional tread tire is mounted on a towed vehicle or on a dead axle, it is mounted so that the open part of the 7 meets the ground first.

An insignificant little thing, but absolutely necessary, is the valve cap. This cover keeps dirt, water, and grit out of the valve and provides the final seal against air escaping from the tube. For speed and convenience in inflating, valve stems should be readily accessible. They should be positioned to prevent rubbing against the brake drum and to extend through the wheel hand holes. Ends of valves on front wheels and inside duals point away from the vehicle. Valves on outside duals point toward the vehicle. On dual wheels, valves are placed 180° apart for convenience in checking pressure and inflating.

Rims and rim flanges should be checked regularly to be sure that they are in good condition and fit properly. Since the flange comes in direct contact with the bead which supports the tire, flanges that are bent, broken, chipped, or of the wrong size put a terrific strain on the bead and lead to early tire failure.

Most of the larger wheels and rims used on equipment are the lockring type. The use of the lockring makes tire changing much easier and faster than on the one piece rim of the same size. The principle of the lockring is simple, requiring only that the lockring be firmly seated in the gutter of the rim base. When this is done, the tire and wheel will perform equally as well as the one piece riri. While there is a high safety factor built into the tire and rim assembly, danger results from carelessness or negligence in assembly. Before starting the inflate, make sure that all rim parts are correctly assembled and interlocking. It is recommended that inflation cages, safety chains, or some other safety device be used during inflation. Rims and lockrings should be inspected periodically for damage. A damaged rim or lockring should be replaced immediately as this will create a safety hazard and may ruin a tire. A displaced lockring may spring loose and can result in serious injury or death to personnel who may be in the vicinity.

When should we replace worn tires? This is a very important question because tires worn beyond the prescribed limit cannot be recapped. If you cannot grip the tread with your thumb and index finger, ask your supervisor for technical assistance to determine if replacement is required. When the tread design is worn off in the center so that the tire is smooth across the center, the tire should be replaced.

Make careful checks for damage due to vehicle obstructions. Spring clips, fender bolts, exhaust pipes, etc. may be set in a satisfactory location when the vehicle is at a standstill. But under unusual operating conditions, the body movement may cause these units to contact the tire and cause severe abrasion. The tires of low bed trailers and trailer-mounted air compressors are highly susceptible to this type damage.

Rocks or dry caked mud should be removed from between dual assemblies as soon as possible. Extensive tire damage can also be caused by snow and ice packed between duals or under fenders and cross braces in winter operation. Any such materials coming in contact with tires while they are in operation can cause severe cuts or abrasions.

FUNDAMENTALS OF AUTOMOTIVE POWER TRAINS AND CHASSIS

CONTENTS

		Page
I.	POWER TRAIN COMPONENTS	1
II.	BRAKE SYSTEMS	12
III.	SUSPENSION SYSTEMS	19
IV.	FRAME	22

BASIC FUNDAMENTALS OF AUTOMOTIVE POWER TRAINS AND CHASSIS

The mechanism that transmits the power of a vehicle's engine to the wheels and accessory equipment is called the power train. In a simple situation, a set of gears or a chain and sprocket could perform this task, but automotive vehicles are not designed for simple operating conditions. They are designed to have pulling power as well as to move at high speeds, to travel in reverse as well as forward, and to operate on rough terrain as well as on smooth roads. To meet these varying demands, a number of units have been added including clutches, transmissions, propeller shafts, universal joints, differentials, and live axles.

The chassis is the assembly of mechanisms that make up the major operating part of the vehicle. It usually includes everything except the vehicle body. This assembly includes the engine, the frame which supports the engine and the power train, the steering and braking systems, and the suspension system.

This chapter provides information on the various components, or subassemblies, that make up the automotive power train and chassis. In effect, it establishes the relationship between these various parts and shows how they work together in the automotive vehicle. To maintain and service these components, or subassemblies, you must know where to find them on a vehicle. You must also understand their purpose and how they operate. This chapter contains a general discussion of these subject; the operation and maintenance manuals which accompany each piece of equipment will give you more detailed information.

I. POWER TRAIN COMPONENTS

The common elements of the power train system assembled in a typical vehicle are shown in the following figure. The main components of the power train are described as follows:

CLUTCH.
By means of the clutch, the operator can disconnect the engine from the remainder of the power train. This is essential when starting the engine, thus allowing the vehicle to stand motionless while the engine is running. It also allows gradual engagement of the engine to the power train and gear ratio changing to meet varying road conditions.

TRANSMISSION.
An internal combustion engine cannot develop appreciable torque at low speeds; it develops maximum torque only at one speed, and the crankshaft of an engine must always rotate in the same direction. Because of these limitations, a transmission is necessary in automotive vehicles. The transmission provides the mechanical advantage that enables the engine to propel the vehicle under adverse conditions of the load. It also provides the operator with a selection of vehicle speeds while the engine is held at speeds within the effective torque range, and it allows disengaging and reversing the flow of power from the engine to the wheels.

PROPELLER SHAFT.
A propeller shaft is used to transfer the power from the transmission located near the front of the vehicle to the differential near the rear.

UNIVERSAL JOINTS.

It is necessary to provide flexibility in the power train if springs are to be used on the vehicle. As the load is increased or decreased, and as the vehicle travels over uneven surfaces, the vertical distance between the transmission output shaft and the axle will change. This flexibility is provided by the use of universal joints which permit transfer of torque at an angle.

SLIP JOINTS.

As the load is changed, and as the vehicle travels over uneven ground, the distance from the axle to the transmission varies. Slip joints allow for this variation.

DIFFERENTIAL.

A differential is required to compensate for the difference in distance the rear wheels travel when the vehicle rounds a turn. The differential permits application of power to the rear wheels while allowing each wheel to turn at a different speed when the vehicle is rounding a curve.

AXLES.

An axle is a shaft supporting a vehicle on which the wheels turn. A *live axle* is one that supports part of the weight of a vehicle and also drives the wheels connected to it. A *dead axle* is one that carries part of the weight of a vehicle, but does not drive the wheels. The usual front axle of a vehicle is a dead axle and the rear axle is a live axle. In four-wheel drive vehicles, both front and rear axles are live axles, and in six-wheel drive vehicles, all three axles are live axles.

TYPICAL POWER TRAIN

THE CLUTCH

A clutch in an automotive vehicle is the mechanism in the power train that connects the engine crankshaft to, or disconnects it from, the transmission and thus the remainder of the power train. Since the internal combustion engine does not develop a high starting torque, it must be disconnected from the power train and allowed to operate without load until it develops enough torque to overcome the inertia of the vehicle when starting from rest. The application of the engine power to the load must be gradual to prove smooth engagement and to lessen the shock on the driving parts. After engagement, the clutch must transmit all the engine power to the transmission without slipping. Further, it is desirable to disconnect the engine from the power train during the time the gears in the transmission are being shifted from one gear ratio to another.

Clutches are located in the power train between the engine and the transmission assembly.

Clutches transmit power from the clutch driving plate to the driven member by friction. In the disk clutch, the driving plate or member, which is secured to the engine flywheel, is gradually brought into contact with the driven member (disk), which is attached to the transmission input shaft. The contact is made and held by strong spring pressure controlled by the operator with the clutch pedal. With only light spring pressure, there is little friction between the two members and the clutch is permitted to slip. As the spring pressure increases, friction also increases, and less slippage occurs. When the operator removes his foot from the clutch pedal and full spring pressure is applied, the speed of the driving plate and driven disk is the same, and all slipping stops. There is then a direct connection between the flywheel and transmission input shaft.

Malfunction Detection. Several types of clutch troubles that may be encountered during vehicle operation are: slipping, chattering or grabbing when engaging, spinning or dragging when engaged, and clutch noises. As an operator, you would explain the malfunction on the Operator's Trouble Report and turn the report into the maintenance shop for corrective action.

Clutch Lubrication. Although some clutches do not require lubrication, there are other types of clutches that require it at periodic intervals. The clutch-pedal control shaft and clutch linkage are among some of the lubricating points that would be greased at normal regular servicing intervals in accordance with the manufacturer's lubrication manual.

MANUAL TRANSMISSIONS

The transmission is part of the power train. It is located in the rear of the engine between the clutch housing and the propeller shaft. The transmission transfers engine power from the clutch shaft to the propeller shaft, and allows the operator a means of varying the gear ratio between the engine and the rear wheels.

Dual ratio, or two-speed, rear axles are sometimes used on trucks. They contain two different gear ratios which can be selected at will by the driver, usually by a manual-control lever. A dual-ratio rear axle serves the same purpose as the auxiliary transmission, and like the latter, it doubles the number of gear ratios available for driving the vehicle under the various loads and road conditions.

Operator's Maintenance. It is the operator's responsibility to check with the manufacturer's instruction manual for instruction on the proper type and amount of recommended lubricant to be used in the transmission case. You must maintain the lubricant at the proper level. The normal level of lubricant to be placed in a transmission is usually at the bottom of the filler plug opening. By maintaining the proper level, gear teeth are protected, foaming is reduced, and thus the transmission will continue to perform properly.

Malfunction Detection. Several types of transmission troubles that may be encountered in vehicle operation are: hard shifting into gears, transmission slips out of *first* or *reverse*, transmission slips out of *second*, transmission slips out of high, no power through transmission, transmission noisy in gear, gear clash in shifting, and oil leaks. As an operator, you would explain the malfunction on the Operator's Trouble Report enabling the mechanic to check out the possible cause of trouble reported.

AUTOMATIC TRANSMISSION

The transmissions described previously are manual transmissions; that is, they require a clutch and a lever for shifting gears. The automatic transmission is used in almost all types of automotive and construction equipment. Automatic transmissions are composed of a fluid coupling or hydraulic torque converter and a system of planetary gears controlled automatically.

Fluid Couplings. Fluid couplings are widely used with automatic transmissions. By slipping at idling speeds and by holding to increase power as engine speed increases, fluid couplings act as a sort of automatic clutch. There is no mechanical connection between the engine and transmission, but power is transmitted through the use of oil.

The principle of fluid drive can best be illustrated through the use of a pair of electric fans facing each other. If one fan is operated with power, the air blast from this fan will cause the other fan to rotate.

There is considerable power loss through slippage at low speeds, but at intermediate or high driving speeds the power loss is very small. It ranges from 1 percent at 25 miles per hour to one-quarter percent at 60 miles per hour.

Torque Converters. A torque converter is a special form of fluid coupling. It is one of the most common types of automatic transmissions and is widely used in the latest models of automotive and construction equipment.

The torque converter consists of three basic elements: the pump (driving member), the turbine (driven member), and the stator (reaction member). All of these members have curved vanes. The stator is placed between the load and the power source to act as a fulcrum and is secured to the torque converter housing. The pump throws out oil in the same direction in which the pump is turning. As the oil strikes the turbine blade, it forces the turbine to rotate, and the oil is directed toward the center of the turbine. Then the oil leaves the turbine and moves in a direction opposite to that of the pump. As the oil strikes the stator, it is redirected to flow in the same direction as the pump, thereby adding its force to that of the pump. Torque is multiplied by the velocity and direction given to the oil by the pump, plus the velocity and direction of the oil entering the pump from the stator.

Planetary Gears. Automatic transmissions use a system of planetary gears to enable the torque from the torque converter or fluid coupling to be used as efficiently as possible.

Planetary units are the heart of the modern automatic transmission. An understanding of the power flow through the planetary units is essential to an understanding of the operation of the automatic transmission.

Four basic parts make up the planetary gear system. These basic parts are the sun gear, the ring (or internal) gear, the planet pinions, and the planet carrier.

The sun gear is so named because it is the center of the system. The term *planet* is used to describe these pinions and gears because they rotate around the sun gear. The ring gear, or internal gear, is so called because of its shape and because it has internal teeth.

There are several advantages inherent in the planetary gear system. One of the advantage is the compactness of the system. Another advantage is that there is more tooth contact to carry the load, in that each gear of the planetary system is usually in contact with at least two other gears of the system. The gears are always in mesh. There can be no tooth damage due to tooth clash or partial engagement. The big advantage is the one which makes it so popular: namely, the ease of shifting gears. Planetary gear sets in automatic transmissions are shifted without any skill on the part of the driver.

There are various ways in which power may be transmitted through the planetary gear set. shaft from the engine may be connected to drive the sun gear, it may be connected to drive the planet carrier, or it may be connected to drive the ring gear. The propeller shaft also may be connected to any of these members. However, only power can be transmitted in the planetary gear system when (1) the engine is delivering power to one of the three member, (2) the propeller shaft is connected to one of the other members, and (3) the remaining member is held against rotation. All three conditions must be satisfied for power to be transmitted in the system. Automatic transmissions provide the means for holding a member through hydraulic servos or spring pressure.

Operation. Most automatic transmissions are basically the same. They combine a fluid torque converter with a planetary gear set, and control the shifting of the planetary gears with an automatic hydraulic control system.

To start the engine, the selector lever must be in the Neutral or Park position. It is good practice to apply the service brakes before starting the engine and keep them applied after the engine is running. In the automatic transmission, the fluid torque converter is attached to the engine crankshaft and serves as the engine flywheel. This means that whenever the engine runs, engine power flows into the converter and drives the converter output (turbine) shaft. There is no neutral in the torque converter. Neutral is provider in the planetary gear set by the release of bands and clutches.

With the engine running, you can *feel* the transmission go into gear and into neutral as the selector level is moved from Park or Neutral to Drive, Low, or Reverse. If the engine is running at fast (cold) idle, the vehicle will start to move as soon as the transmission goes into gear, unless the parking or service brakes are applied. If the engine is idling at normal (hot) idle, the vehicle will not move. You can, however, *feel* the transmission go into gear. Part of this *feel* is the audible decrease in engine rpm. The engine is now running under a load. The torque converter and the planetary gear set are actually transmitting engine torque to the driveshaft. The torque applied, however, is not sufficient to move the vehicle.

For all normal forward driving, the selector is moved to Drive. As the throttle is advanced from the idle position, the vehicle will start off smoothly and accelerate steadily. The transmission is designed to operate at a steady-throttle position. Most drivers depress the accelerator pedal to definite position and hold it there steadily until the desired speed is attained. Depending on the accelerator pedal position, the transmission will upshaft automatically to intermediate and then to high.

The transmission automatically multiplies and/or transmits engine torque to the driveshaft as driving conditions demand. The speeds at which the coupling point and the gear shifts occur are controlled partially by the driver. The driver has only a partial control in the Drive position, because the transmission in the Drive position will shift the planetary gear set into the higher gear to prevent engine overspeeding regardless of throttle position.

The transmission can multiply engine torque as much as 5.4 times. The torque converter can multiply engine torque as much as 2.2 times. The planetary gear set in low gear multiplies the torque converter output torque 2.46 times. The maximum engine torque multiplication in the transmission is 2.2 x 2.46 or 5.41 times. This means that the transmission can receive an engine output torque of 100 ft-lbs and deliver 541 ft-lbs torque to the driveshaft. Of course, frictional losses have to be subtracted from the 541 ft-lbs.

The driver can force downshaft the transmission from high to intermediate at speed up to about 65 mph. A detent on the downshift linkage warns the driver when the carburetor is wide open. Accelerator pedal depression through the detent will bring in the downshift.

With the throttle closed, the transmission will downshift automatically as the vehicle speed drops to about 10 mph. With the throttle open at any position up to the detent, the downshifts will come in automatically at speeds about 10 mph and in proportion to throttle opening. This prevents engine lugging on steep hill climbing.

When the selector lever is moved to L (low) with the transmission in high, the transmission will downshift to intermediate or to low depending on the road speed. At speeds below about 25 mph, the downshift will be from high to low.

With the selector in Low position, the transmission cannot upshift. On some vehicles the Low position is called Hill Control, since low gear provides maximum engine braking. When maximum engine braking is desired, the transmission must not upshift, because an upshift will reduce engine braking effort. When the selector is moved to Reverse, the hydraulic control system shifts the planetary gear set to reverse. When the selector lever is moved to Park, a spring force is applied against a pawl to engage the parking pawl with a parking gear on the output shaft. When the pawl is engaged, the transmission output shaft (and, therefore, the rear wheels) is mechanically locked to the transmission main case.

In summary:
1. An automatic transmission has the torque converter to act as an automatic clutch. This automatic clutch permits the vehicle to stand still at engine idle, but automatically

goes to work at a full-throttle start so that the transmission can take maximum engine torque, multiply it more than four times and deliver it to the driveshaft.
2. It is practically impossible to *kill* the engine under any driving condition.
3. At a start, engine speed is fast and vehicle speed is slow. With a steady throttle, engine speed remains fairly constant while vehicle speed increases to 65 mph. You found that the torque converter and planetary gear set *know* when engine torque should be multiplied, how much to multiply it, and when to transmit it to the driveshaft.
4. The ratio changes (shifts) occur at full-engine torque within a fraction of a second and without extreme harshness.

Operator's Maintenance. Periodic service by the operator includes checking the transmission oil level when the engine is idling and at normal operating temperature, the vehicle is level, and the transmission control lever is in Park. Remove dipstick and note oil level. If it is low, and sufficient transmission fluid (the oil used in all automatic transmission is special and is composed of mineral oil and additives). In the transmission, it is used as a combination power-transmission medium, hydraulic control fluid, heat transfer medium, bearing surface lubricant, and gear lubricant. In all cases, the manufacturer's recommendations should be followed when servicing and filling the transmission with transmission fluid.

Caution: Do not overfill the transmission because overfilling will cause foaming and shifting troubles.

Malfunction Detection. Several types of automatic transmission troubles that may be encountered during vehicle operation are: No drive in any selected position; engine speed accelerates on standstill starts but vehicle acceleration lags; engine speed accelerates during upshifts; transmission will not upshift; upshift harsh; closed throttle (coast) downshift harsh; will not downshift; vehicle creeps excessively in drive; vehicle creeps in neutral; no drive in reverse, improper shift points; unusual transmission noise; and oil leaks. As an operator, you must explain the malfunction on the Operator's Trouble Report and turn the report into the maintenance shop for corrective action.

AUXILIARY TRANSMISSIONS

Auxiliary transmissions are mechanisms mounted in the rear of the regular transmission to provide an increased number of gear ratios. The types most commonly used, normally have only a low and a high (direct) range, incorporated into a transfer assembly. The low range provides an extremely low gear ratio on hard pull. At all other times, the high range is used, and the power passes through the main shaft. Gears are shifted by a separate gearshift lever in the driver's cab.

Transfer Cases. Transfer cases are placed in the power trains of vehicles driven by all wheels. Their purpose is to provide the necessary offsets for additional propeller shaft connections to drive the wheels.

Transfer cases in heavier vehicles have two speed positions and a declutching device for disconnecting the front driving wheels. Two speed transfer cases serve also as auxiliary transmissions.

Some transfer cases are quite complicated. When they have speed changing gear, declutching device, and attachment for three or more propeller shafts, they are even larger than the main transmission.

Some transfer cases contain an overrunning sprag unit (or units) on the front output shaft. (A sprag unit is a form of overrunning clutch; power can be transmitted through it in one direction but not in the other.) On these transfer cases, the transfer is designed to drive the front axle slightly slower than the rear axle. During normal operation, when both front and rear wheels turn at the same speed, only the rear wheels drive the vehicle. However, if the rear wheels should lose traction and begin to slip, they tend to turn faster than the front wheels. As this happens, the sprag unit automatically engages so that the front wheels also drive the vehicle. The sprag unit simply provides an automatic means of engaging the front wheels in drive whenever additional tractive effort is required. There are two types of sprag-unit-equipped transfers: a single-sprag-unit transfer and a double-sprag unit transfer. Essentially, both types work in the same manner.

Power Takeoffs. Power takeoffs are attachments in the power train used for obtaining power to drive auxiliary accessories. They are attached to the transmission, auxiliary transmission, or transfer case.

Malfunction detection and operator maintenance for auxiliary transmissions are similar to those for the manual transmission.

PROPELLER SHAFT ASSEMBLY

The propeller shaft assembly consists of a propeller shaft, a slip joint, and one or more universal joints. This assembly provides a flexible connection through which power is transmitted from the transmission to the live axles.

The propeller shaft may be solid or tubular. A solid shaft is somewhat stronger than the hollow or tubular shaft of the same diameter, but the hollow shaft is stronger than a solid shaft of the same weight. Hollow shafts are used in the open.

A slip joint is provided at one end of the propeller shaft to take care of end play. The driving axle, being attached to the springs, is free to move up and down while the transmission is attached to the frame and cannot move. Any upward or downward movement of the axle, as the spring are flexed, shortens or lengthens the distance between the axle assembly and the transmission. To compensate for this changing distance, the slip joint is provided at one end of the propeller shaft.

The usual type of slip joint consists of a splined stub shaft, welded to the propeller shaft, which fits into a splined sleeve in the universal joint.

A universal joint is a connection between two shafts that permits one to drive the other at an angle. Passenger vehicles and trucks usually have universal joints at both ends of the propeller shaft.

Universal joints normally do not require any maintenance other than lubrication. Some universal joints (U-joints) have grease fittings and should be lubricated when the vehicle has a preventive maintenance inspection. Others may require disassembly and lubrication periodically. When lubricating U-joints that have grease fittings, use a low pressure grease gun to avoid damaging seals.

FINAL DRIVES

A final drive is that part of the power train that transmits the power delivered through the propeller shaft to the drive wheels or to sprockets, in the case of tracklaying equipment. Because it is encased in the rear axle housing, the final drive is usually referred to as a part of the rear axle assembly. It consists of two gears called the ring gear and pinion. These are beveled gears, and they may be spur, spiral, or hypoid.

The function of the final drive is to change by 90 degrees the direction of the power transmitted through the propeller shaft to the driving axles. It also provides a fixed reduction between the speed of the propeller shaft and the axle shafts and wheels. In passenger car this reduction varies from about 3 to 1 to 5 to 1. In trucks, it can vary from to 1 to as much as 11 to 1.

The gear ratio of a final drive having bevel gears is found by dividing the number of teeth on the driven or ring gear by the number of teeth on the pinion. In a worm gear final drive, the gear ratio is found by counting the number of revolutions of the worm gear required for one revolution of the driven gear.

Most final drives are of the gear type. Hypoid gears are used in passenger cars and light trucks to eliminate the rear seat propeller shaft tunnel or to permit a lower body design. They permit the bevel driven pinion to be placed below the center of the ring gear, thereby lowering the propeller shaft. Worm gears allow a large speed reduction and are used to a limited extent on larger trucks. Spiral bevel gears are similar to hypoid gears. They are used in both passenger cars and trucks to replace spur gear that are considered too noisy.

DIFFERENTIALS

Associated with the final drive and contained in the rear axle housing is the differential. The purpose of the differential is easy to understand when you compare a vehicle to a company of men marching in mass formation. When the company makes a turn, the men in the inside file must take short steps, almost marking time, while men in the outside file must take long steps and walk a greater distance to make the turn. When a motor vehicle turns a corner, the wheels on the outside of the turn must rotate faster and travel a greater distance than the wheels on the inside. This causes no difficulty for front wheels of the usual passenger car because each wheel rotates independently. However, in order to drive the rear wheels at different speeds, the differential is needed. It connects the individual axle shaft for each wheel to the bevel drive gear. Therefore, each shaft can turn at a different speed and still be driven.

To overcome the situation where one spinning wheel might be undesirable, some trucks are provided with a *differential lock*. This is a simple dog clutch, controlled manually or automatically which locks one axle shaft to the differential case and bevel drive gear. Although this device forms a rigid connection between the two axle shafts and makes both wheels rotate at the same speed, it is used, very little. Too often the driver forgets to disengage the lock after using it. There are, however, automatic devices for doing almost the same thing. One of these, which is rather extensively used today, is the high-traction differential. This does not work, however, when one wheel loses traction completely. In this respect, it is inferior to the differential lock.

With the no-spin differential, one wheel cannot spin because of loss of tractive effort and thereby deprive the other wheel of driving effort. For example, one wheel is on ice and the other wheel is on dry pavement. The wheel on ice is assumed to have no traction. However, the wheel on dry pavement will pull to the limit of its tractional resistance at the pavement. The wheel on ice cannot spin because wheel speed is governed by the speed of the wheel applying tractive effort.

AXLES

A live axle is one that supports part of the weight of a vehicle and also drives the wheels connected to it. A dead axle is one that carries part of the weight of a vehicle but does not drive the wheels.

In 4-wheel drive vehicles, both front and rear axles are live axles, and in 6-wheel drive vehicles, all three axles are live axles. The third axle, part of a *bogie drive* is joined to the rearmost axle by a trunnion axle. The axle trunnion is attached rigidly to the frame. Its purpose is to help in distributing the load on the rear of the vehicle to the two live axles which it connects.

There are four types of live axles used in automotive and construction equipment. They are: plain, semifloating, three-quarter floating, and full floating.

The plain live axle, or nonfloating rear axle, is seldom used in construction equipment today. The axle shafts in this assembly are called nonfloating because they are supported directly in bearings located in the center and ends of the axle housing. In addition to turning the wheels, these shafts carry the entire load of the vehicle on their outer ends. Plain axles also support the weight of the differential case.

The semifloating axle that is used on most passenger cars and light trucks has its differential case independently supported. The differential carrier relieves the axle shafts from the weight of the differential assembly and the stresses caused by its operation. For this reason, the inner ends of the axle shafts are said to be floated. The wheels are keyed or bolted to outer ends of axle shafts and the outer bearings are between the shafts and the housing. The axle shafts, therefore, must take the stresses caused by turning or skidding of the wheels. The axle shaft in a semifloating live axle can be removed after the wheel and brake drum have been removed.

The axle shafts in a three-quarter floating axle may be removed with the wheels, which are keyed to the tapered outer ends of the shafts. The inner ends of the shafts are carried as in semifloating axle. The axle housing, instead of the shafts, carries the weight of the vehicle because the wheels are supported by bearings on the outer ends of the housing. However, axle shafts must take the stresses caused by the turning, or skidding, of the wheels. Three-quarter floating axles are used in some trucks but in very few passenger cars.

The full floating axle is used in most heavy trucks. These axle shafts may be removed and replaced without removing the wheels or disturbing the differential. Each wheel is carried on the end of the axle tube on two ball bearings or roller bearings and the axle shafts are bolted to the wheel hub. The wheels are driven through a flange on the ends of the axle shaft which is bolted to the outside of the wheel hub. The bolted connection between axle and wheel does not make this assembly a true full floating axle, but nevertheless, it is called a floating axle. A true full floating axle transmits only turning effort, or torque.

MAINTENANCE

There are very few adjustments that must be made to the power train during normal operations. As an operator, your primary duties will be limited to lubrication of the power train. You can reduce repairs by proper lubrication and periodic inspection of these power train units.

Proper lubrication depends upon the use of the right kind of lubricants which must be put in the right places in the amounts specified by the lubrication charts. The charts provided with the vehicle will show what units in the power train will require lubrication, and where they are located.

In checking the level of the lubricant in gear cases, keep these two important points in mind:

First, always carefully wipe the dirt away from around the inspection plug and then use the proper size wrench to remove the inspection plugs. A wrench too large will round the corners and prevent proper tightening of the plug. For the same reason, never use a pipe wrench or a pair of pliers for removing plugs.

Secondly, be sure the level of the lubricant is right—usually just below or on a level with the bottom of the inspection hole. Before checking the level, allow the vehicle to stand for a while on a level surface so the gear oil can cool and find its own level. Gear oil heated and churned by revolving gears expands and forms bubbles. Although too little gear oil in the gear boxes is responsible for many failures of the power train, do not add too much gear lubricant. Too much oil causes extra maintenance.

Excessive oil or grease can find its way past the oil seals or gear cases. It may be forced out of a transmission into the clutch housing and result in a slipping clutch; or it may get by the rear wheel bearings from the differential housing to cause brakes to slip or grab. Always clean differential and live axle housing vents to prevent leaking seals.

Universal joints and slip joints at the ends of propeller shafts are to be lubricated if fittings are provided. Some of these joints are packed with grease when assembled, others have grease fittings. Do not remove these plugs until you consult the manual or your chief for instructions.

Some passenger cars and trucks have a leather boot or shoe covering the universal and slip joints. The boot prevents grease from being thrown from the joints and it also keeps dirt from mixing with the grease. A mixture of dirt and grease forms an abrasive that will wear parts in a hurry. Never use so much grease on these joints that the grease will be forced out of the boot. The extra grease will be lost and the added weight of the grease will tend to throw the propeller shaft out of balance.

When you are to give a vehicle a thorough inspection, inspect the power train for loose gear housings and joints. Look for bent propeller shafts that are responsible for vibrations, and examine the gear housing and joints for missing crews and bolts. Check to see that the U-bolts fastening the springs to the rear axle housing are tight. A loose spring hanger can throw the rear axle assembly out of line, and place additional strain on the propeller shaft and final drive. When making these inspections, always check the steel lugs for tightness.

After tightening the gear housing, loose connections, and joints, road test the vehicle to see if the various units in the power train are working properly. Shift the gears into all operating speeds and listen for noisy sounds. Report all improper operation of the power train units on the Operator's Trouble Report enabling the mechanic to check out possible causes.

DRIVING WHEELS

Wheels attached to live axles are the driving wheels. The number of wheels and number of driving wheels is sometimes used to identify equipment. Wheels attached to the outside of the driving wheels make up dual wheels. Dual wheels give additional traction to the driving wheels and distribute the weight of the vehicle over a greater area of road surface. They are considered as single wheels in describing vehicles. For example, a 4x2 (four by two) could be a passenger car or a truck having four wheels with two of them driving. A 4x4 indicates a vehicle having four wheels with all four driving. In some cases, these vehicles will have dual wheels in the rear. You would describe such a vehicle as a 4x4 with dual wheels.

A 6x4 truck, although having dual wheels in the rear, is identified by six wheels, four of them driving. Actually, the truck has ten wheels but the wheel attached to each driving wheel could be removed without changing the identity of the truck. If the front wheels of this truck were driven by a live axle, it would be called a 6x6.

II. BRAKE SYSTEMS

Good brakes are an absolute necessity for the safe operation of a motor vehicle. The modern day vehicle is capable of moving at extremely high speeds, and this results in an ever increasing demand for more efficient braking systems. Braking systems must not only be able to stop the vehicle, but must stop it in as short a distance as possible.

Friction is the resistance to relative motion between two surfaces in contact with each other. Thus, when a stationary surface is forced into contact with a moving surface, the resistance to relative motion or the rubbing action between the two surfaces will slow down the moving surface. In nearly all brake systems, the brake drums provide the moving surface and the brake shoes provide the stationary surface. The friction between the brake drums and the brake shoes slows the drum, wheel, and the friction between the tires and the road surface slows the vehicle, eventually bringing it to a complete stop.

INDIVIDUAL BRAKES

On modern equipment individual service brakes are provided for each wheel and are operated by a foot pedal. The equipment also has an emergency or parking brake. The parking brake is operated by a separate pedal or a hand lever.

Individual brakes are classified into three types: external contracting brake, internal expanding brake, and disk brake.

External Contracting Brakes. External contracting brakes are sometimes used for parking brakes on motor vehicles and for controlling the speed of auxiliary equipment drive shafts.

In operation, the brake band (or shoe) of an external contracting brake is tightened around the rotating drum by moving the brake lever. The brake hand is made of comparatively thin, flexible steel, shaped to fit the drum, with a frictional lining riveted to the inner surface. This flexible brake band cannot withstand the high pressure required to produce the friction that will stop a heavily loaded or fast moving vehicle, but works well as a parking brake.

In an external contracting brake, the brake band is anchored opposite the point where the pressure is applied. In addition to supporting the band, the anchor proves a means for adjusting brake lining clearance. Other adjusting screws and bolts are provided at the ends of the band.

Internal Expanding Brakes. Internal expanding brakes are used almost exclusively as wheel brakes. This type of brake permits a more compact and economical construction. The brake shoe and brake operating mechanism are supported on a backing plate or brake shield which is attached to the vehicle axle. The brake drum, attached to the rotating wheel, acts as a cover for the shoe and operating mechanism and furnishes a frictional surface for the brake shoe.

In operation, the brake shoe of an internal expanding brake is forced outward against the drum to produce the braking action. One end of the shoe is hinged to the backing plate by an anchor pin, while the other end is unattached and can be moved in its support by the operating mechanism. When force from the operating mechanism is applied to the unattached end of the shoe, the shoe expands and brakes the wheel. A retracting spring returns the shoe to the original position when braking action is no longer required.

The brake-operating linkage alone does not provide sufficient mechanical advantage for positive braking. Some means of supplementing the physical application of the braking system has to be used to increase pressure on the brake shoes. A self-energizing action is very helpful in accomplishing this, once setting of the shoes is started by physical effort. While there are variations of this action, it is always obtained by the shoes themselves, which tend to revolve with the revolving drum.

When the brake shoe is anchored (see figure below) and the drum revolves in the direction shown, the shoe will tend to revolve with the drum when it is forced against the drum. As a result, the shoe will exert considerable pressure against the anchor pin. Since the pin is fixed to the brake shield, this pressure will tend to wedge the shoe tightly in between the pin and the drum as shown. As the initial braking pressure is increased on the cam, the wedging action increases and the shoe is forced still more tightly against the drum to increase the friction. This self-energizing results in more braking action than could be obtained with the actuating pressure alone. Brakes making use of this principle to increase pressures on the braking surfaces are known as self-energizing (or servo) brakes.

External contracting brake

Internal expanding brake

It is most important that the operator control the total braking action at all times; therefore, the self-energizing action should increase only upon application of additional "actuating" pressure at the brake pedal. The amount of self-energizing action available depends mainly on location of the anchor pin. As the pin is moved toward the center of the drum, wedging action increases until a point is reached where the shoe will automatically lock. The pin must be located outside this point so that the operator can control the braking.

When two shoes are anchored on the bottom of the backing plate, self-energizing action is effective on only one shoe. The other shoe tends to revolve away from its pivot, which reduces its braking action. When the wheel is revolving in the opposite direction, the self-energizing action is produced on the opposite shoe.

Two shoes are usually mounted so that self-energizing action is effective on both. This is accomplished by pivoting the shoes to each other and leaving the pivot free of the backing plate. The only physical effort required is for operating the first, or primary, shoe. Both shoes then apply additional pressure to the braking surfaces with no increase in the pressure on the operating linkage. The anchor pins are fitted into slots in the free ends of the brake shoes. This method of anchoring allows the movement of the shoes necessary to expand against the drum when the shoes are forced against the drum, and the self-energizing action of the primary shoe is transmitted through the pivot to the secondary shoe. Both shoes will tend to revolve with the drum and will be wedged against the drum by the one anchor pin. The other anchor pin will cause a similar action when the wheel is revolving in the opposite direction.

The operating mechanism for wheel brakes differs with the brake systems, and so do the brake shoe adjusting devices. The brake drums and brake shoes, however, are similar in all wheel brakes.

Most modern automotive brakes have a self-adjusting feature that automatically adjust the brakes when they need it as a result of brake lining wear.

Disk Brakes. The disk brake has a metal disk instead of a drum, and a pair of flat pads instead of curved brake shoes. The figure below shows a sectional view of a typical disk brake assembly. The two flat pads are located on the two sides of the disk. The assembly in which the flat pads are held is called the caliper assembly. In operation, the pads are forced against the two sides of the disk by the movement of pistons in the caliper assembly. The pistons are actuated by hydraulic pressure from the master cylinder. The effect is to clamp the rotating disk between the stationary pads as illustrated below. This is the same action you get when you pick up a piece of paper; our fingers and thumb clamp on both sides of the paper to hold it. In the same way, the pads apply friction to the disk and attempt to stop its rotation. This provides the braking action.

Sectional view of disk brake in released and applied position.

MECHANICAL HANDBRAKES

In most automotive vehicles, the handbrake has its own hookup. Either external contracting brake bands are located on the drive shaft or some type of mechanical linkage operates the rear wheel brakes.

HYDRAULIC BRAKE SYSTEMS

A hydraulic brake system is primarily a liquid connection or coupling between the brake pedal and the individual brake shoes and drums. The system consists of one master cylinder connected by pipes and flexible tubing to the wheel cylinders. The wheel cylinders control the movement of the brake shoes at each wheel.

The brake fluid in hydraulic systems is composed of alcohol and caster oil or glycerin. This liquid neither freezes nor boils at temperatures encountered in year-round operations. When the brake pedal in a hydraulic brake system is depressed, the hydraulic fluid forces the pistons in the wheel cylinder against the brake shoes. The shoes expand against the brake drum and stop the vehicle. Hydraulic brakes are self-equalizing brakes. If the actuating pistons were all the same size, each brake in the hydraulic system would receive an identical hydraulic force when the brakes are applied because a force exerted at any point upon a closed liquid is distributed equally through the liquid in all directions. Some brake systems have larger wheel cylinders in the front than in the rear. This is because, when stopping, more of the vehicle's weight is felt in front and, therefore, more front wheel braking effort is required.

The mechanical advantage of any brake system is the relation between the pressure applied by the operator on the brake pedal to the pressure exerted on the braking surfaces.

The master cylinder has two functions. It is a reservoir for the brake fluid, and it contains the piston and the valves which change mechanical force to hydraulic pressure when the brake pedal is depressed. The pressure on the brake pedal moves the piston within the master cylinder, forcing the brake fluid from the master cylinder through tubing and flexible hose to the wheel cylinders. As pressure on the pedal is increased, greater hydraulic pressure is built up within the brake cylinders, and thus greater force is put forth against the ends of the brake shoes. When pressure on the pedal is released, the springs on the brake shoes return the wheel cylinder pistons to their released positions. This action forces the brake fluid back through the flexible hose and tubing to the master cylinder.

Most older model cars are equipped with the single system master cylinder. This system is, however, being replaced with dual system master cylinders.

The operation of a dual system master cylinder is basically the same as a single master cylinder. The dual system master cylinder, however, has two pistons, two separate fluid reservoirs, and two output ports. Thus, the dual system master cylinder has two separate hydraulic pressure systems. One of the hydraulic systems normally is connected to the front brakes, and the other system is the rear brakes. If either the front or rear hydraulic system fails, the other system remains operational.

The master cylinder, like other parts in the brake system, is subject to wear, leaks, and deposits or corrosion on the cylinder wall and piston. Master cylinder reservoir fluid level should be checked periodically and clean brake fluid added, as needed, to maintain fluid level approximately ½" from the top of the reservoir.

The brake lines transmit fluid and pressure from the master cylinder to the wheel cylinders, which in turn change the hydraulic pressure into mechanical force. The wheel cylinders are mounted on the brake backing plate. Inside each cylinder are two pistons that move in opposite directions by hydraulic pressure, which pushes the brake shoes against the brake drum. The brake shoes are made of iron, steel, or cast aluminum. They support the brake lining and transmit force to the lining, which is attached to the face of the shoe and make contact with the inner surface of the brake drums. During contact with one another the lining and the drum create the frictional surface that gives the braking effect.

AIRBRAKE SYSTEMS

Air, like all gases, is easily compressed. Compressed air exerts pressure and this pressure will be equal in all directions. Air under pressure can be conveniently stored and carried through lines or tubes. Considerable force is available for braking since operating air pressure may be as high as 100 psi. All brakes on a vehicle, and on a trailer (when one is used), are operated together by means of a brake valve.

The compressor is driven from the engine crankshaft or one of the auxiliary shafts. The three common methods of driving the compressor from the engine are gear, belt, and chain.

The compressor may be lubricated from the engine crankcase or be self-lubricated. Cooling may be either by air or liquid from the engine.

The purpose of the compressor governor is to automatically maintain the air pressure in the reservoir between the maximum pressure desired (100-105 psi) and the minimum pressure required for safe operation (80-85 psi) by starting and stopping compression.

The two steel tanks which are components of most air brake systems are called reservoirs. These tanks are used to cool, store, and remove moisture from the air and give a smooth flow of air to the brake system.

A safety valve consists of an adjustable spring-loaded ball check valve in a body. It is used to protect the system against excessive pressures and is usually mounted on a reservoir. The safety valve is normally set at 150 psi but can be varied to suit the vehicle requirements.

A pressure gauge is attached to any line which registers reservoir pressure and is mounted to the dashboard of the vehicle.

The brake valve is the operator's control of the air brake system. When the brake valve is engaged, air from the reservoir flows through the valve to the brakes. The three types of brake valves used in the air brake systems are pedal, treadle, and hand. When you press the pedal of an airbrake system, air under pressure in a reservoir is released to the brake lines by an air valve. This air goes to the brake chambers located close to the wheel brakes, which contain flexible diaphragms. The force of the air admitted to these chambers cause the diaphragms to operate the brake shoes through a mechanical linkage.

An air pressure gage will let you know if you have proper air pressure within the reservoir (60 lbs. pressure is minimum). This gage is usually found on the instrument panel of a truck or bus. If the pressure fails to build up or exceeds the maximum limits after building up, secure the truck until the fault is corrected.

Independent control of trailer brakes is valuable under adverse conditions when it is sometimes desirable to apply the brakes on the trailer without applying the brakes on the truck or tractor. The independent trailer control valve, conveniently located in the cab, provides the operator with perfect control of his trailing load at all times.

VACUUM BRAKES

In the vacuum brake system, depressing the brake pedal opens a valve between the power cylinder, which contains a piston, and the intake manifold to which the power cylinder is connected. To apply the brakes, air is exhausted from the cylinder ahead of the piston, while atmospheric pressure acts on the rear side of the piston to exert a powerful pull on the rod attached to the piston.

When the brake valve is closed, the chamber ahead of the piston is shut off from the intake manifold and is open to the atmosphere. The pressure is then the same on both sides of the piston; therefore, no pull is exerted upon the pull rod. The brake shoe return springs then release the brakes and return the piston to its original position in the power cylinder.

Hydrovac is a trade name for a one-unit vacuum power braking system. It combines into one assembly a hydraulic control valve, a vacuum power cylinder and a hydraulic slave cylinder. This assembly is connected to both the master cylinder and the wheel brakes, eliminating the need for mechanical connections with the brake pedal.

When you press the brake pedal, fluid is forced from the master cylinder through the check valve to the slave cylinder and on to the wheel cylinders. The foot pedal pressure, acting through the master cylinder, acts also against the slave cylinder piston, assisting the vacuum pistons and push rods to press upon the brake shoes.

OPERATOR MAINTENANCE

Periodic brake service by the operator includes the use of proper brake fluid; checking brake fluid level; inflating tires properly; checking for loose connections or parts; checking for leaks in the system; draining air reservoirs daily; and checking the self-contained lubricating oil system of air compressors daily.

MALFUNCTION DETECTION

The types of brake trouble that may be encountered in vehicle operation are: brake pedal goes to the floorboard with no resistance; one brake drags; all brakes drag; vehicle pulls to one side when braking; soft or spongy pedal; excessive pedal effort required; noisy brakes; air in the system; loss of brake fluid; brakes heat up during driving and fail to release; leaky brake cylinder; grabbing brake action; and brake pedal can be depressed without slowing the vehicle. As an operator, you must explain the malfunction on the Operator's Trouble Report and turn it into the maintenance shop for necessary correction.

STEERING MECHANISMS

All steering mechanisms have the same basic parts. The steering linkage ties the front wheels together and connects them to the steering gear case at the lower end of the steering column, which in turn connects the gear case to the steering wheel.

The arms and rods of the steering linkage have ball or ball and socket ends to provide a swivel connection between them. These jointed ends are provided with grease fittings, dust seals or boots, and many of them have end-play adjustment devices. These joints and devices must be adjusted and lubricated regularly.

The tie-rod is usually located behind the axle and keeps the front wheels in proper alignment. To provide for easier steering and maximum leverage, the tie-rod may be separated into two lengths and connected to the steering gear near the center of the vehicle.

The drag link between the steering arm and the pitman arm may be long or short, depending on the installation.

The pitman arm, splined to the shaft extending from the steering gear case, moves in an arc, its position depending on which way the steering wheel is turned. It is approximately vertical when the front wheels are straight ahead. Therefore, the length of the drag link is determined by the distance between the steering arm and the vertical position of the pitman arm. Unlike the tie-rods, the length of the drag link is not adjustable.

The steering gear case contains the gears that control the movement of the pitman arm and steering linkage.

POWER STEERING

Power steering has been used for a number of years on heavy-duty applications, but it is only in recent years that power steering has been applied to any extent on automotive vehicles. The principle of power steering is very simple. A booster arrangement is provided which is set in operation when the steering wheel is turned. The booster then takes over and does most of the work of steering. Power steering has used compressed air, electrical mechanisms, and hydraulic pressure. Hydraulic pressure is used on the vast majority of power-steering mechanisms today.

In the hydraulic power-steering system, a continuously operating pump provides hydraulic pressure. As the steering wheel is turned, valves are operated to admit this hydraulic pressure to a cylinder. Then, the pressure causes a piston to move—and the piston does most of the steering work.

There are actually two general types of power-steering systems. In one, the integral type, the power operating assembly is located in the steering gear case. In the other, the linkage type, the power operating assembly is part of the steering linkage.

In the linkage-type power-steering system, the power cylinder or booster cylinder is not part of the steering gear. Instead, the power cylinder is connected into the steering linkage. In addition, the valve assembly is included in the steering linkage, either as a separate assembly or united with the power cylinder.

WHEEL ALIGNMENT

Steering control depends greatly upon the position of the wheels in relation to the rest of the vehicle and the surface over which it travels. Any changes from the specified setting of the wheels affect steering and the riding control of the vehicle. Therefore, the proper wheel alignment is important for vehicle control.

Steering geometry is the term manufacturers use to describe steering and front wheel alignment. Steering geometry includes pivot inclination, wheel caster, wheel chamber, toe-in and toe-out. These terms refer to angles in the front wheel alignment which may change because of driving over rough terrain, striking stationary objects, and accident damage.

OPERATOR MAINTENANCE

Doing maintenance servicing by the operator, the service that the steering linkage normally requires is periodic lubrication of the connecting joints between the links which contain bushings.

When vehicles are equipped with manually operated steering, check the steering gear housing for sufficient lubrication and add recommended manufacturer's gear lubricant, if necessary. For vehicles equipped with power steering, check belt tension which can cause low oil pressure and hard steering. Check fluid level. If the fluid level is low, add fluid to bring it up to the recommended level. Use only special power steering fluid recommended. If the level is low, the possibility exists that there is a leak. Check all hose and power-steering connections for signs of leaks. Leakage may occur at various points in the power-steering unit if the seals are defective. Report conditions to the maintenance shop for replacement of any defective seal, or it may only be necessary to tighten the connections to eliminate leaks.

MALFUNCTION DETECTION

The types of steering trouble that may be encountered in vehicle operation are: excessive play in the steering system; hard steering; vehicle wanders; vehicle pulls to one side when braking; front wheel shimmy at low speeds; front-wheel tramps (high speed shimmy); steering kickback; tires squeal on turns; improper tire wear; and noises. As an operator, you would explain the malfunction on the Operator's Trouble Report and turn it into the maintenance shop for corrective actions.

III. SUSPENSION SYSTEM

A suspension system is a system of anchoring and suspending the wheels or tracks from the frame by means of springs. The suspension system is an important feature of military vehicles; it supports the weight and allows them to be driven under varying loads and speed conditions over bumpy roads and rough terrain without great risk of damage.

The usual components of a suspension system are the springs and shock absorbers. Some suspension systems also have torsion bars.

SPRINGS

Springs support the frame and the body of the vehicle, as well as the load the vehicle carries. They allow the wheels to withstand the shocks of uneven road surfaces and provide a flexible connection between the wheels and the body. The best spring is the one which absorbs road shock rapidly and returns to its normal position slowly. Such a spring, however, is very rare, if not an impossibility. Extremely flexible, or soft springs, allow too much movement of the vehicle superstructure, while still, hard springs do not allow enough movement.

The springs do no support the weight of the wheels, rims, tires, and axles. These parts make up the unsprung weight of the vehicle. The unsprung weight decreases the action of the springs and is, therefore, kept to a minimum to permit the springs to do the job of supporting the vehicle frame and load.

The three types of spring suspension usually found in vehicles are: the longitudinal, the lengthwise mounting, which is the most common; the independent, which is generally used in front suspensions; and transverse, which is the crosswise mounting.

The multiple leaf spring consists of a number of steel strips or leaves of different lengths, fastened together by a bolt through the center. Each end of the largest or master leaf is rolled in an eye which serves as a means of attaching the spring to the spring hanger and spring shackle. Leaf rebound clips surround the leaves at two or more intervals along the spring to keep them from separating on the rebound after the spring has been depressed. The clips allow the spring leaves to slide but prevent them from separating and throwing the entire rebound stress on the master leaf. Thus, the spring acts as a flexible beam. Leaf springs may be suspended lengthwise (parallel to the frame), or cross-wise.

When installed lengthwise, both ends of the spring are attached to the frame and the center is clamped to the axle or spring seat. In some trucks and cars the rear springs are clamped under the axle, instead of over it to lower the center of gravity. A low center of gravity will help prevent a heavily loaded truck from upsetting.

Springs installed crosswise have the ends attached to the axle, and the frame rests on the center of the spring. Torque arms or radius rods are required with this type of spring suspension to absorb the driving thrust of the wheels. The driving thrust and brake action of wheels tend to twist the springs from the spring hangers and shackles connecting them to the frame or axles.

Spring hangers are fittings to which the spring ends are attached. A bolt or pin passes through the bushing in the spring eye and is secured to the spring hanger on the frame. The bushing and shackle bolt or pin, therefore, provide the bearing surface which supports the load on the spring.

The spring bushings may be made of bronze or rubber. They may be pressed or screwed into the spring eye, depending on the design. The steel bolts or pins that pass through the bushing are also either plain or threaded. Threaded bushings and shackle bolts offer a greater bearing surface and are replaced more easily when they become worn.

When a leaf spring is compressed, it must straighten out or break. Therefore, spring shackles are required at one or both ends of the spring. Spring shackles provide a swinging support and allow the spring to straighten out when compressed. One shackle is used in either the front or rear support of springs installed lengthwise. Two shackles are used in supporting springs installed crosswise.

You will see many types of spring shackles. The link shackle and U-shackle are the most common. Link shackles are used in heavy vehicles, and the U-type is more common for use on passenger cars and light trucks.

You will find link shackles used to support a transverse spring on the dead front axle of some wheeled tractors. Most wheeled tractors do not even have springs, and all load cushioning is obtained through large, low pressure tires.

Track-type tractors are equipped with one large leaf spring supported without spring shackles. It is fastened to the engine support and rests on the frames supporting the tracks and rollers. Brackets on the track frames keep the spring from shifting. The main purpose of the spring is to relieve the running gear of stresses during operation.

Some vehicles are equipped with leaf springs at the rear wheels only; others are so equipped both front and rear.

Coil springs are most generally used on independent suspension systems. They provide a very smooth riding quality. Their use has normally been limited to passenger vehicles. Recently, however, they have been used to a limited extent on trucks. The spring seat and hanger, shaped to fit the coil ends, hold the spring in place. Spacers made of rubberized fabric are placed at each end of the coil to prevent squeaking. The rubber bumper, mounted in the spring supporting member, prevents metal to metal contact when the spring is compressed. Most vehicles are equipped with coil springs at the two front wheels, while some other have them at both front and rear.

SHOCK ABSORBERS
Springs alone are never satisfactory in a light vehicle suspension system. A stiff spring gives a hard ride because it does not flex and rebound when the vehicle passes over a bump. On the other hand, too flexible a spring rebounds too much, and the vehicle rides roughly. To smooth the riding qualities of the vehicle, shock absorbers are used. They prevent excessive jolting of the vehicle by balancing spring stiffness and flexibility. They allow the springs to return to rest slowly after having been compressed. Although single-acting shock absorbers check only spring rebound, double-acting shock absorbers check spring compression as well as spring rebound, permitting the use of the more flexible springs.

FRONT AXLE SUSPENSION
Most passenger car front wheels are individually supported with independent suspension systems. The ones you are likely to encounter are the coil spring and the torsion bar suspension systems. These are used with independent front axles and shock absorbers.

REAR AXLE SUSPENSION
Driving wheels are mounted on a live driving axle that is suspended by springs attached to the axle housing. Leaf springs are generally used for suspending live axles. Coil springs are used on a number of passenger cars with torque tube drive.

OPERATOR MAINTENANCE
Under normal operation, and given proper maintenance, suspension systems would not need adjustments or replacement for many miles. The spring assemblies of the suspension system should be checked regularly to ensure that shackles are tight and that bushings within the shackles are not worn excessively or frozen tight. Occasionally, spraying lubricating oil on the spring leaves helps to prevent squeaking at the ends of the spring leaves. Following the lubrication chart furnished for a particular vehicle, check and lubricate the front suspension system including linkage, kingpin, and ball joints. During your checks you may find shock absorber bushings worn; if so, it is best to have the bushings replaced, or in some instances a complete replacement of the shock absorbers is needed.

MALFUNCTION DETECTION
Some types of suspension troubles that may be encountered in vehicle operation are: hard steering, vehicle wander, vehicular pulls to one side during normal driving, front-wheel shimmy, front-wheel tramp (high speed shimmy), steering kickback, hard or rough ride, sway on

turns, spring breakage, sagging springs, and noises. As an operator, you would explain the malfunction on the Operator's Trouble Report and turn the trouble report into the maintenance shop for corrective action.

IV. FRAME

The chassis is the assembly of mechanisms that make up the major operating part of the vehicle. It is usually assumed to include everything except the vehicle body. The individual operating assemblies are mounted on the frame, which must be strong enough to support the weight of the vehicle and its rated load without distortion. The frame must be rigid enough to keep the units of the vehicle in proper alignment and to protect them against the stresses and strains of road and surface shocks.

The frame is generally constructed of cold-rolled open-hearth steel, but sometimes of alloy steel to lighten the weight of the vehicle. The side members or rails are the heaviest parts of the frame. The cross members are fixed to the side members rigidly enough to prevent weaving and twisting of the frame. Angular pieces of metal called gusset plates are riveted or welded at the point where members are joined for added strength.

The number, size, and arrangement of cross members depend on the type of vehicle for which the frame is designed. Usually, a front cross member supports the radiator and front end of the engine as well as stiffens the frame. The rear cross members furnish support for the fuel tanks and rear trunk on passenger cars, and the two-bar connections for trucks. Additional cross members are added to the frame to support the rear of the engine and power train and to secure the rigidity required.

The cross members of most small vehicles are designed in either X or K form. The front cross members are wider and of heavier construction than the back members because they support the engine and the front wheels. The side members are shaped to accommodate the body and support its weight. They narrow toward the front of the vehicle to permit a shorter turning radius for the wheels and widen under the main part of the body where the body is secured to the frame. Trucks and trailers usually have frames with straight side members to accommodate several designs of bodies and to give the vehicle added strength to withstand heavier loads. Heavy duty trucks and trailers have I-beam frames.

Brackets and hangers which are bolted or riveted to the frame to support the shock absorbers, fenders, running boards, and springs are usually made of case or pressed steel.

GLOSSARY OF TECHNICAL TRUCKING TERMS

CONTENTS

	Page
AGGREGATED SHIPMENTS……….CARTAGE (LOCAL)	1
CLAIM……….CONNECTING CARRIER	2
CONTAINER……….FLAMMABLE LIQUIDS	3
FORKLIFT……….INTERLINE FREIGHT	4
INTERSTATE COMMERCE ACT……….NATIONAL FREIGHT CLAIMS COUNCIL	5
OILFIELD HAULER……….SEMITRAILER	6
SHIPPING ORDER……….UNCLAIMED FREIGHT	7
VALUATION, ACTUAL……….WET GOODS	8

GLOSSARY OF TECHNICAL TRUCKING TERMS

A

AGGREGATED SHIPMENTS: Consolidated shipments from various shippers enroute to a single consignee or receiver and treated as one shipment.

AMERICAN TRUCKING ASSOCIATIONS, INC. (ATA): A national federation of fifty-one independent and autonomous state trucking associations, each representing various classes and types of truck operation, and thirteen independent and autonomous conferences, each of which represents a special class or type of truck operation.

ANNUAL REPORTS OF THE INTERSTATE COMMERCE COMMISSION: Yearly reports of the Commission summarizing its activities and offering recommendations for legislative changes effecting interstate commerce.

A.P.U.: Authorized pick-up.

ARRIVAL NOTICE:
A notice, furnished to consignee, of the arrival of freight.

ASTRAY FREIGHT: Freight separated from the waybill but marked to indicate origin and destination.

AUTOMOBILE TRANSPORTER: Any company authorized to transport motor vehicles by hauling them on special vehicles or driving them (drive-away).

AXLE WEIGHT: Amount of weight carried by one axle.

B

BELT DRIVEN: Tractor with tandem axles. Belts connected to powered front-axle transmit power to the rear axle.

BILL OF LADING: An itemized list of goods contained in a shipment.

BILLS OF LADING ACT: 1917 Act of Congress pertaining to the preparation and negotiability of bills of lading.

BLANKET BOND: A bond covering a group of persons, articles, or properties.

BLOCKS: Supports used in trailers to prevent shipments from shifting during transportation.

BLUE LABEL: Atomic material shipment.

BONDED WAREHOUSE: A warehouse approved by the Treasury Department, used for storing goods until duties are paid or goods are otherwise properly released.

BREAK BULK: To separate a composite load into individual shipments and route to different destinations.

BULK FREIGHT: Freight not in packages or containers.

C

CAB: Driver's compartment of a truck or tractor-trailer.

CARGO: The freight carried by a vehicle.

CARRIER: An individual, partnership, or corporation engaged in the business of transporting goods or persons.

CARTAGE (LOCAL): Hauling between locations in the same town, city, or suburb.

CLAIM:
1. A demand made upon a transportation company for payment, due to loss or damage of freight alleged to have occurred while shipment was in possession of carrier.
2. A demand upon a transportation company for refund of an overcharge.

CLASSIFICATION RATING: The class to which an article is assigned for the purpose of applying transportation charges.

CLASS I MOTOR CARRIERS: Common or contract motor carriers of property that have average gross operating revenues of $1,000,000 or more annually from motor carrier operations.

CLASS II MOTOR CARRIERS: Common or contract motor carriers of property that have average gross operating revenues of $300,000 or more, but under $1,000,000 annually from motor carrier operations.

CLASS III MOTOR CARRIERS: Common or contract motor carriers of property that have average gross operating revenues of less than $300,000 annually from motor carrier operation.

CLASS TARIFF: A published schedule of class rates.

CLEAR RECORD: A record which shows that a shipment was handled without loss or damage.

COMBINATION: Motor truck or truck tractor coupled to one or more trailers (including semitrailers).

COMBINATION RATE: A rate made by combining two or more rates published in different tariffs.

COMMODITY: Any article of commerce. Goods shipped.

COMMODITY, EXEMPT: Goods that may be transported in interstate commerce without operating authority or published rates.

COMMON CARRIER: A transportation business that offers service to the general public. Interstate common carriers must hold a franchise issued by the Interstate Commerce Commission which limits service to a specific geographical area.

COMMON CARRIER, IRREGULAR ROUTE: A common carrier whose routes and schedules are not regulated by government agencies.

COMMON OWNERSHIP: Ownership of one mode of transportation by another. Such ownership is restricted by federal law.

COMPETITIVE RATE: A charge established to meet the competition of another transportation line.

CONCEALED DAMAGE: Damage to the contents of a package which is apparently in good condition externally.

CONCEALED LOSS: Loss or damage that cannot be determined until the package is opened.

CONCENTRATION POINT: A place where small shipments are consolidated into larger shipments.

CONCRETE MIXER: Truck body designed to mix concrete.

CONFERENCE: An independent and autonomous organization within the American Trucking Associations representing a special class or type of motor carrier operation. The thirteen conferences are: National Automobile Transporters; Common Carrier Conference —Irregular Route; Contract Carrier; Film Carriers; Heavy and Specialized Carriers; Local and Short Haul Carriers National; American Movers Conference; Munitions Carriers; National Tank Truck Carriers; Oilfield Haulers; Private Carriers; Regular Common Carrier; and the Steel Carriers Conference of ATA.

CONNECTING CARRIER: A carrier which interchanges trailers with another for completion of shipments.

CONTAINER: Anything in which articles are packed.
CONTAINERIZATION: Shipping system based upon large cargo-carrying containers that can be easily interchanged between trucks, trains, and ships, without rehandling of contents.
CONTRACT CARRIER: A company that engages in for-hire transportation of property under individual contract or agreement with one or a limited number of shippers.
COUNCIL (AMERICAN TRUCKING ASSOCIATIONS, INC.): A self-sustaining group within the American Trucking Associations composed of individuals who specialize in some particular aspect of trucking operations. The Councils are: Council of Safety Supervisors, National Accounting and Finance Council, National Freight Claims Council, Sales Council, and the Operations Council.
CUBIC FOOT: A common measure of the capacity of a truck.
CUBIC CAPACITY: The carrying capacity of a truck measured in cubic feet.

D

DIFFERENTIAL ROUTE: Route for which there is no published rate. The rate must be computed from existing published rates.
DISPATCHING: The scheduling and control of truck pickup and delivery.
DOCK: A platform where trucks are loaded and unloaded.
DOLLY:
  1. An auxiliary axle assembly equipped with a fifth wheel used to convert a semitrailer to a full trailer. This is called a trailer converter dolly.
  2. Small platforms on rollers or wheels used to handle freight in a warehouse.

E

ELKINS ACT: A law providing penalties for various violations of the Interstate Commerce Act.
ENROUTE: On the way.
E.T.A.: Estimated Time of Arrival.
EXCLUSIVE USE OF TRUCK: A request made by a shipper, on the bill of lading, for the complete use of a vehicle.
EXEMPT CARRIERS: Trucks hauling certain commodities are exempt from Interstate Commerce Commission economic regulation. The largest portion of the exempt carriers transport agricultural commodities or seafood.
EXPEDITING: To accelerate transportation. Expedited freight service is usually faster than normal service. An example is dispatching less than truckload quantities, on a single truck, for quick delivery.

F

FEEDER SERVICE: Short transportation truck routes from terminals into nearly areas, to collect and distribute freight to a main truck line for long haul deliveries.
FILM CARRIER: Any for-hire company authorized to transport films.
FIXED CHARGES: Carrier costs that do not vary with an increase or decrease in traffic. An accounting classification.
FLAMMABLE LIQUIDS: Liquids that give off vapors capable of burning.

FORKLIFT: A machine used to move goods loaded on pallets or skids.
FREE TIME: The time period freight is held before storage charges are applied.
FREIGHT: Any commodity being transported.
FREIGHT BILL: Document for a common carrier shipment. Gives description of the freight, its weight, amount of charges, taxes, and whether collect or prepaid. Charges paid in advance are called prepaid freight bills. Charges collected at destination are called destination or collect freight bills.
FREIGHT FORWARDER: A company that assembles small shipments, from various shippers, into larger shipments to form a full truck or car load. Forwarders send the consolidated freight to a station where it is disassembled and routed to the proper destinations.
FULL TRAILER: Truck trailer with wheels on both ends (as compared to a semi-trailer in which the front rests on the rear of the power unit).

G

GATEWAY: A point where freight moving from one territory to another is interchanged between transportation lines.
G.B.L.: Government Bill of Lading.
GROSS TON: 2,240 pounds; more commonly called a long ton.
GROSS WEIGHT:
1. The weight of an article together with the weight of its container and the material used in packing.
2. As applied to a truck, the weight of a truck together with the weight of its entire contents.

H

HEATER SERVICE: Heat protection of freight that would be damaged by freezing.
HEAVY SPECIALIZED CARRIERS: A trucking company franchised to transport articles which, because of size, shape, weight, or other inherent characteristics, require special equipment for loading, unloading, or transporting.
HIGH-CUBE: A truck body with above-average cubic content. Usually constructed with low floors and thin walls.

I

ICING CHARGE: A charge made for cooling perishable freight.
INITIAL CARRIER: The transportation line that picks up a shipment from the shipper.
INSULATED VAN BODY: Van body designed primarily for transportation of commodities at controlled temperatures. It may be provided with equipment for refrigeration or heating.
INSURANCE FREIGHT: Insurance that protects shippers if goods are accidentally damaged during transportation.
INTERLINE FREIGHT: Freight which moves from point of origin to destination over the lines of two or more transportation companies.

INTERSTATE COMMERCE ACT: An act of Congress regulating the practices, rates, and rules of transportation lines engaged in handling interstate traffic.
INTERSTATE COMMERCE COMMISSION (ICC): The federal body charged with enforcing acts of Congress affecting interstate commerce.
INTRASTATE TRAFFIC: Traffic having origin, destination, and entire transportation within the same state.

J

JACKET: A cover placed around such containers as cans and bottles.

L

LADING: That which constitutes a load; the freight in a vehicle.
LESS THAN TRUCK LOAD (LTL): A quantity of freight less than that required for the application of a truckload rate.
LINE HAUL: Movement of freight between cities, excluding pickup and delivery service.
LOG BOOK: A book carried by truck drivers, which contains daily records of hours, route, etc. They are required by Interstate Commerce Commission regulations.

M

MINIMUM RATE: The lowest lawful rate that may be charged for transporting a shipment.
MIXED TRUCKLOAD: A truckload of different articles combined into a single shipment.
MOTOR FREIGHT ASSOCIATION: A non-profit motor carrier organization that prepares, files, and distributes tariff material for member carriers in a specified territory.
MISSILE CARRIER: Flatbed truck body designed for hauling rockets and other lengthy cargo.
MOVER (HOUSEHOLD GOODS CARRIER): A company that transports household goods by motor vehicle.
MUNITIONS CARRIER: A company that transports munitions by motor vehicle.

N

NATIONAL ACCOUNTING AND FINANCE COUNCIL: A self-sustaining subordinate group within the American Trucking Associations, composed of individuals who specialize in motor carrier accounting and finance.
NATIONAL FREIGHT CLAIMS COUNCIL: A self-sustaining subordinate group within the American Trucking Associations, composed of individuals who specialize in freight claims matters.

O

OILFIELD HAULER: Any company authorized to transport oilfield equipment.

OPERATIONS COUNCIL, THE: A self-sustaining subordinate group within the American Trucking Associations, composed of individuals who specialize in terminal, city, and line haul operations.

OVERAGE: Excess freight over the quantity believed to have been shipped, or more than the quantity shown on a shipping document.

P

PACKING LIST: A detailed inventory of items contained in shipment.

PERISHABLE FREIGHT: Freight subject to decay or deterioration.

POINT OF ORIGIN: The terminal at which freight is received from the shipper.

POLE TRAILER: Truck trailer which uses a rigid pole as a structural member connecting the axle unit to the truck pulling it. They are used to haul long, rigid loads such as logs, poles, and pipe.

PREPAID: A term denoting that transportation charges have been or are to be paid at shipping point.

PRIVATE CARRIER: A company which maintains its own trucks to transport its own freight.

PROOF OF DELIVERY: Delivery receipt copy of freight bill signed by receiver at time of delivery.

PUBLISHING AGENT: A person authorized by transportation lines to publish tariffs.

PUSHER-AXLE: Non-powered rear axle on tractor.

R

RATE: The charge for transporting freight.

REFUSE BODY: Truck body designed for loading and hauling rubbish.

REGULAR COMMON CARRIER: Any company authorized to serve the public and to transport general commodities over set routes.

RESTRICTED ARTICLES: Commodities that can be handled only under certain specific conditions.

S

SAFETY SUPERVISORS (COUNCIL OF): A self-sustaining subordinate group within the American Trucking Associations, composed of individuals who specialize in motor carrier safety.

SALES COUNCIL: A self-sustaining group within the American Trucking Associations, composed of individuals who specialize in customer relations and sales management matters for the motor carrier industry. (See COUNCIL – AMERICAN TRUCKING ASSOCIATIONS, INC.)

SEDAN DELIVERY BODY: Small panel truck body used on a passenger car chassis.

SEMITRAILER: Truck trailer equipped with one or more axles and constructed so that the front end rests upon a truck tractor.

SHIPPING ORDER: Instructions to carrier for transportation of a shipment, usually a copy of the bill of lading.
SHORTAGE: When quantity actually receives is less than that shown on the waybill.
STATE TRUCKING ASSOCIATION: An independent and autonomous association representing all classes and types of truck operation in a state. American Trucking Associations, Inc. is a federation of these state trucking associations.
STEERING AXLE: An axle through which directional control of the vehicle is applied. It may be powered or non-powered, and there may be more than one steering axle on a single unit.
STRAIGHT TRUCK: A truck with the body and engine mounted on the same chassis. (As contrasted to a combination unit such as a tractor semitrailer)

T

TACHOGRAPH: A device used in a cab to automatically record miles driven, number of stops, speed, and other factors during a trip; a registering tachometer.
TAG: An identifying card or label attached to an article or its container.
TANDEM AXLE: An assembly of two axles, either of which may be powered.
TANK TRUCK CARRIER: Any for-hire carrier that serves the general public and is authorized to carry petroleum, chemical, liquid, or dry commodities in bulk, by means of specialized tank truck units.
TANK TRAILER: Enclosed truck trailer designed solely for the transportation of fluid commodities in bulk.
TARE WEIGHT: The weight of a container and the material used for packing. Also, as applied to a loaded truck, the weight of the truck, exclusive of its contents.
TERMINAL: A building for the handling and temporary storage of freight pending transfer between locations.
THROUGH RATE: A rate applicable for transportation of commodities from point of origin to destination.
TOLL: A charge made for the use of a facility such has a bridge or turnpike.
TRACER: A request that a carrier locate a shipment to speed its movement or to establish proof of delivery, or a request for an answer to a previously filed claim.
TRANSPORT: To move freight from one place to another.
TRUCK MILE EARNINGS: Income determined by dividing the gross freight revenue by miles operated.
TRUCK TRACTOR: Motor vehicle designed primarily for pulling truck trailers and semitrailers; constructed to carry part of the weight and load of a semitrailer.
TRUCK TRAILER: Freight-carrying vehicle designed to be pulled by a truck or truck tractor.
TRUCKLOAD:
   1. Quantity of freight required to fill a truck.
   2. When used in connection with freight rates, the quantity of freight necessary to qualify a shipment for a truckload rate.

U

UNCLAIMED FREIGHT: Freight which has not been called for by the receiver or owner, or freight that cannot be delivered due to improper address.

V

VALUATION, ACTUAL: True value of goods required to be shown on bill of lading, when rate to be applied is dependent on that fact.

W

WAYBILL: Description of goods sent with a common carrier freight shipment.
WEIGHT SHEETS: Itemized list of articles furnished by shippers to weighing bureaus.
WET GOODS: Liquids.